§✧§

BY THE SAME
AUTHOR

THE CHICAGO TRIBUNE, Volume I, 1847–1865

A history of Chicago's oldest newspaper from its foundation to the end of the Civil War.

Alfred A. Knopf. Price, $5.00.

LIBERTY AND THE PRESS

An account of the Chicago Tribune's *fight to preserve a free press for the American people.*

The Chicago Tribune. Price, $2.00.

THE CHICAGO TRIBUNE

VOLUME II

JOSEPH MEDILL

*As he looked in 1880 which marked twenty-six years of executive
association with the* Chicago Tribune. *In 1874 Medill acquired control of a majority of the newspaper's stock.*

The Chicago Tribune

Its First Hundred Years

BY

PHILIP KINSLEY

Volume II

1865 ✻ 1880

1945

The Chicago Tribune

FIRST EDITION

PREFACE

This is Volume II of the history of the *Chicago Tribune*. The first volume was published in May of 1943 and it is intended to continue the record in this way in commemoration of the centennial year of this newspaper, 1947.

The preface to Volume I gave the purpose and scope of this work in some detail. The story was told of the beginnings of the paper in 1847, its early struggles and uncertain course, and the beginning of its real history with the coming of Joseph Medill in 1855. The first volume carried the *Tribune's* history through the Civil War and into the period of its stability and maturity as a newspaper. It gave special emphasis to its intimate relation to the birth of the Republican party and its responsibility in the making of Abraham Lincoln the President of the United States.

In the present volume the story is continued from the death of Lincoln to 1880. These periods mark distinct epochs in the history of the nation, the city of Chicago and this newspaper. The history of the paper is one with that of its readers, the real opinion-makers of democracy, and therefore we attempt here what is something like a moving picture, a narrative of the times as mirrored in the day by day *Tribune*.

In reality things do not happen in the quick and orderly fashion which memory retains or which the reading of the major events of history gives. Public opinion is a changing emotion, a feeling, and man acts from immediate and interested motives as well as from the pressure of ideals, the mysterious divine in his heart. In a daily newspaper we get a panorama of the good and bad, the action of released forces. Life becomes something of a slow obstacle race, with the good dimly discerned, the motives indistinct, with accomplishment, it seems, always around the corner. Then things clear and the great event is recorded.

The material for this work was taken almost exclusively from the files of the *Tribune*, which, however, always gave the arguments of its opposition. In the early days the *Tribune* considered that it voiced the political opinion of the best part of the old Northwest Territory citizenship. It called itself also the business barometer of Chicago, the expanding young city which had become the center and pathway of trade for the great western empire built since the foundation of the paper. The history of the paper is almost coincident with the western movement of the United States. Its guiding star was set always in the West. The paper, like the city, passed to a new economy, a metropolitan position, during this second epoch. Its local news coverage increased 100 per cent, its telegraph and cable news 900 per cent. Its staff and mechanical equipment were likewise improved. Its stock paid an eight per cent dividend. In the meantime other papers in Chicago were dropping by the wayside. The record here shows the strong foundations of the *Tribune*, its standards of independence and integrity, and how it built stone by stone a stronger house.

The major problems of the nation and the city, with which the news and editorials dealt and on which the *Tribune* always took a strong position, are shown here in the process of formation. We begin with the Reconstruction days, the decade of bitterness following the war. The nation that had been built out of the war presented problems in paternalism. Tariff and monopolies, scandal in high political places, and the reign of boodlers in Chicago occupy much attention. The Chicago fire, the Henry Ward Beecher scandal, the Grant administration and the gold scandals, and the election of Garfield are some of the historic events shown here as they occurred. There are new sidelights on Lincoln constantly cropping up, and much on the rise of union labor, prohibition, woman suffrage and other social changes. Despite political mismanagement or business selfishness, Chicago opened its doors to new intellectual and artistic impulses as well as to great material achievements.

The major change in the *Tribune* itself was the passing of Horace White as editor-in-chief and the return of Joseph Medill after nine years to complete control of the paper. Thereafter his was the guiding mind of the *Tribune* until his death.

CHRONOLOGY OF THE CHICAGO TRIBUNE
1847 — 1865

A CHRONOLOGY of the early proprietors of the *Tribune* during the period covered by the first volume of the history of the newspaper (1847–1865) gives the reader an idea of the paper's early struggles. It follows:

June 10, 1847 — First issue of the *Tribune;* circulation 400. James Kelley, John E. Wheeler and Joseph K. C. Forrest are proprietors.

July 24, 1847 — Kelly sells his interest to Thomas A. Stewart.

September 27, 1847 — Forrest sells his interest for $600. Wheeler and Stewart take charge.

August 23, 1848 — John L. Scripps buys an interest.

July 7, 1851 — Wheeler sells his interest to Thomas J. Waite, who becomes business manager.

June, 1852 — Scripps sells his interest to a syndicate of Whigs. General William Duane Wilson becomes political editor and Stewart the local editor.

August, 1852 — Mr. Waite dies of cholera. The interest of the Waite heirs is purchased by Henry Fowler. Wilson, Fowler, and Stewart are the publishers. Truman C. Stickney is collector and bookkeeper. W. H. Austin is foreman of the news room; and Sam Beach foreman of the job printing room.

March 23, 1853 — General Wilson retires, Henry Fowler & Co. purchasing his interest. Timothy Wright and Captain James D. Webster are silent partners. (Captain Webster later became a general in the Union army.)

July, 1854 — Fowler retires because of failing health and T. A. Stewart & Co. are the publishers.

May, 1855 — Joseph Medill of Cleveland, Ohio, buys an interest in the paper. Timothy Wright joins as a general partner with the firm name becoming Wright, Medill & Co. In July, Mr. Stewart sells his interest to Wright and Webster. Medill acts both as managing editor and business manager. He organizes his staff as follows:

Dr. Charles H. Ray of Galena, Illinois, editor-in-chief; John C. Vaughan of Cleveland, editorial writer; Alfred Cowles of Cleveland, clerk and cashier of the counting room; Conrad Kahler of Buffalo, chief pressman, with Jack Woodlock as assistant; another Buffalo man, Thomas, foreman of the news room; John Dean, foreman of the job room, with Charles Day as his assistant; William Peck, local editor; Clarendon Davison, commercial editor.

At the time of Medill's reorganization an inch of space for an advertising card and a copy of the paper were furnished the advertiser for $15 a year. This policy is changed by Medill. The cost of the card advertisment is fixed at 50 cents an insertion and does not include the paper. The daily circulation at the time is 1,200 by carrier and 240 by mail; the weekly circulation is about 1,000. The editorial office is rented for $220 a year, and other offices in proportion. The next year the business office is moved to the street level at a rental of $1,200 a year which is considered a great extravagance.

August 29, 1856 — The corporate name of the firm owning the *Tribune* is changed from Wright, Medill & Co. to Vaughan, Ray and Medill (who each own a one-fifth interest on a basis of a $50,000 valuation). Vaughan and Ray are announced as editors. Vaughan retires the following year and the firm becomes Ray, Medill & Co. The only other member of the "company" is Alfred Cowles.

1858 — Ray, Medill, and Cowles purchase the interests of Wright and Webster and become exclusive proprietors of the paper.

July 1,1858 — Consolidation of the *Tribune* and the *Democratic Press*, bringing in John L. Scripps, William Bross, and Barton W. Spears. Scripps becomes senior editor, James F. Ballyntine commercial editor, and Henry Martyn Smith, city editor. Horace White becomes political reporter.

November 1, 1860 — The name *Press and Tribune* is dropped and the paper becomes *The Chicago Tribune* again.

February 18, 1861 — The *Tribune* Company is incorporated at Springfield, Illinois. The owners are John L. Scripps, William Bross, Charles H. Ray, Joseph Medill, Alfred Cowles, and William H. Rand, then head of the mechanical department. Scripps is president of the company; Bross, vice-president; Cowles, secretary and treasurer, and Medill the editorial superintendent. The original capitalization is for 200 shares of stock with a par value of $1,000 a share.

July 26, 1861 — The *Tribune* absorbs the *Daily Democrat*, owned by "Long John" Wentworth.

November, 1863 — Dr. Ray retires and Medill becomes editor-in-chief.

April, 1865 — Medill retires from editorial management of the Tribune, retaining his financial interest and keeping up some editorial and business activity. (He returned to take complete control in 1874.) Horace White becomes editor-in-chief. The circulation on the day of Lee's surrender is 53,000; normal for the time, 40,000.

CONTENTS, VOLUME II
1865-1880

ILLUSTRATIONS, VOLUME II

ILLUSTRATIONS

1865 ❖ 1880

Chapter One

EMERGING FROM THE WAR

THE DECADE following the Civil War and the assassination of President Lincoln was a period of steady growth for the *Tribune* as an institution. It made many mistakes, lost many battles, but in the war for newspaper supremacy in Chicago and the Middle West it emerged into a position from which it has never been shaken. It increased its local staff and telegraph news coverage, enlarged its mechanical facilities several times to meet business demands, gained a circulation which was claimed to be as great as that of all the other English-language newspapers in the city combined, and was constantly crowded with advertisments. The size of the paper was increased to 8 pages daily and 16 on Sunday. It became especially the leading want ad medium of its territory.

This decade was marked by the move from the old home on Clark Street to a new building of its own at Madison and Dearborn Streets. The new home was destroyed by the fire of 1871 but was promptly rebuilt and the paper never lost its stride. Its political orientation was definitely changed during this period.

Joseph Medill, who had been the dominant editorial figure of the *Tribune* since he bought a one-third interest in the paper in 1855, resigned as editor-in-chief in 1865, following a

3

disagreement as to policies with Horace White and Alfred Cowles, who controlled the majority of the stock. He was out of power on the paper until November of 1874, when he bought stock control. From that time until his death in 1899 he impressed it with his own policies and made it a power in the political world.

This change was a sharp one, for Editor White, a free trade liberal, had made the *Tribune* so independent of parties that it almost fell into opposition to the Republican party which Medill had helped to found and which he held so deeply in his affection. Under White and Cowles the *Tribune* supported Horace Greeley for president and attacked the Grant administration vigorously. With the new advent of Medill the paper retained its independence on men and issues, but declared itself the firm defender of Republican party principles forever.

While out of the *Tribune* management, Medill was active in the Illinois Constitutional Convention, on which he was asked to serve as chairman. He became Mayor of Chicago immediately after the great fire. He spent a year in travel and close observation in Europe.

Three former *Tribune* editors died during the first decade after the war. They were Dr. Charles H. Ray, who had bought into the paper with Medill and who sold his stock and returned as editorial writer in 1865; John L. Scripps, former postmaster of Chicago and Lincoln biographer, who had sold his stock to White; and the Rev. Henry Ward Fowler, one of the earlier editors.

This decade gave rise to many questions which were to affect the future of America profoundly and which were reported and debated in the *Tribune* from day to day. These included woman suffrage, prohibition, the rise of Socialism and Communism, the eight-hour work day, as well as the ever present Negro problem and the reconstruction of the South.

It was a time of great upheaval and of great scandals and crimes. Darwinism had cast its shadow over orthodox religion and old creeds were falling. Henry Ward Beecher furnished the great clerical scandal of the age, as well as much of its spiritual inspiration and new religious liberalism. The modern world began to emerge in the rise of the German empire and in revolutionary changes in Japan. Railroads united the American continent and the Atlantic cable brought the news of Europe and its troubles immediately to our shores.

The shape of the world to come may be found in the *Tribune* of this post-war decade. It became a great educational institution, opening its columns to all sides of political, religious and economic questions, holding firmly, however, in its editorials to the principles which it believed were the best guide for social change. It remained frankly partisan. Under Editor White it lost many old friends and much patronage, but its leadership was soon regained under Medill. Before 1866 one editorial manager handled all the work outside of the writing of editorials, but the expansion brought by the war and which continued in the news department, called for a division of labor and a managing editor was appointed in 1866. James H. Goodsell was the first managing editor. Succeeding him were Sydney Howard Gay in 1868; Henry Martyn Smith in 1872, James B. Runnion in 1873, and then came Samuel J. Medill, Joseph Medill's youngest brother, who remained at the news helm of the *Tribune* until his death in 1883 at the age of forty-two.

"President Johnson starts out well," said the *Tribune* on April 18, 1865, "in his policy of dealing kindly with the mass of the people in the South but visiting punishment on the guilty leaders. That's the talk. Lincoln was going to pardon the guilty leaders and restore them to property and citizenship. He intended to forgive all the crimes they had committed. He sought to conquer them by kindness and clemency and to effect peace and reconciliation at the expense of justice and retribution. But they would not be reconciled and treacherously and foully slew him.

"Johnson's little finger will prove thicker than Abraham Lincoln's loins. While he whipped them gently with cords, his successor will scourge them with the whip of scorpions. Nothing will be done vindictively or from the spirit of revenge but justice must be meted out and justice demands that treason be treated as a crime and the leaders of the rebellion shall be punished."

On the suggestion of the *Chicago Times* (a Copperhead contemporary) that Booth was insane, the *Tribune* said: "Booth was just as insane as Jeff Davis, Robert E. Lee, C. L. Vallandigham and the editor of the *Times*. It was the demoniac spirit of proslavery Copperheadism which put the pistol to his [Lincoln's] head and fired it. Let the responsibility rest where it belongs."

Lincoln's last speech on Reconstruction, printed April 12 was reprinted on April 19.

The Republican ticket swept to victory in the Chicago municipal elections that spring. The Republican majority was reported at 5,600 in a light vote. There were 24 Republicans elected to the council and eight Democrats. "This is glory enough," said the *Tribune* on April 19. "No comments needed."

Chicago was in mourning over Lincoln's death. German citizens held a mass meeting and resolved that it was their solemn duty to support President Johnson and to leave the party to which the assassin belonged. The Lincoln funeral cortege was to be in Chicago on May 1, 1865.

"Let it live," said the *Tribune* in referring to the *Times*. "The course of the secession sheet in this city since the assassination of the President is diabolical and incendiary and the feeling against it is so intense that a spark would send the concern into Lake Michigan. But we entreat the people to preserve their tempers and tolerate the reptile. Don't touch

The historic funeral train which entered Chicago on May 1, 1865 carrying the body of Abraham Lincoln. From five o'clock until midnight Chicagoans thronged to the Court House, where his body lay in state, to look on the face of the dead president.

it and before another year has rolled around under the effect of its treasonable utterances the Democratic party of the city of Chicago will give up the ghost and will die a natural death."

There were four columns on the memorial services in Chicago. "The day was dim and dark and dreary. At times the falling rain seemed like the weeping of nature over the loss of her noblest son."

The *Tribune* suffered from an epidemic of verse. In three days it had received 160 pieces of poetry beginning either "Toll, toll, ye mourning bells," or "Mourn, mourn, ye tolling bells."

Booth was being hunted. Davis had fled. Anderson had hoisted his old flag over Sumter. The funeral train moved out of Washington and preparations were made to receive the body at the end of Lake Park opposite Park Row. Colonel R. M. Hough was made chief marshal.

"The Copperhead journals," said the *Tribune* on April 24, "wince and complain because they say THE CHICAGO TRIBUNE connects the Democratic party with Booth's crime. This we have never done. There is a faction of Copperheads who style themselves Democrats and these we have connected and shall continue to connect with Booth's crime, not by assertions but by proofs."

A special correspondent telegraphed graphic details daily of the progress of the funeral train. The *Tribune* asked contributions to the Lincoln Monument Association just formed. The body was to be placed at rest in Springfield on May 6.

The *Tribune* scolded General Sherman for his armistice terms with Johnston, in which the rebel soldiers were to be allowed to go home with arms and the rebel state recognized. "It was a dangerous, pernicious thing to do," said the *Tribune*. However, Sherman was a great captain and they did not charge him with being a traitor.

It was reported on April 26 that Mrs. Lincoln was to make her home in Chicago and that she had wanted her husband's

7

body buried near that of Douglas in Chicago but that Springfield friends had won out.

The funeral procession, it was announced, was to move up Michigan Avenue to Lake Street and then to Court House Square where the body was to lie in state. Lieutenant Governor Bross was to be one of the pall bearers. A committee of 100 was to go to Michigan City to meet the train.

Reconstruction could be safely entrusted to President Johnson, the *Tribune* said on April 27. "He is a providential man for the time. He will protect the South from being kept under the heel of her slave owning aristocracy. He will raise up the weak and place the power of each state in Union hands. He will build on unconditional Unionism in men for the work."

The death of the assassin Booth in a burning barn was reported on April 28. "He is dead, but the murderer is still at large," said the *Tribune* on April 29. "This is Copperheadism."

It quoted the *Chicago Times* of July 1, 1864, in the following reference to Lincoln: "He could not be more worthless dead than he is living, but would be infinitely less mischievous, and his corpse, repulsive as it would be in its freshest state and richest and most graceful habiliments, would yet be the most appropriate sacrifice which the insulted nation could offer in atonement for its submission to his imbecility and despotism."

On May 1, the day that Lincoln's body arrived in Chicago, the *Tribune* in an editorial, "In Memoriam," recalled the Lincoln nominating convention. "The contrast with the scene of today," it said, "is solemn beyond anything in our history, or perhaps in any history.

"The significance of the contrast lies in the fact that Lincoln was nominated to be President and nominated to be murdered at the same instant of time. Lincoln was for peaceful rather than vindictive measures toward his enemies. He would throw away the implements of war. The majority of his countrymen demanded exemplary punishment for treason. Whether he was right or they the next generation can determine better. The memory of the last great martyr is embalmed forever in the hearts of the American people. Looking upon his remains today, let us consecrate ourselves anew to the great cause of Freedom and Union, for which he yielded up his life."

The recent severe outbreak of poetry, the *Tribune* complained, "has completely overwhelmed one of our most athletic editors, who is seriously considering the expediency of resigning his chair and adopting the situation of a coal heaver or some other light occupation involving less physical and more intellectual labor than is required in reading five pecks of manuscript pomes per diem."

At a meeting in Bryan Hall, addressed by Schuyler Colfax and J. Y. Scammon, a plan was offered for a Lincoln Institute in Chicago, similar to the Cooper Union in New York. Lieutenant Governor Bross moved for action in this and a committee was appointed. Colfax, an Indiana politician, was chairman of the Committee on Postoffice and Roads and was on his way to see the western mining country. He had been one of the last men to see Lincoln, who had speeded him on his journey to this "treasury of the world." He was to be accompanied on this trip by Bross, who had visited Lincoln during the darkest days of the war and who had been commissioned by the President to tell his old Illinois friends his determination to stick it through and remain at his post whatever happened.

The entire back page of the May 2 issue was given to the Lincoln obsequies. There were 20,000 words of description of this scene. "These streets," said the writer, "that five years ago this very month blossomed with flags and echoed with the booming of cannon and the jubilations of assembled thousands as the news was announced that Abraham Lincoln had been nominated for President, are now clad in parti-colored

9

emblems of mourning, and echo only the solemn tolling of the bells."

The casket was opened in the Court House and from 5 o'clock until midnight the people looked on the face of Lincoln. "His countenance was somewhat discolored from the gunshot wound," said the reporter, "but exhibited a natural and life-like appearance more as if slumbering than in the cold embrace of death."

The May 2 edition of the *Tribune*, 40,000 copies, was exhausted before the demand for it ceased. Additional copies of the *Tri-Weekly Tribune* were printed, containing descriptions of the event. The funeral cortege started for Springfield. The story of Abraham Lincoln in his tomb was given three and a half columns. The first evening edition of the *Tribune* was issued on May 8. By this time the paper was back to normal with four columns of advertisments on the first page.

In an editorial on "Political Journalism" on May 8 the *Tribune* said: "If it is essential to political journalism that a newspaper shall set up some politician or clique as a predestined idol of its servile worship, whose acts it must applaud whether wise or otherwise, then THE CHICAGO TRIBUNE has never been a partisan journal and unless it sinks into the hands of men of very different views from those of its present conductors, it never will be.

"There is a lower order of mind, which, being unable to comprehend a principle, must pin its faith to the skirts of some individual man. We do not belong to that strata. We believe in principles; and in men only as they wisely comprehend and adapt themselves to those principles.

"At most times we have been in advance of public sentiment but from six months to a year has brought the reconciliation. Nearly all the measures we have pressed upon the administration had the opposition of adipose matter and the approval of the brains of the country."

These measures were enumerated as the removals of Frémont, Halleck, Buell and McClellan, the emancipation policy,
the use of Negroes as soldiers, the enactment of the confisca-
tion law, the punishment of treason, the elevation of Grant to
command, the elevation of Chase to the Supreme Court and
that of McCulloch to the Treasury, the establishment and
amendment of the national banking laws, the wiping out of
wildcat banks, and the renomination of Lincoln.

"While journalist lackeys and toadies have frequently tried
to curry favor with the late President by representing their
time-serving subserviency to individuals as greater than ours,
and to make capital out of our independent, honest and out-
spoken devotion to principle, they have at all times been
rebuked by the truthful statement from the lips of the President himself, that he believed he had no better or truer friends
in the country than the editors of THE CHICAGO
TRIBUNE."

The capture of Jefferson Davis was reported on May 9,
1865.

A new feature, the family market table, giving the retail
prices of leading articles of food for the week, began on
May 13.

Davis was captured by the Fourth Michigan Cavalry in
Georgia, it was reported in detail on May 15. He was said to
have been clad in his wife's clothes. "He has forfeited his
guilty life a thousand times, but the avenging sword of justice has overtaken him at last," said the *Tribune*.

Tribune advertising rates were higher than those of other
papers, because, as the *Tribune* stated on May 16, its circulation was double that of all the other papers together. "THE
TRIBUNE is read by everybody in Chicago except a few
Copperheads and the majority of these read it clandestinely.
It circulates in profusion all over the Northwest and thousands who do not fully agree with all of its views patronize
it for its boldness and independence and patriotism and

because it is the leading business paper of this section and they cannot do without it."

The average circulation for May was 46,999 for the daily paper. The Sunday paper of May 18, with the story of Davis' capture, had a circulation of 18,000. The *Tribune* announced it was enlarging to ten columns at a cost of $100 a day extra in white paper. The expected slump after the war had not materialized.

Full particulars of the capture of "Old Lady Jeff Davis" betrayed by his whiskers and No. 13 boots, were printed on May 22. Preparations for a great Chicago Fair were going on. Union Hall had been built in Dearborn Park as the chief exposition center. This extended for a block, holding all sorts of agricultural and artistic trophies.

The corner opposite the Sherman House on Court House Square, which had once echoed to the anvil chorus of a blacksmith shop, was now the home of a "business palace," A. H. Miller's jewelry store, four stories high, with a mansard roof and much plate glass and marble.

Conspiracy trials began in Washington and there was a grand review of the Union army there, lasting three days. The army was to be disbanded and cut to 100,000 men.

"Will the government of the United States, under the pretense of states rights, again become a party to the crime of oppression?" asked the *Tribune*. "What shall be the fate of Davis? It is a question of restoring these men, reeking with blood, to all political rights. Jehovah, after having quelled the rebellion in Heaven, did not compromise with the infernal serpent, but

> ' *Him the Almighty Power*
> *Hurl'd headlong flaming from the ethereal sky,*
> *With hideous ruin and combustion, down*
> *To bottomless perdition, there to dwell*
> *In adamantine chains and penal fire?'* "

A first-page advertisment, with special reference to Georgia, called for "Southward Ho!" It furnished information on business investments. Inquiries were referred to W. H. Rand, the *Tribune* office.

On May 24 the soldiers were arriving home and Camp Douglas prisoners were going south. *Tribune* correspondents ranged the South, telling of conditions there. "THE TRIBUNE desires to live at peace with these and help them make a good living. Remember, we are brothers."

The shawl and waterproof cloak in which Jeff Davis was captured were said to be on the way to the Chicago Fair on May 26. Vice-President A. H. Stephens of the Confederacy was in Fort Warren. Indians were still threatening stage coach travel in the West. A London paper called President Johnson a "drunken mechanic." Rebel leaders were fleeing to Latin America. The Iron and Steel Association met in Chicago. The question of free trade was debated. The *Tribune* was for a tariff for revenue only. The steel industry, the paper said, must survive under its present protection. To prohibit foreign iron would put the American people under a monopoly. No political party could survive that. The *Tribune* printed the food prices, wholesale and retail, and said the restaurants were charging prices far too high.

Dr. Ray, who had been resting for several months, returned to the editorial staff of the *Tribune*, it was announced on May 29. The ice people, smarting under the *Tribune's* attack on the price of ice, asked why the Tribune had raised its price during the war. The *Tribune* explained that its dispatches were 900 per cent more than before the war, that its commercial, general and local news was 100 per cent more and the paper one-fifth larger.

"Before the war," said the *Tribune*, "the papers had not got into the habit of taking many special dispatches. THE TRIBUNE did not average half a column a day in large, leaded type. It now takes three to four columns a day in small, solid type, making more than ten times as much, as our files prove. Before the war we published less than 3 columns of market reports. Now we publish 5 to 6 columns a day in small type. The local matter has increased from two columns in minion leaded to four and sometimes eight in nonpareil solid. The space to accommodate this increase was obtained by crowding out several columns of advertisements and by increasing the size of THE TRIBUNE, the use of smaller type and less leading. We charge more for advertisements because we have less space and our circulation is four times greater."

The Northwestern Fair opened in Chicago on May 30, 1865. The *Tribune* approved of the President's amnesty proclamation, saying that it kept the leading rebels within reach of the law and was no step backward toward slavery. "An Aristocracy Ruined" was the subject of editorial comment:

"From Cairo to New Orleans the land is practically a desert, the slaves gone, great estates abandoned, domestic animals used up in war. Gins and sugar houses are going to decay. The work of the sheriff will soon begin on foreclosures. This is the goal that the lords of the lash have reached. This is the logical, expected and natural result of the heretical teaching that has endeavored to erect crime into a political system and to sanctify it with the approval of Democracy and Christianity.

"Secure in the triumph of the better gospel of Freedom, the country, save to the ringleaders in wickedness, can afford to be magnanimous in its mercy. But some must hang. The world needs an example and a warning."

Opening day of the great Fair was reported in many columns on May 31. There was a procession, an address by the Governor and an inaugural ode by T. Buchanan Read which took up nearly a column. A carload of roses had been sent from Springfield. A Lincoln log cabin from Macon

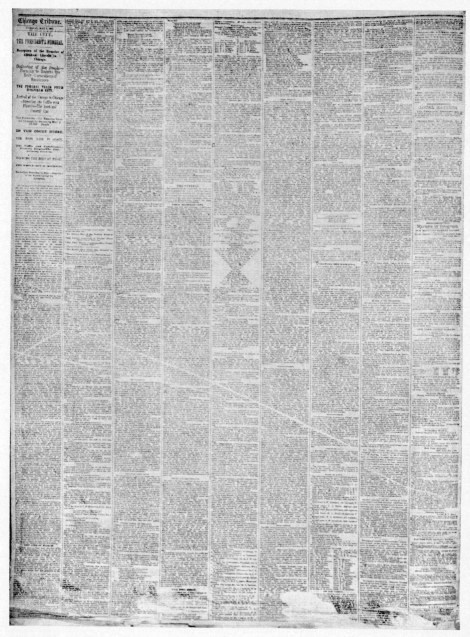

Back page of the special memorial edition which the Tribune *printed on May 2, 1865, the day on which Lincoln's remains reached Chicago on their way to Springfield, Illinois.*

County had been erected on Randolph Street and Wabash Avenue. Grand opera was to open soon. The Chicago Driving Park was to inaugurate a race series. General and Mrs. Grant and General Sherman were coming to the Fair. Grant's old claybank warhorse, Jack, ridden from the time he entered the army as Colonel of the Twenty-first Illinois Volunteers, was to be exhibited. This was the contrast that Chicago presented to the prostrate South.

Military governments were good enough for the South until order was established, the *Tribune* said on June 1. All sorts of Reconstruction plans were offered. The editors said their tables were loaded with plans, that forbearance, charity and forgiveness were needed, that this problem of Reconstruction was the most difficult problem ever presented to the human intellect. President Johnson could be trusted, they then thought, to help the poor whites and the freed blacks of the South into greater economic security and their fair share of political power. The editors, however, were soon to change their minds on this and they never got through wondering why Johnson had disappointed their hopes and had gone over, as they thought, to the old slave-owning aristocracy which they had always blamed for bringing on the war.

On June 6 the *Tribune* announced that it was for a moderate system of Negro suffrage. On the presidential situation it was prophesied that the struggle would be between the friends of Grant and Johnson. "If Johnson displays the wisdom we think he possesses," the *Tribune* stated, "in reorganization, management of foreign affairs and the administration of finance, the call for keeping him at the helm will be imperative. Grant will continue to smoke his pipe and keep up a great thinking."

Chapter Two

EMANCIPATION NULLIFIED

THE latter half of the year 1865 brought to a close one era of American civilization and ushered in another. The great plantations of the South were in ruins, the slave-holding aristocracy broken. The North emerged in new industrial strength and with greater man power than before the war. Agitation was begun for an eight-hour day for northern labor, a movement which was to result in the rise of labor unions and an epidemic of strikes. This was associated with the spread of Communism and Socialism, social revolution wafted on the seeds of European immigration.

The great political problem of the hour, according to the *Tribune*, was how to "complete the revolution," how to keep the republic, now made secure by the victory of April, on the march "toward universal freedom, equal rights and pure democracy." This had special reference to Negro rights in the conquered territory.

After a satisfactory start, according to the *Tribune*, President Johnson took the wrong direction in handling the Reconstruction problems, and a great struggle with Congress was forecast. In this struggle the *Tribune* took a leading part in support of the Radical Republican policy, led by Thaddeus Stevens of Pennsylvania, a policy which was never completely successful and which was to keep the South in turmoil for years.

General Grant, who had made a quiet tour of the South

to see how things were going, arrived in Chicago on June 11, 1865. He visited the Northwestern Fair, where a poem in his praise was read and a prize ox named for him.

Grant was on his way to his old home in Galena, where a house on a high hill had been presented to him by the citizens. Chicago was filled with thousands of Fair visitors and daily parades of returning soldiers were held. It was apparent that Grant's popularity was great and Republicans, seeing in him the man to displace Johnson, began to lay their plans for the coming political struggle. A reception was held for Grant in Union Hall. The *Tribune* reporter wrote of this scene: "The waving handkerchiefs of the ladies swept over the surging sea of human faces like flecks of foam dancing on the billows of the ocean."

Grant was no speechmaker, but the crowd seemed to like even this quality in him. "I thank you for your welcome," was all he said.

A *Tribune* reporter accompanied Grant to Galena and wrote of the great reception there.

Lee was to be brought to trial for treason, it was reported on June 13. The *Tribune* thought that this would be breaking the pledge that Grant made at the surrender, that though Lee deserved a traitor's doom it was inexpedient to incur the charge of bad faith.

President Johnson had taken the wrong direction, the *Tribune* said on June 15. "His proclamation tends to go back and leave power in the hands of the old rebel leaders. There is danger of 16 bitter Copperhead states making the next President."

The *Tribune* platform, it was stated on June 16, would give suffrage at once to every Negro who had borne arms in the cause of the United States, those who owned real estate and those who could read and write.

It was impossible to forgive Jefferson Davis, the *Tribune* said on June 19. "By the direct agency of Davis and the consent of Lee more men were deliberately starved to death in the last four years in prison pens than were destroyed by the guillotine in France during the revolution. The revolution must not fail."

A third attempt to lay an Atlantic cable was begun on June 20, 1865, with the sailing of the *Great Eastern* for America.

On the question of suffrage the *Tribune* said: "THE TRIBUNE is not in favor of indiscriminate Negro suffrage in the South and had hoped to avoid a struggle on this point. The war of ideas has just begun and the republic was never in more danger from rebel machinations than today. It is a fatal policy that leads the country by Copperhead help back to the ascendency of rebel ideas. The work of reorganization is premature. The President's line has no recognition of the political rights of the colored man. He hopes the blacks are safe in newly washed rebel hands. The premature admission of rebel states, without the safeguard, may overthrow the President."

A new era in railroad travel was seen in "a patent day and night car." A representative of the *Tribune* had journeyed to Joliet with George M. Pullman on a "velvet cushioned divan."

The unity of the Republican party was threatened by the new issues. The *New York Times* had taken the President's side in the matter of suffrage, arguing that he had no power to let the Negroes vote. The *Tribune* would take and use the military power to accomplish this. South Carolina with its 40,000 freed men was the best chance.

Cow stealing was one of the criminal cases tried in the Recorder's court. The Fair had taken in more than a quarter of a million dollars.

How the *Tribune* felt about the ex-rebels and their leaders was expressed in this editorial of June 30. "Let them work or die—it is to us not much matter which. We know that they are many and that hunger will prick and that they are proud, but there is the spade, dig or starve. We do not mean to be hard hearted nor to ignore the claims of women to sympathy and commiseration, but if Mrs. Davis is in want let her take in sewing as many a better woman, whom her husband's crime had first deprived of a protector and then beggared, is doing today, and thinking it no great or unendurable hardship either. General Lee is receiving rations too from the government, whose citizens he has slain by tens of thousands. We are in favor of striking him off the list of recipients or of feeding him in some penitentiary where his work in hammering stone will be some small compensation for the bread he eats. But if he prefers liberty, we will hire him to tote paper in the *Tribune* press rooms provided no Union soldier applies for the job. . . . We are in favor on principle of busting that whole man-selling-and-live-without-work arrangement, which has brought rebellion upon this country."

The execution of William Bell at Waukegan for the murder of Ruth Briden near Lake Zurich was given four columns on July 1. In an editorial on this case the *Tribune* urged a reform in the law which would give the jury the right to say whether the penalty should be death or life imprisonment.

On July 4 the attention of citizens was called to the city's "foul streets, dirty river, inefficient police and bad water."

The income tax for the year in Cook County was two million dollars, three times that of the preceding year. Among the returns were those of Alfred Cowles, $36,179; John B. Drake, $38,027; Wilbur F. Storey, $15,523; William Bross, $22,473.

Henry Winter Davis of Maryland was the chief orator of the Fourth of July celebration. He argued for the reorganization of the South on the basis of free government in which loyal whites and Negroes would vote and the secessionists be denied this privilege. The *Tribune* found this the spirit of the day.

President Johnson's plan of reorganization, which was lenient with the ex-rebels, permitting them to build a civilization on the basis of white votes, even though the Negroes were free in name, was condemned by the *Tribune* on July 10 as certain to lead to "shame and disaster." They did not at this time, however, question his integrity of purpose or his patriotism and said they expected to see him change his plan. They advocated military protection for freedom of press, pulpit and stump to abolitionists of the South. They wanted to see the Southerner "scrambling for black votes."

Medill accompanied Henry Winter Davis and a party of friends on an expedition to the Lake Superior region and wrote a letter about it.

A feat in telegraphing was reported on July 15 when the *Tribune* received 6,800 words on a commercial convention in Detroit, sent in 3 hours and 15 minutes.

The trial of Mary Harris in Washington was first reported on this day. This was the story of a little Chicago Irish girl who had gone to the capital to shoot and kill Adonerim Judson Burroughs, a Treasury clerk there and brother of President Burroughs of the University of Chicago (the first institution of this name). This was a celebrated case of the time, with great advocates on both sides and the plea of insanity, as years later in the Thaw case, was put before the jury. The *Tribune* covered the case in detail and after the verdict of acquittal said that remodeling of the criminal law was called for, as juries would not hang women and they should have a chance to send them to the penitentiary. "This artful, maudlin stuff brings insecurity and disgrace to criminal jurisprudence," said the *Tribune*.

More incomes from the completed tax list were printed on July 18: Eli Bates, $51,015; N. K. Fairbank, $99,400; T. B. Bryan, $26,140; J. V. Farwell, $154,119; Joseph Medill,

$24,330; S. M. Nickerson, $275,648; William B. Ogden, $388,455; C. H. McCormick, $191,309; J. L. Scripps, $16,702.

Farwell, Field & Co. sales for the year were $5,464,000; Bowen Brothers, $4,785,000; Field, Palmer and Leiter, $2,630,-000. These big firms were not then daily advertisers.

A new department appeared in the sports section, with a report on fishing on the St. Croix river by "Viator." A crib for the new lake tunnel was launched on July 24, "one of the wonders of the world in a city which in itself is one of the wonders of the world."

A telegraphic summary of crops in the Northwest was printed on July 25. The paper was sprinkled with patent medicine and quack doctor advertisments, with advertising puffs intermingled with city news paragraphs. "The thanks of THE TRIBUNE boys," said a city note on August 9, "are due to W. H. Bolshaw of the Matteson House saloon for a liberal remembrance last evening in his best style. The saloon is very much improved since he assumed control and is more liberally patronized than ever. He deals in none but the best."

A quarrel with the *Times* flared out over a description of Irish homes and people in squatter territory northwest of the river called "Kilgubbin." This article in the *Times* was called a reflection on the Irish people, and the *Tribune*, which had always been highly critical of the Irish Democrats, attempted to make some capital from this incident.

The cornerstone of the New England Congregational Church on North Dearborn Street was laid on August 10.

On August 15 the *Tribune* called the attention of the President and all in authority to the situation in Alabama where, it was stated, the Emancipation Proclamation had been nullified by the policy of Johnson and a reign of terror existed for the Negroes. "Either let the President restore slavery, so that we can know where we stand and so remove the motive of the slaveholders for murdering slaves, or let him protect the Negro race in their newly conferred freedom."

City printing was again given to the *Tribune* by a vote of 16 to 10 in the council. The *Tribune* charged more, it was said, but the council decided it was worth more.

Alderman Woodward said in the council meeting that business men were willing to pay the *Tribune* $24 for what other papers would insert for $7 because they believed that paper had such an excess in circulation that their terms became practically the cheapest.

The *Journal* disputed the *Tribune* circulation claims and the *Tribune* gave the internal revenue figures for the year ending May 31, 1865. Sales were $353,000 for the *Tribune* and $100,-000 for the *Journal*. Advertisers gave the *Tribune* $190,844 for this period and the *Journal* $69,950.

The trade and commerce report at this time gave the city first place in pork, beef and provisions trade in the West.

Financial panic, failures and defalcations in New York led the *Tribune* to characterize Wall Street as a "school of robbery." In an editorial on representative papers it was stated that the *Tribune* sales were first in the West and the *New York Herald* first in the East. "The *Herald's* principles are as ornamental as a fine lady's flounces," said the *Tribune*, "but it is representative of a changeable, fickle entity, the average people where it circulates. The people of the West are not so superficial as the loungers of New York hotels nor so indifferent to the political welfare of the country as the masses of New York. They have conscience and love the truth."

The census figures for Chicago were reported—60 souls in 1831, 177,956 in 1865. "Clear the track, make way for the car of our inevitable destiny," said the *Tribune*.

Summer travel notes, gossip from watering places and sporting events were given space in August. Many reports were printed from the South and one correspondent was sent on a horseback trip through Mississippi to talk with poor whites and Negroes.

In a discussion of the housing problem on August 22 the

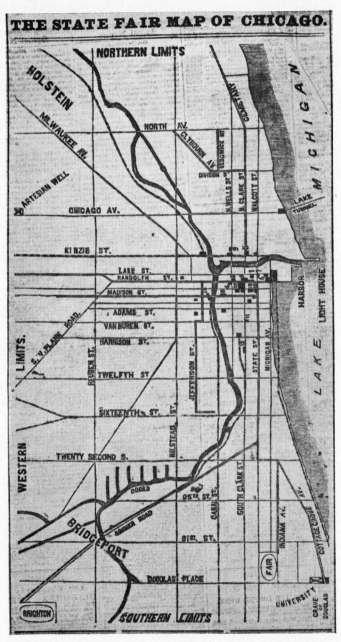

One of the earliest maps of Chicago printed in the Tribune was that published in the issue of September 4, 1865, for the convenience of visitors to the Illinois State Fair.

Tribune forecast the modern apartments. The housing shortage could be solved, the paper said, by "model associate homes, buildings capable of accommodating several families, with privacy for each." Investors were invited to look into this.

The following circulation sales figures were printed on August 26 at the head of the second page editorial column and for many days thereafter:

"Sales for year ending May 31, 1865:

Tribune	$353,600
Times	100,000
Journal	100,000
Post	50,000 "

An unsigned Washington letter of August 25 has the marks of Medill's writing. The writer said that a year ago he had hurried North praying that he would never again be condemned to a summer in that place. He spoke of his discontent in Washington and gave a picture of the job hunters at the executive mansion. He predicted an early and disastrous failure for the President's plan of reconstruction. Unless the President changed his policy, he said, there would be a wide breach in Congress with those who had placed him in power.

"Public opinion here," said the writer, "gives him credit for meaning to do right and as willing to change if his plan is a failure. There is no reason to despond."

It was announced on August 28 that the Illinois and Michigan Canal was to be deepened to six feet below the lowest water level of the lake. A road was to be constructed from the city limits south to the village of Hyde Park. The delivery of letters by carrier was gaining in favor. The new Chamber of Commerce building, "the most magnificent edifice of its kind in the United States," was completed and dedicated with three days of speeches and banquets. The Board of Trade opened a new hall.

In a final editorial on the verdict in the Mary Harris case the *Tribune* said: "The real defense of Miss Harris was not insanity, but curls. The jury in acquitting her committed a crime against justice hardly less flagrant than her own; yet the wrong was not intentionally theirs. The law threw upon them a task which no man was competent to perform, viz: to draw the line between sanity and insanity. They found refuge from the impossibility in a verdict of not guilty."

The Board of Trade banquet of September 1 was marred by a dispute between "the gentlemen of the press" and the officials of the banquet. Reporters wanted seats at the speakers' table so that they could report. When this was refused the reporters left in a body, after some name calling.

The proceedings, said the *Tribune*, "fell as dead as the Sybilline leaves and the impression was created that the affair was a failure. The idea that it is any favor to a reporter to be allowed to put his legs under a pine table and write phonography for two hours, preliminary to writing out his notes five hours later, after the rest of the company had got fuddled and gone to bed, is absurd and can exist only in the lowest form of intellect. We vote to abolish the dead-head system, so that an editor is free to stay at home if he wishes, and is always free to pay his money at the door when he wishes."

The banquet was given a column notice, with the menu described as "a feast fit for the gods," but no speeches were reported.

A murder on Michigan Avenue, in which a stranger was slain and robbed led the *Tribune* to editorialize on September 4: "An era of murder is upon us. The public journals teem with tales of bloodshed. These wild beasts must be hunted down and put to death. Eight years ago there was a similar wave of crime. We appeal now as we did then to the juries who shall be entrusted with the guardianship of society, to strike a blow which the desperados will feel. The war against the public enemy is over. Let the war against the common enemies of mankind be now prosecuted with equal firmness to an equally decisive victory."

The Illinois State Fair was held at the Chicago Driving Park. The *Tribune* printed a map of the city, giving key numbers to public places and hotels, and warned visitors to beware of thieves, drink and bad women.

A new *Tribune* prospectus was printed on September 5, 1865:

"After four years of desperate conflict, the principles, for which THE TRIBUNE in common with patriotic soldiers and citizens has contended, have achieved their enduring triumph. The Union men and women of the great republic have won the most important victory since the dawn of the Christian era. The rebellion is crushed and soon the foot of no slave will crush American soil. The future is full of the promises of greatness to the American nation. It is the duty of every citizen to see to it that there are no steps backward —that the march of the Republic toward universal freedom, equal rights and pure democracy, shall be onward and upward. The newspaper is the greatest educator of the age and if conducted in the interest of public virtue is the principal safeguard of liberty and law."

The *Tribune* then listed its features as in other years. Its sales for the year were given as $370,270. Eight columns of advertisments were printed on the first page on September 7. The paper announced that it had had to defer printing 10 columns of advertising.

Publication of the official history of the war was begun on September 8. A warning was given to President Johnson on September 14 as follows: "President Johnson has gone far enough to get his feet wet in a Rubicon which we hope he will not cross, for if he proceeds it will prove a Red Sea to him and his small host. The plain question is whether he will cross over to the Rebels, now called Southern Unionists, or keep faith with Union men who elected him. That which crushed out the rebellion can hardly quail before a single man — though he be Andrew Johnson."

The *Tribune* criticized the speculators of the Board of Trade on September 15 and said that "business as at present conducted there is training our young men to be gamblers rather than merchants."

Agitation for an eight-hour work day was reported at a trades union meeting on September 18. The *Tribune* commented that if this prevailed over the United States the cost of living would rise one-fifth.

The question of the Reconstruction policy of the President entered into Republican politics at this time and was reflected in state conventions. New York had a Republican rebel group calling for the elevation and perpetuation of citizenship to all the people of the Southern states. The *Tribune* said it echoed this and insisted that the Republican party stick to its principles.

The *Tribune's* Washington correspondent wrote that there was great public dissatisfaction with the President's policy but that it was not taking much form, the Eastern press not being up to the job. "It is no small satisfaction to all true men here," he wrote, "to know that the old, tried and ever faithful champion of the truth and justice, THE CHICAGO TRIBUNE, is again leading the van in the urgently needed counter current of public opinion."

Careless driving caught the attention of the city editor. It was reported on September 23 that a man attempting to cross Clark Street at Randolph was knocked down by the careless driver of a swill wagon. Such accidents were becoming frequent, it was noted. A cow was reported stolen on Ohio Street.

The correspondent from Montgomery, Alabama, wrote of the poor prospect of the Union men there and the "retrograde policy" of the President. "He has pardoned the most bitter, malignant and influential class of rebels, men whom he can use as tools."

Lincoln's letter in which he stated that he would favor universal suffrage, in the event of success in war, on the basis of military service and intelligence, was reprinted on September 27. "Had he lived," said the *Tribune*, "the ballot would have been given to at least some portions of the four million he made free. Every day now stealthily and insidiously reverses Emancipation by restoring its enemies to power. At Memphis Federal troops are getting $5 a day for stealing Negroes away from employment at $2 a day and selling them to planters where they get $8 a month."

The trial of Reuben T. White at Waukegan for killing his wife, Phoebe, was featured at this time. The defense was insanity. Among the doctors who testified were N. S. Davis and R. N. Isham.

A four-column report on a radical union convention in Wisconsin was given on September 28.

A circulation war was on in Chicago. The *Tribune* printed daily at its editorial masthead circulation figures showing its supremacy. The *Post* referred to the *Tribune* editors as juveniles and said that "Deacon" Bross ought to take a rod to them when he got back from his western jaunt.

Tribune files for this period show a gap until November 10, when a $40,000 express robbery was reported at Clark and Lake Streets, a forerunner of big crime.

The November election in Cook County, as referred to at this time, reveals a split in the Republican ranks and in the *Tribune* family. The *Chicago Journal* called attention to this by the comment: "Our friend Medill of the Tribune has had much to say lately about a new system of spelling. About as bad a spiel as any man has ever made was his recent spiel as a bolter of the Union nominations."

The straight Republican or Union ticket, it appears, was not to the liking of Medill because it did not present the names of old soldiers he wanted to support. An organization of 4,000 bolters was ineffective against the straight party ticket, which mustered a majority. Medill said that the Republican party could not stand such a strain again. "I would as soon think of striking a woman or a minister," he was quoted, "as to snatch an office out of the fingers of the surviving defenders of the Union belonging to my party."

The *Tribune* had supported the straight party ticket. It was explained in an editorial that Medill had resigned as managing editor six months before, but that he retained a chair in the *Tribune* office and had considerable pecuniary interest in its property.

"The Question of the Age — Who Edits the *Tribune*," was the subject of an editorial on November 14. The purpose was to show how the paper was being advertised by its rivals. "THE CHICAGO TRIBUNE is a great institution," it began. "We are compelled to the making of this observation by a variety of irresistible circumstances. One of them is that THE CHICAGO TRIBUNE wherever it makes its appearance, and there are few places in the world where it does not appear, always puts every newspaper into a terrible flutter, like a hawk among a brood of young pullets. They scatter in every direction and set up such a terrible cackle that everybody rushes out to see what is the matter. The chickens cackle louder and scream 'TRIBUNE, TRIBUNE,' with all their might, whereupon of course, everybody rushes out to get hold of the terrible hawk that has created such a disturbance in the barnyard. This is nature — it is the effect of advertising.

"Another circumstance is that THE TRIBUNE builds up and pulls down and turns inside out all political parties, just as it pleases. At least this is what the newspaper pullets say it does, and we do not find it in our heart to charge them with lying about it. Some years ago, or to speak more precisely, in 1854, when THE TRIBUNE stood alone in advocating the formation of the now powerful Republican party, the pullets of all sizes and colors set up a furious cackle and accused it of the intention to smash all the old parties and build up a new one which should get possession of the government, monopolize all offices and make old politicians turn their coats.

"It was THE TRIBUNE which produced the war, moved the army to Bull Run, appointed generals or laid them on the shelf, liberating and arming the Negroes, and everything that happened. The people naturally came to the conclusion that a newspaper of such power was a great institution."

Chicago was threatened with a cholera epidemic. The Robbins block at Wells and Water Streets was raised to grade, 27½ inches, including the sidewalks, without a crack. More than 1,500 jacks were used in the project.

Mrs. Lincoln visited at the Clifton House in November Tad was in public school, Robert in the law office of Scammon, McCagg and Fuller.

A column of editorial comment from other papers on the *Tribune's* prospectus was printed on November 21. The *Tribune* was more truly exponent of the great West than any other paper published at the time, the *Galena Gazette* said, adding: "The managing editor is Horace White, who has been connected with the paper for nearly ten years. He is a ripe scholar with a wide knowledge of politics."

The *Tribune* still insisted that Davis should be tried before a tribunal and hanged. Five columns were given on November 22 to a farmers' convention at Morris, Illinois. Cheaper transportation to the seaboard and direct trade with Liverpool were demanded.

The *Tribune* was running about six columns of want advertising daily at this time and in December illustrated display advertisments began to appear on the first page, among them those of Field, Palmer and Leiter.

A joint committee of Congress took up the problems of

Reconstruction. The *Tribune* called on that body to assert itself against the policy of Johnson in the matter of the rights of Negroes. "Johnson assumes," it was stated, "that the colored have no rights except what the political minority in these states chooses to give them in a constitutional convention. This is an undemocratic blunder and will convert the south into another Jamaica [there had been a recent insurrection there], a scene of slow torture for the black man and of continued despotism and terror to the white. It will condemn the south to hopeless poverty, crime and violence.

"We do not ask that any ignorant, depraved pauper, whether black or white, shall vote, but we do ask that intelligent, moral, self-supporting men of whatever color shall not be excluded by law from any avenue to influence or usefulness to which their abilities and the votes of their fellow citizens would raise them. We demand this in the name of the Republican party and the Declaration of Independence. We ask it as the proper fruit of the war, the completion of the work of emancipation. We ask it in the name of the martyred Lincoln."

There was much destitution in Chicago that winter. The Citizens Executive Relief committee organized a campaign for funds. "Deacon" Bross returned from his transcontinental trip and began to lecture on the West.

Queen Victoria returned to public life and opened Parliament in person.

"Equal Justice to All — Fair Wages for Honest Labor," was the *Tribune* slogan for 1866. The prospectus stated that the *Tribune* was now the largest daily in the United States.

Repeal of the income tax was discussed in Congress. The *Tribune* said the tax was confiscatory and the reason for it, the war, had passed. It suggested 3% on incomes under $5,000 and 5% on larger incomes, as all that was necessary.

As the year closed the *Tribune* asked: "Has the Republican party force and power enough to complete the work

Chicago Tribune.

VOL. XIX.   CHICAGO, SATURDAY, JUNE 2, 1866.   NUMBER 343.

One of the sensational events of 1866 was the invasion of Canada from the United States by the Fenians, members of a secret Irish organization pledged to destroy English rule in Ireland.

of the abolition of slavery or is it about to divide, leaving the work half done? " It talked of Republicans who were "mere white-washed Copperheads, going astray after false gods."

The annual report of the city, showing its improvements, its records of various departments, the condition of labor, crime, the record of the courts, etc., was printed on December 29.

"The road is open," said the *Tribune* on December 30, 1865. "Skill, integrity, economy, sobriety, will rise. There is opportunity for every man. If he fails to rise through moral weakness, idleness, dissipation or other folly, he must not blame society or capitalists, but himself."

Chapter Three

" WE, THE PEOPLE, OR I, ANDREW JOHNSON "

THE YEAR 1866 brought a complete break between the *Tribune* and President Andrew Johnson, representing two opposing forces that sought to bring the southern states into harmony with the Union again, by different roads.

The immediate issues were the extension of the life of the Freedman's Bureau, which had been created on March 3, 1865, and the increase of its power in forcing the rehabilitation of the freed slaves. Tied in with this was the Civil Rights act, which anticipated the Fourteenth Amendment and which sought to give the Negro political power by military force.

To the *Tribune* the struggle between Congress and the President over these bills was merely a continuation of the war, a Copperhead plot. In supporting the Radical Republican element which controlled Congress the editors of the *Tribune* thought they were carrying out the purposes for which the war was fought. The elements which sided with the President were in many cases the same as those which had denied the necessity of war. From this point of view, which has the support of many recent historians, the war could have been avoided and the tragic years of Reconstruction made unnecessary. It was simply good against evil to the *Tribune*, Christ against Satan.

The *Tribune* in this year began its long struggle against monopolies, such as railroads and coal. It became a free trade advocate. Joseph Medill, who had resigned as editor-in-chief, found himself in the unique position of writing letters to the *Tribune* from the outside, opposing its policies on the tariff. This debate in the *Tribune* attracted the attention of the famous philosopher and economist John Stuart Mill in England, and he entered the controversy.

Both sides in the Reconstruction struggle invoked the memory of Abraham Lincoln and sought to read his mind into their policies. Talk of impeachment began, a move which the *Tribune* at first supported and the wisdom of which it doubted later. Underneath it all was the opening of the presidential struggle of 1868 and the effort to keep the South from winning the war politically after losing it by the military road.

Two pages reviewing the trade and commerce of the year were printed on January 1, 1866. This annual business review became an increasingly important function of the paper and one editor, Elias Colbert, devoted months to its preparation. The government had been the chief buyer of goods for the last four years and this report reflected a change from a war to a peace footing. Industrial and commercial classes had never enjoyed greater prosperity, it was reported, although they had been told that revolution and disaster would follow the war. Gold, the basis of all values, had fallen from 285 to 128¼. "In our city," said the *Tribune*, "not a single merchant has failed and rarely has trade been so prosperous."

There were thirteen national banks in the city with aggregate capital of $5,110,000 and private banks with capital of $8,820,000. It was reported that the city had 150 patrolmen and eight detectives. Allan Pinkerton's detective agency had its central office here, with 125 employes.

"We shall not see such another year," said the *Tribune* of 1865. "It is not given to a single generation to witness more than one such victory of the good over the evil, of Christ over Satan. The darkness is past and the dawning of a more glorious day than the world ever saw gilds the horizon of our national life."

A one-page review was given to lumber, provisions and grain trade.

It was announced on January 3 that John L. Scripps had left the *Tribune*.

The *Tribune* began a quarrel with the *New York Times* and Thurlow Weed, New York Republican boss, on the question of supporting Congress or the President on Reconstruction. "The world will never be at rest," the *Tribune* said on January 4, "until every mind and conscience, in some way, has its fair vote."

A letter which President Lincoln had written to General Wadsworth, in which he declared for Negro suffrage based on intelligence and military service, was reprinted at this time to support the position of the *Tribune*. "God has strong, silent forces working out His Will," said the *Tribune*.

A tariff debate occupied much attention at this time and the *Tribune* "family" found itself divided on the issue. Horace White and Dr. Charles H. Ray were on the free trade side of the question while Medill, writing from the outside, signed a series of letters with the name "Protection."

John Bright, British economist and free trade advocate, contributed a letter to the *Tribune* on January 5 in which he argued that protection benefited only the capitalist and said that the tariff issue was taking the place of the slavery issue in the United States. The *Tribune* also took up the war of the farmers against high freight rates. "THE TRIBUNE favors the people as against the rights of the corporations to do as they please," it was stated on January 8. "They [the corporations] must do right."

Organization of a Free Trade League was announced in Chicago on January 17, with Dr. Ray as president and Thomas Hoyne, old political opponent of the *Tribune*, as one of the vice-presidents. The league meetings were given much publicity in the *Tribune* and Medill met this with letters in favor of a revenue tariff. Francis A. Eastman, a member of the league, answered "Protection's" letters and the debate was continued during the early part of the year. One of Medill's letters was in reply to a radical free-trader of Winona, Minnesota, which was to be the place, many years later, of a tariff speech which is supposed to have decided the political fate of President Taft. Another letter dealt with Dr. Ray's speech as president of the Free Trade League. On February 10 Medill published the following "card" in the *Tribune*:

"The Tribune Company having opened their columns for a full discussion of the tariff question pro and con, I have availed myself of the privilege offered to others, and have written a number of articles signed 'Protection,' in behalf of the protective policy. As many persons have ascertained the name of the writer, I deem it useless to further employ an anonymous signature, and, hereafter, while the question remains an open one to correspondents, I shall write over my own signature."

President Johnson had forfeited claims to Republican support in order to get Southern support for re-election, the *Tribune* said on February 6. A new reactionary party was seen in the making, composed, according to the *Tribune*, of "Copperheads, Rebels and Republican trimmers like Raymond [Henry J. Raymond, editor of the *New York Times* and member of Congress]."

The population of Chicago had reached 200,000, it was announced on February 11. Seventeen thousand were counted in the churches on that Sunday. " What is the matter with the churches? " was debated in the *Tribune*.

President Johnson was under the spell of the slavery abettors, the *Tribune* said on February 13, stating: "Universal suffrage for the colored race, perpetual disfranchisement of all inveterately disloyal citizens, and immediate trial and punishment of Davis for his manifold crimes, are the three planks of the new platform upon which all loyal citizens must now unite, in order to put an end, for all time to come, to the supremacy of Southerners and Southern ideas in the councils of the nation."

A five-column oration on "God In History," given by George Bancroft, historian, before Congress, was printed on February 14. "That God rules in the affairs of men is as certain as any truth of physical science," was his thesis.

The Evangelical Ministerial Association and the *Tribune* engaged in a discussion of the Sunday paper issue on February 15 and 16. The *Tribune* was charged by the ministers with violating God's law. The *Tribune* wanted to know if the laws of the Hebrew Sabbath (Saturday) now applied by divine authority to the first day of the week.

As if in answer to this question, with the answer in favor of the ministers, a cogwheel in the *Tribune's* eight-cylinder press was broken on the following Saturday night, while the Sunday edition was being printed. The *Tribune* had to finish printing on the *Journal* press. The *Times*, inveterate enemy of the *Tribune* in politics, offered the use of its machinery and was courteously thanked. This did not settle the Sunday question, however, as the Rev. D. X. Junkin preached a two-column sermon on the subject and the *Tribune* continued to editorialize.

President Johnson vetoed the new Freedman's Bureau bill and favored the immediate admission of the southern states with full rights in the Union. Grant suppressed the *Richmond Examiner* for sedition. The *Tribune* had no comment on this act, but suggested the removal of Johnson from office, declaring he was self-impeached.

The *Tribune* gave the "sad tidings of the defection of Lincoln's successor," and summoned the people "to come to the rescue and prevent the achievements of the battlefield from being blasted and nullified by the perverseness of the Executive."

A Protection mass meeting with more than 5,000 attending was reported on February 23. Medill was one of the secretaries of the meeting and made a speech which was given three and one-half columns in the *Tribune*. The organization was "for the defense of home labor against the raids of foreign free trade." The organization was called the American Industrial Union and Medill was made president. In an editorial on "The Impending Crisis" on February 24, the *Tribune* said the 1868 presidential campaign had been opened at Washington:

"The President's policy is defined as the immediate admission of southern states on a white basis, the colored people being free but excluded from all political privileges. It is backed by the South and the Copperhead party of the North. The only way to break the political strength of the ex-slaveholders is to educate and elevate the poor whites and give the ballot to the Negro."

A mass meeting of "those who sustain the reconstruction policy of Congress as opposed to that policy which proposes to restore red-handed and unrepentant rebels to power" was announced for an early date. The meeting was called for the old Board of Trade Hall and had 150 signatures in its call, including Medill, Julian S. Rumsey, D. K. Pearson, John L. Hancock, Horace White and E. C. Larned.

"We owe it to the memory of Lincoln and the blood of our heroes, owe it to God and posterity, to save the country from the new calamity threatening," said the *Tribune* on February 25. "Deacon" Bross was one of those who addressed the meeting, which was held on February 26, and was described as "one of the most intense, enthusiastic and determined expressions of public opinion ever held in Chicago."

The Washington correspondent of the *Tribune* said early in March that the Union party was threatened with demoralization as a result of the President's policy. The *Tribune* hammered away at the President in daily editorials, sometimes two or three in one day.

A display advertisment in which an illustration was used was printed on the first page on March 10. This was the picture of a "tonsorial palace" on Washington Street opposite the Court House, and told of how "Spanish lustral cures baldness." One hundred feet on Michigan Avenue was sold for $3,250 and 2½ acre lots on Cottage Grove Avenue went for $2,000 each.

The President was referred to as "Andrew the First" and compared with William of Prussia. England was agitated by the Reform bill and by the insurrectionary Fenian movement in Ireland. The Fenians were also active in the United States and in Canada. The *Tribune* saw this as a back wave of the American Civil War and compared the land monopolists of England with the slaveholders.

Eight columns of advertising appeared on the first page on March 17. City news was held down to a few hundred words. (The *Tribune* page of this period contained ten columns.)

The London correspondent sent in a two-column letter from John Stuart Mill on free trade, which was printed on March 18. The discussion of this subject in the *Tribune* was exciting interest in England, the letter stated. Mill was a

Member of Parliament and a free trader. Medill replied to him in an article which was given space on March 23.

The *Tribune* said at this time that it was embarrassed with an excess of advertising. In the renewed circulation war the *Journal* said that when they had the pleasure of printing the *Tribune* (during the latter's press breakdown) they struck off 16,000 copies. The *Tribune* said their books showed that on that morning, February 19, the edition was 23,150, the smallest edition in months; that its circulation had increased from 2,000 to 3,000 since that spring, and that the *Journal* was in no sense a competitor.

An 18-inch refractor telescope, the largest in the world, was added to Dearborn Tower of the University of Chicago, it was announced on March 24.

Grant was about to sail for Europe, it was announced. The *Tribune* regretted this, as in the event that Johnson was impeached the most important man in the country would be the commander of the army. The President had vetoed the Civil Rights bill and the pot was simmering in Washington. Emancipation had been nullified, the *Tribune* said. It was recalled that Illinois lost 28,842 in dead and wounded in the war. "Let us see who are the masters of this country, we, the People, or I, Andrew Johnson," said the *Tribune* on March 28.

"Should the President be impeached?" The *Tribune* asked on March 31. "We believe he deserves to be impeached by the House, tried by the Senate, convicted and removed from office for treason, bribery and other high crimes and misdemeanors, for his attempts to secure admission to Congress of representatives of states with which the government is still at war."

Whittier's *Snow-Bound, a Winter Idyll*, was reviewed in this issue and an advertisment on page one featured a great sale of paper collars.

The President issued a formal declaration of peace on April 1, 1866. "The Radical Republicans were victorious in an election in Connecticut, against the combined hosts of Copperheadism and Andrew Johnsonism," according to the *Tribune*. Governor A. G. ("Parson") Brownlow of Tennessee, speaking to Unionists there, said the overwhelming majority of Southern people were as traitorous as ever and their purpose was to break up the government. Ward H. Lamon was attacked by the *Tribune* for his statement that Lincoln would have approved the Johnson policy.

Locally, the *Tribune* called for the election of good men to the council, "an economic and wise rule in the interests of cleanliness and morality, one that will not interfere needlessly with the great business interests on which the prosperity of the city depends, also candidates who will stand against open rebellion and for good loyal governments for the reconstructed states and for the Federal Union and who want a treacherous President firmly rebuked."

A city news item told of a surprise party for the Rev. W. C. Jackson, pastor of the First United Presbyterian Church. He was given a "basket of good things and a liberal supply of greenbacks." "Such acts make glad the heart of the faithful laborer in the Lord's vineyard," the reporter added.

Gift and prize concerts were advertised on page one. For one concert 500,000 tickets were offered, with the first prize $30,000. The *Tribune* said it was time to put the lottery laws into effect.

The question of the jurisdiction of Congress over Reconstruction was argued at this time. Senator Trumbull's address on the President's veto of the Civil Rights bill was given two and one-half columns. "The President's policy must be overcome by Congress or slavery is practically restored and the country is again drifting into civil war," said the *Tribune* on April 6. "The way out is to make the freedman wholly free and give him all the rights necessary to defend his freedom. Fail in this and peace is hollow."

The *Chicago Times* said General Grant agreed with the

President. "We know General Grant's opinion on one subject," said the *Tribune*. "He is in favor of suppressing the *Chicago Times*."

John L. Scripps called a meeting of the Republican Central Committee of the city. The Civil Rights bill was passed in the Senate over the President's veto. Montgomery Blair formed a National Johnson Club at Washington. "The accumulated filth of states rights and pro-slavery fallacies, which we all deemed thoroughly cleansed by the hardships of war, is now reproduced with all its vile stench by Andrew Johnson, and all the copperhead vermin in the land are now gathering around the reconstructed stable," said the *Tribune* on April 7, 1866.

Germany was moving toward national unity. Thirty duchies and principalities were united and the face of the modern world began to come out of the shadows.

The Washington correspondent reported that Alexander H. Stephens, vice-president of the Confederacy, visited with Theodore Tilton, editor of the *New York Independent* and with Joseph Medill of the *Chicago Tribune* in Tilton's room at Washington. Stephens was for admission of the states on the basis of the President's policy, it was reported. Tilton insisted that political equality of the Negro must be a condition, and "Mr. Medill, viewing the question from the lower ground of Radical supremacy, argued that the Black Republicans of the South must be allowed to vote as an offset to the ex-rebel Democrats."

The Civil Rights bill was repassed in the House by a vote of 122 to 41. The *Chicago Tribune* assured the *New York World* that it had had no consultation with the 33 Radical Senators or the 119 Radical members of the House on the question of the impeachment of Johnson. "We take our own course, now as we have always done." The *New York Tribune* sided with the President in his proclamation of peace.

Medill, writing from Washington on April 14, told how Johnson had fallen into the hands of the Copperheads and betrayed the Republicans who had elected him Vice-President. "Now Congress is master of the situation," Medill wrote, "and the Johnson policy of reconstruction will be summarily set aside. The loyal millions of the North are not to be diverted from their purpose to readjust the Union of those states upon foundations of eternal justice, which will endure to the end of time — the President's bread-pill, soothing-syrup policy to the contrary notwithstanding."

Spring fashions occupied much space. "For party and opera dress," said the *Tribune* fashion writer, "the modistes are determined on the decollete style, but such does not seem to meet with much favor. A pair of them were seen a short time ago at one of our fashionable places of amusement, the wearers having their hair powdered a la Martha Washington, but the impression made on the audience was one of digust rather than admiration."

The Church of the Messiah at Wabash Avenue and Hubbard Court was dedicated, with the Rev. Robert Laird Collyer as pastor.

The re-passage of the Civil Rights bill had laid the foundations for Reconstruction deep and strong, Medill wrote from Washington on April 18. "All men are now equal before the law in their civil rights. It only remains for Congress to secure to them their political rights." The Reconstruction Committee of Congress was about ready to make a report.

In the local elections the *Tribune* advised a straight Republican ticket. The results were 10 Republicans and 6 Democrats for the new council. The total vote was 11,945.

A new tax of 5% on all incomes over $1,000 was passed.

Publication of Victor Hugo's *Toilers of the Sea* was begun in the *Weekly Tribune* on May 1.

The Reconstruction Committee of Congress reported. The *Tribune* said it was a policy of proscribing rebels rather than extending the suffrage. "A freedman without a vote is no freedman. This disfranchisement of labor is a libel on our Republican form of government." The report was described as "like Hamlet with Hamlet left out."

Another civil war was declared possible, with the Southern press, "as boldly defiant as on the birthday of secession." A Kentucky convention asked the withdrawal of the Freedman's Bureau and the military. General Sheridan testified that it was necessary for the military to remain in New Orleans and Texas, as loyal people were not safe otherwise. Outrages on Negroes were reported. There were riots in Memphis and in an effort to make a new state out of East Tennessee. The Reconstruction report was adopted by a vote of 128 to 37. Jefferson Davis was reported indicted at Norfolk for treason.

The *Tribune* sent a writer to tour the South from Cairo to New Orleans. His letters were unsigned. At Memphis, he wrote, he was called upon to lead the Congregational Church in worship in the courthouse, as the pastor was ill.

The *Tribune* paid tribute on May 16 to Congressman Thaddeus Stevens of Pennsylvania, leader of the Radical Reconstructionists, who was ill. "May he outlive all his enemies and their policies."

The *Tribune* supported the Reconstruction bill but still hoped for improvement in "impartial suffrage."

Four hundred guests were taken on a ride in the new Pullman cars to Aurora, Illinois. This was said to be the finest train of cars in the world.

The *Tribune* was made the corporation paper of the year by a vote of 29 to 2 in the city council.

General Grant's views on the situation were given on May 31. "He does not see things in the rose colored light of Johnson and Seward. He thinks the rebels now regard themselves as masters of the situation. Their leaders think that treason will triumph by politics if not by war. This change was brought about by Johnson."

Fifteen hundred Fenians (members of a secret Irish revolutionary organization) invaded Canada in June. "The Irish farce is becoming a tragedy," said the *Tribune* on June 1, asking the Chicago Fenians to keep out of it. The liberals in Mexico under Juarez accomplished a massacre. War threatened in Europe.

A committee headed by Thomas Hoyne asked President Johnson to speak at the Douglas monument ceremony in Chicago.

The Fenian war with Canada became worse. Chicago headquarters were established in the European Hotel, State and Lake Streets.

The *Tribune* on June 5 advised those who wanted to read an "honest, straight Republican paper" to read the *Evening Post*. "It is making progress as a Radical paper."

Gift prizes were found amenable to the lottery laws, and the *Tribune* hoped this would "put a stop to the demoralizing business." Concert advertising disappeared from the first page.

The Fenian invasion of Canada ended with the arrest of the leaders by the United States government on charges of violation of neutrality.

The report of the Reconstruction Committee was printed on June 10, 1866. It left the question of extension of suffrage open, but was not yet prepared to give the rebel states power in representation. The *Tribune* said this would stand as the platform and leading campaign document of the Union party at the next election, in opposition to the President's message.

Horace Greeley appeared in Washington as the friend of Jefferson Davis. The *Tribune* correspondent said Greeley was rapidly becoming a public nuisance.

Congress expressed itself in favor of a protective tariff and was considering a moderate increase in iron, wool, and other schedules. "The iron people want 60% protection from foreign wares," said the *Tribune* on June 21. "They are heading to destruction. The people will want to know what becomes of all the money taken from them by exorbitant tariff."

A constitutional amendment putting representation on the basis of voters, an indirect way of extending suffrage, and outlawing the rebel war debt, was opposed by President Johnson at this time. The *Tribune* gave much attention to the war situation in Europe. Germany was mobilizing against Austria, the first trial of the new confederation. Foreign news was still sent by steamer and, therefore, was two weeks or more late. The protectionists won in the House tariff committee fight. "The new tariff bill is a monstrosity," said the *Tribune* on June 28. "It is to wring money from the many and give it to the few."

The *Tribune* advised the President not to make his Douglas monument trip an electioneering tour for his third party. It was predicted on June 28 that Grant would be nominated by the Republicans.

On July 1 the Tribune came out against the city gas monopoly and advocated the city supplying itself with gas as well as water. It suggested buying the Chicago Gas Company, whose contracts would expire in 1869.

A list of incomes for 1865 was printed on July 3. Among these were: Alfred Cowles, $40,163; R. T. Crane, $18,529; J. B. Drake, $50,926; John V. Farwell, $52,046; G. H. Phelps, $197,867; Thomas Hoyne, $14,600; L. Z. Leiter, $28,799; C. H. McCormick, $153,135; Joseph Medill, $24,688; W. H. Rand, $22,491; Horace White, $20,419; Peter Schuettler, $199,772. The income of William B. Ogden, said to be the largest, had not been returned to the assessor's office.

The *Journal* said the *Tribune* stole the tax list from the assessor's office. The *Tribune* said the *Journal* stole all but one copy, which the *Tribune* got 9 hours in advance.

General John A. Logan opened the Illinois campaign on July 4, 1866. The *Tribune* made his speech a campaign document. The new tariff bill passed the House by 94 to 53. The

Tribune said the vote showed the West was against it and expressed the belief that money had put it through the House. The Senate postponed consideration.

The *New York Tribune* called the *Chicago Tribune* a "rattle-pated concern that disgraces the name of Tribune." The *Tribune* devoted a column and a half to discussion of this on July 13, recalling much political history. The New York paper, it was stated, had never loyally supported the Republican organization.

"In the great senatorial contest between Lincoln and Douglas it advised the Republicans of Illinois to renominate Douglas instead of bringing out Lincoln. The editors of THE TRIBUNE believed that the Republican party, whether strong or weak, should nominate Republican candidates. We therefore held repeated personal conferences with Mr. Lincoln, who had then been several years in retirement, who had almost abandoned his ambition for public life and who was not politically popular in his own section of the state. We pressed on him and on the people the bolder Republican policy of running a Republican.

"In the Chicago convention, while we favored Lincoln for President, the New York Tribune aired its sagacity by nominating old Bates of Missouri. Where would the country have been if the New York Tribune's wisdom had prevailed over our 'rattle-pated' policy and Mr. Bates elected President instead of Mr. Lincoln?

"With a field a tenth as large as our New York rival, we have about the same daily circulation, we make a vastly better newspaper in every department, we make more money, and today our establishment is worth more and will sell for more in the open market than the New York Tribune. We exert a ten-fold greater and healthier influence, and stand today, despite all disadvantage of geographical situation, as compared with that of our rival, the foremost Republican paper in this country."

Chapter Four

RADICAL REPUBLICANS VICTORIOUS

With the opening of the Atlantic cable, bringing news from Europe in one day instead of two weeks, and the rapid extension of the railroad to the Pacific coast, the *Tribune* news columns reflected new horizons in the latter half of 1866. It kept pace in its own development with Chicago itself, which spread rapidly into suburbs and tunneled lake and river in the effort to supply water and transportation to an ever increasing population.

Carrying the fight with President Johnson into the fall elections, picturing the President as presenting a "dictator threat," the *Tribune* found its principles vindicated in the results at the polls and declared that Congress had control of the nation. It began a new campaign for a reconstructed Union, based "on equal rights and exact justice to all men," invoking the principles of the Declaration of Independence in support of its demand for "impartial suffrage." Ten states were still out of the Union and to be whipped into submission to Negro suffrage.

In its efforts to provide the West with a wider and more complete news coverage the *Tribune* led the break with the New York Associated Press, "a news oligarchy," and aided in forming the Western News Association. After slavery, the *Tribune* declared, the next great war to be fought was that against monopolies. In an editorial the editor of that day gave what was considered as the secret of the success of the *Tribune*.

46

On November 4, 1868 the Tribune reported Grant's election to the presidency in a story occupying nearly 5 columns on its front page.

A convention of loyal Unionists of the South was called for September of 1866 in Philadelphia. The *Tribune* said the Southern wing of the Republicans should be sustained. "The South must no longer be permitted to run to waste as a sort of political desert in which Republicanism cannot grow. There should be no hamlet there where Northern orators cannot speak."

A disastrous fire of July 17 called attention to the many fires during the year. The *Tribune* said this was because Chicago was built in a hurry.

A new Freedman's Bureau bill was passed over the President's veto. "Let the President resign," said the *Tribune* on July 19. "He has been voted down as in England, where a Liberal ministry has just fallen. If this paragraph should fall under the eye of Andrew Johnson we desire it to assure him that from Maine to California and from the lakes to the Gulf of Mexico, he has among all the men who voted for him at the last election not as many friends who would vote for him today as might stand in the east room of the White House. He is the most friendless public man in America. The whole people are in two classes, those who avow contempt for him and those who conceal it."

A city ordinance making the district south of 22nd Street a cow pasture was defeated.

The age of baseball had begun, the *Tribune* said on July 22, 1866. Tennessee ratified the new constitutional amendment and was admitted as a state. A first-page story and editorial on July 30 announced the success of the Atlantic cable. European news as late as July 28 was printed. The *Tribune* at that time had no special correspondents in Europe, relying on the New York papers for European news.

A riot and massacre in New Orleans engaged attention early in August. The *Tribune* called for the avenging of the killing of carpet baggers.

Senator Lyman Trumbull came home and the Republican

state campaign opened. Medill was at work as an organization secretary.

The Asiatic cholera made its appearance in Chicago. The *Tribune* told how to avoid the disease. "The cleanly person, who drinks water, eats plain and wholesome food, sleeps between clean sheets, bathes regularly, avoids excitement of all kinds, eats the bread of honest labor, owes no man, loves his neighbor and his God, may live above the cholera in the worst cholera season that ever prevailed."

The Republican national convention was called for Philadelphia in September. The *Tribune* talked about "the Copperhead-Johnson party" and said a third party was threatened. In Chicago a Republican meeting considered direct voting on candidates instead of the delegate and convention system. A letter from Medill was read in which he favored giving this plan a chance and outlining a method by which it could be referred to the people.

President Johnson was referred to in the *Tribune* frequently during this period as a "dictator, usurper and despot." It was held that loyal men had the right to dictate terms on which conquered rebels might participate in government.

The *Tribune* put in a new coupon press for printing tickets which required numbering. "This is the most recent sign of our determination ever to be in advance," it was announced.

Governor Brownlow of Tennessee talked of the "next civil war" and President Johnson went on a tour. The *Tribune* broke with John Wentworth again over the "Court House gang" and the job of sheriff. It announced that it would have no part in making Wentworth the Republican nominee for Congress in the fall. He had been intoxicated while in Congress, it was charged, and did not vote on the most important bills.

"The veteran volunteer who has done his duty in the field and stands by his guns in peace is the noblest work of God," said the *Tribune*.

Cable news of the previous day was printed on September 2 for the first time. The Johnson tour to the Douglas tomb was reported from each city by Press Association. Grant was with him but was silent on politics.

A committee of ten was appointed, of which Medill was one, to confer with the Republican state central committee on a method of putting the direct primary question to the people. General Hasbrouck Davis, publisher of the *Chicago Evening Post*, was also a leader in this movement.

Five hundred Southern Union delegates were at the Philadelphia convention, which was specially reported in the *Tribune*. The Johnson tour was subordinated to this convention news. "In the contrast between the reception of the patriots at Philadelphia and that of the apostate president, let Andrew Johnson read his doom," said the *Tribune* on September 4. In this issue the *Tribune* printed an editorial which become known as a classic of its kind. It was written by James A. Sheahan. The subject was "Coming to the Funeral" and it said in part:

"The President is coming to the funeral. He comes with music and cannon and fireworks. He comes with speeches and processions. He comes vaunting his own glories, shouting his own praises, singing his own paeans, threatening honest officials who do not swear fealty to him, and holding out bribes in the way of public offices to other men to do violence to their consciences. He is coming to the funeral distributing his advertising cards. He is coming to the funeral of a patriot and on the way is threatening civil war; he is coming to the funeral of a Senator, threatening to dissolve the Senate by the sword. He is coming to the funeral of a freeman, asserting how easily he may declare himself a dictator; he is coming to the funeral of an Illinoisan, declaring that Illinois shall declare the inferiority of her sons. He is coming to the funeral of a statesman, belching forth at every station the duty of a nation to accept his acts as law. He is coming to the funeral of one of the people, proclaiming as he comes that there is tyranny in the rule of the many, freedom only in the rule of one."

General Grant, Admiral David G. Farragut, and William H. Seward were among those with the President. He was escorted to the Sherman House by a Knights Templar band and a crowd.

The *Tribune* described this as the "progress of the Egoist" and said the procession was short and the crowd unruly. "The people cry aloud for Grant and do not want to hear A. J.," said a heading of September 5.

Despite the lack of enthusiasm the *Tribune* gave 10 columns to the Douglas monument ceremonies on September 7. Major General John A. Dix delivered the eulogy. The Presidential party left soon after for St. Louis on the palatial Pullman car Omaha, with caterer H. M. Kinsley of the Opera House restaurant in charge of the commissary. A demonstration for Grant was reported at Bloomington. On September 8 the President's visit to the grave of Lincoln was reported. The President, it was said, was incensed at the repeated cheers for Grant.

The Maine election went Republican on September 10. Lieutenant Governor Bross of Illinois was made chairman of a reception committee to Southern loyalists, journeying from Philadelphia on October 1.

A new institution developed at the opening of the Buffalo saloon at Clark and Lake Streets. This was a free lunch counter.

The story of the New Orleans massacre of July 30, when several Unionists were killed, was made a campaign document by the *Tribune*. This was called a reign of terror by wealthy planters.

Grant and Farragut let it be known that they had been on the Presidential tour by orders and were not in sympathy with Johnson policies.

A park, a quarter of a mile wide and fourteen miles long, around the Chicago city limits, was to be proposed to the legislature.

"General Grant," the *Tribune* said on September 14, "is worthy of the fullest confidence of the Union party. There is not a drop of Copperhead blood in his veins."

The death of John L. Scripps was reported on September 22, 1866. The *Tribune* said of him: "No man ever labored more earnestly, and few more effectively, to impress right principles upon the public mind through the medium of the press. A large share of the success achieved by THE TRIBUNE during his connection with it was due to his thoughtfulness, earnestness and unwearied perseverance."

A murder at the Chicago Driving Park led the *Tribune* to complain that racing had degenerated into gambling in the hands of a tough sporting fraternity.

Grant, in a letter printed September 27, said no man could commit him to a political policy and asked every man to vote his own judgment.

Governor Brownlow of Tennessee was in Chicago and big plans were made for the visit of the Southern loyalists, whose tour formed a part of the campaign. On October 2 a four-column story of the reception to the Southerners was printed, with the following lead: "A mean, bad man like Andrew Johnson, who plays humble while puffed up with personal pride, feels even more keenly as insults the successes of others than the slights to himself, and a more glorious success than the reception last evening to the men whose loyalty makes them Andy's enemies, could not be imagined."

The *Tribune* gave nine columns to this visit on October 3 and said in an editorial: "This is the most prodigious exhibition of political feeling that Chicago has witnessed since the great Wide Awake procession of 1860."

On October 6 three columns were printed on a libel suit of Gerrit Smith of New York against the *Chicago Tribune*.

This was in the United States Circuit Court, with Wirt Dexter and John Van Armen for the defendant and W. W. Farwell for the plaintiff. The alleged libel was based on an article which appeared on June 31, 1865, in which it was stated: "Gerrit Smith stands indebted to his sire for a feeble intellect and a large fortune."

Smith was a former member of Congress, an abolitionist whose money had been used to help the schemes of John Brown. He had recently come out with a plea for Jeff Davis, and wanted no punishment, no more war or bloodshed. The *Tribune* article stated that on the arrest of Brown, Smith had fled from the wrath of the Buchananites, taken refuge in an insane asylum and remained there until the inauguration of Lincoln.

The defense raised the question in court that the insanity referred to was feigned and that the article must be so understood. This was not a libel, it was pleaded.

Republican victories were reported on October 10 in Pennsylvania, Indiana, Iowa and Ohio. The *Tribune* said that Congress had been sustained. Norman B. Judd defeated Wentworth in the Illinois primaries for Congress. The nomination of Judd was made unanimous in the Republican convention.

"The elections," said the *Tribune* on October 11, "virtually settled the great issues involved in the controversy between the people and the president. Carry this on in Illinois and other states."

The *Chicago Times* attacked Dr. Charles H. Ray, then a canal trustee, for the payment of certain claims by that body. The *Tribune* on October 16 defended the payment but said that Dr. Ray had not been connected with the *Tribune* for more than three years except for two months the previous year.

The *Tribune* came out for General Beveridge for Sheriff, against the nominee of the old Court House ring.

General Ben F. Butler of Massachusetts came to Chicago,

calling for the impeachment of the President in an address, and also urging a ship canal between Chicago and New York.

General Beveridge won the nomination for Sheriff. During the latter part of October the *Tribune* campaigned against the so called live stock ring, "which seeks to suppress market reports and cheat the farmers."

The *Tribune* called for a great Republican majority in the November elections. Medill went west with a party of excursionists celebrating the extension of the Union Pacific. He sent back daily reports of the countryside scenes, and wrote of Pullman comfort, on the way to Omaha. He wrote of the service of caterer Kinsley, who provided famous dinners. One meal, described as the finest ever served on a railroad train, included game, fish, fowl, meats, salads, jellies, grapes, pears, and wines.

On November 6, the close of the campaign, the *Tribune* said: "Close up the ranks. The eyes of Christendom are upon us. This is the Gettysburg of the war — the turning point of the rebellion. Every man is a soldier today. When the polls close let us see the backs of the enemy walking away to the other side of the Potomac."

Emperor Maximilian abdicated the throne of Mexico, and his wife, Carlotta, was said to be insane.

"Magnificent Republican victories," were reported on November 7 in Illinois, Michigan, Wisconsin, New York and Massachusetts. The majority in Illinois was given as 40,000, with a Republican gain of 5,000 in Cook County. "The returns proclaim with a vehement force the indignation of a free and intelligent people against a faithless executive," said the *Tribune*, "Chicago is now the banner Republican city of the Union."

The state Republican majority grew with later returns to 50,000 and the *Tribune* said on November 9: "The elections are over and if any external proposition may be said to have received popular approval, it is that the impeachment of

Andrew Johnson has been authorized by the American people."

The new House, it was found, would have a Republican majority of 81, with ten states unrepresented. The *Tribune* said that Congress could now do what it wanted, but must proceed with impeachment carefully, according to law, that it was a question of proof.

In a real estate review, November 10, it was stated that 9,000 new buildings had been erected during the year and lots on Michigan and Wabash Avenues as far south as Polk Street were selling at $400 a front foot. A new Bridewell was to be built, and a building for the Chicago Historical Society.

The *Tribune* continued to press for "impartial suffrage" in the South. On November 13 the *Chicago Times* advised the Democratic party to rid itself of Johnson and accept qualified Negro suffrage. This, it was argued, was the only hope for the party and would cut the ground from under the Radical Republicans. The *Tribune* acknowledged this late conversion to its policies and gave the *Times* for the first time in years a kind word. The *Times* said this was the way to kill "the worst political party that ever existed on the globe."

Cholera made its appearance in Chicago in a mild way and the *Tribune* said the city needed a sanitary board and efficient board of health.

The 1867 prospectus, which was printed on November 21, said: "Now, when the wicked rebellion is crushed, the oligarchy conquered and slavery abolished, THE CHICAGO TRIBUNE insists that the legitimate fruits of our victory shall not be yielded back to the vanished rebels by an apostate executive who has perfidiously betrayed the loyal people who entrusted him with presidential powers.

"THE TRIBUNE opens a new campaign to secure to the Union an enduring peace and a Reconstruction based on equal rights and exact justice to all men. It advocates impartial suffrage, irrespective of color or birthplace. No scheme of Reconstruction will prove satisfactory or enduring that denies equal civil and political rights to any class of loyal citizens. The South can never be truly free, prosperous or happy until all its citizens are recognized as equal before the law and equal in making the laws, which they must obey, regardless of color or position.

"THE CHICAGO TRIBUNE sincerely believes in the principles of the Declaration of Independence and is therefore Radical in its aims, impulses and endeavors, and is confident of witnessing, at an early day, the acceptance and adoption of the beneficent doctrines of Republicanism in every section and division of our common country.

"The readers of THE TRIBUNE will bear testimony that the policies it has opposed have generally been discarded; the measures it has supported have nearly all been adopted, and that its predictions have been singularly verified. The secret of its influence on public affairs, is, that it espouses what is Right, earnestly, and combats what is Wrong, boldly; and the glass with which it sees into the future is implicit Faith in the power of Truth, and the ultimate triumph of the Right."

The two-mile tunnel under the lake, "the eighth wonder of the world," was reported completed on November 28.

It was announced in a first-page story on November 29 that the press of the West, by action of a special committee of which Horace White, editor of the *Tribune*, was a member, "have disconnected themselves from the New York Associated Press and will hereafter receive news from the United States and European News Association."

The Western press would "resist the arbitrary and dictatorial assumptions of the ring, which consists of six morning journals of New York." D. H. Craig was made manager of the new association.

Editor White, in New York on this business, took occasion to write a column of impressions on seeing Adelaide Ristori, world-famous Italian actress, in the title role of Schiller's *Mary Stuart*. It was reported on December 2 that

Charles A. Dana, former editor of the *Chicago Republican*, was to establish a 2¢ Radical daily in New York.

The President's message was characterized as a mild affair on December 4. The national balance sheet showed receipts above expenditures. The *Tribune* began a column under the heading "Feuilleton," consisting of notes on music and literature. The war against the "New York press gang" was carried on daily.

On December 7 the *Tribune* declared a campaign against monopolies, saying: "After the settlement of the slavery question, the next great problem for the American people to grapple with will be that of monopolies."

The fight between the Western Associated Press and the "arrogant New York Associated Press" furnished an instance of the monopoly danger, the *Tribune* declared. Prosperity of the Western press, it was stated, could only be reached "by freeing ourselves from the tyranny of a monopoly in telegraph news."

The New York papers, the *Tribune* said, printed a page of Washington news each day and sent the Western press only half a column. "They kept the cream and sold the skim milk."

Special dispatches to the *Tribune* during the year, it was stated, had cost the paper $800 a week.

The official opening of the new municipal water crib was made the occasion for an excursion on the lake and an ode of triumph written by George T. Stansbury, an employe of the Board of Public Works. The achievements of City Engineer E. S. Chesbrough were celebrated in a poem which began:

> *God all gracious! Thou whose kindness*
> *Guards us now from awful death;*
> *Thou who dost care to mind us,*
> *Could'st destroy us with a breath;*

Thou it is whose will has brought us
All this power from our birth,
That we have a belt of waters,
Passing through a belt of earth.

The *Tribune* proposed on December 8 that 12 millions be spent on canals, the enlargement of the Illinois and Michigan Canal to Joliet and then building a new one from La Salle or Hennepin to the Mississippi. This would be taken out of a state tax and would serve to keep the profits now going to the railroads in the hands of producers.

Tribune advertisments grew in size and in number, with many sales and bargains noted. The relation between the headings of news stories and the subject matter continued mysterious. Sometimes it was necessary to search out a few lines far down in a story, to find the basis of the headline. Editing and news writing, as they are known today, had hardly begun. All sorts of items were dumped under a New York heading or a heading of "News by Telegraph." There was no clarification or pointing of the news in heads of stories.

The Western Associated Press held a meeting in Crosby's Opera House, reported on December 11, 1866. There was debate over the action of the committee in separating from New York. The organization by a vote of 23 to 3 finally declared its independence of the New York monopoly. "Henceforth," said the *Tribune* on December 14, "the Western press will be managers of their own affairs, subject to dictation of nobody. They will provide for collection and transmission of their own telegraph news, and will introduce a republican form of government among the newspapers of the West. They have liberated the press of the country from an intolerable despotism."

Horace Greeley was spoken of as a presidential candidate and the *Tribune* commented: "He is ambitious and vindictive, an eccentric and ill-balanced mind." He had a hold on the rebels, it was stated, through his efforts to free Davis.

At the final meeting of the Western Associated Press, Medill moved to ask Congress to repeal a tax on advertising. A committee, of which Horace White was a member, was to seek to organize a United States Associated Press.

The murder case of Mollie Trussell, keeper of a bawdy house, who killed her husband, George Trussell, a gambler, occupied much attention at this time. The woman was described as "robed in ball costume, bedizened with brilliant diamonds, the accumulated results of a life of disgrace." The killing took place at Price's livery stable on Randolph Street, where Trussell kept his celebrated trotting horse, "Dexter." The woman was found guilty of manslaughter and given one year in prison.

Medill's address on the New York press monopoly, given at the Western Associated Press meeting, was printed on December 17. The New York association, he asserted, was a monopoly in the worst sense of the word. "The New York ring is not vice-regent of the Almighty. They will open their eyes to the fact that if the sun does rise in the east it does not set there, but in the west."

Commenting on action of citizens who sought to break the gas monopoly in Chicago, the *Tribune* said on December 17: "Let the city of Chicago manufacture its own gas and furnish it at cost. This would make a direct saving to each customer of $54 a year in the gas bill."

Commenting on murder trials on December 18 the *Tribune* said: "The principle was established a couple of years ago, in the Mary Harris case, that it is no offense for a virtuous young woman to kill a virtuous young man. It is now shown that it is a misdemeanor punishable by one year's imprisonment, for a harlot to kill a gambler. That is certainly a gain."

The *Tribune* approved a bill to permit Negroes to vote in Illinois.

A column of dramatic, musical and art criticism by "Peregrine Pickle" (George P. Upton) became a regular feature. Articles by Petroleum V. Nasby were reprinted from the *Toledo Blade*. In the Wabash Avenue Methodist Church the Rev. R. M. Hatfield said that eternal hell was not too severe for a lifetime of sin. *Mugby Junction*, a Christmas story by Charles Dickens, and part of a new poem by Robert Browning appeared in the holiday issues. The suffering of the poor and homeless was noted. It was reported on December 30, 1866 that 24 missions and churches had been begun or completed during the year, five public schools and a new union passenger station on Van Buren Street. The Washington Street tunnel had been begun, the suburbs were growing and many large buildings were projected.

Chapter Five

PERSONAL LIBERTY AND THE PURITANS

PROHIBITION, woman suffrage and labor unions began to take form as national issues in 1867. The *Tribune* took a definite stand against the use of force to compel men to abstain from drinking intoxicating liquor, declaring that freedom is as vital to morality as to pure religion. "The rights of the ladies" were not treated seriously at this time. The *Tribune* advised laboring men to use co-operatives instead of strikes as a method of improving their economic condition.

Congress was the master of the national political field during this year and the Radical Republicans that controlled it had to take the responsibility for action in the South. The

Republican party could only live in that section by the aid of Negro votes, and this justified the iron hand, according to the northern Republicans.

The *Tribune*, which increased its circulation greatly during the year, looked upon the political problem as a question whether those who saved the Union should rule it or whether it should be allowed to pass back into the hands of those who had sought to destroy it. The opposition, those who sided with President Johnson, were identified with treason.

With the removal of Secretary of War Stanton by the President, the *Tribune* called for his impeachment, but warned that his guilt must be legally established. The impeachment resolutions presented in Congress were found unsatisfactory by the *Tribune* and when they failed of passage the paper said a source of mischief had been ended.

The Sunday closing of saloons was a question that greatly stirred Chicago politics, in which the German vote was most powerful. The issue was presented as that of personal liberty against the Puritans. This was to trouble the *Tribune* for many years, as the issue was complicated by that regard for "law and order" for which the paper always contended.

The Democrats won the fall elections in many parts of the country, making it necessary, according to the *Tribune*, that Grant should be called on to head the 1868 ticket. Whether Grant stood with the Copperheads or the Radicals was still a question, but the *Tribune* trusted that he was on their side.

In a review of the year on January 1, 1867, the *Tribune* said: "The past year on the whole has seen the recognition of the rights of the individual, of the vitality of the people and the sympathy of mankind."

The population of the city was reported at 200,418, with an increase in property values of 33%. Holiday sales of jewelry, furs, music, books and notions were estimated at $475,000. A record of the courts was printed on January 7. The *Tribune* supported a bill in the legislature to permit the city to manufacture its own gas, also an act to protect the city streets from railroad companies. A metropolitan board of health was urged.

Many columns were devoted during the month to the Hart L. Stewart divorce case. On the question of the impeachment of "A. J.," as the headliners referred to the President, the *Tribune* cautioned on January 21: "Johnson has been impeached by the people and action at this time is not necessary in Congress. It might give the opposition an argument in the election. There must be definite proof, not mere accusations."

There was great excitement over the drawing of the Crosby Opera House prizes. Two hundred and ten thousand tickets had been sold at $5 each. There were 302 prizes, from $100 to $600,000. There were many famous paintings thrown into the lottery, which was supervised by a committee of citizens headed by J. D. Dore, president of the Board of Trade. The opera had been a great success but the owner had failed. Clubs were formed to buy tickets. It was first reported that "Shanghai," a hack driver, had won the grand prize, then rumor gave it to the owner of Meyer's saloon. A crowd gathered to have free drinks at Meyer's expense but he stopped the flow of beer by saying he had "no ticket in the damn place at all." The big prize finally went to A. H. Lee, a miller of Randolph County.

The *Tribune* kept after the tariff lobby which was at work on a Senate bill increasing duties.

Files of the paper are missing until July 1 of this year when it was noted that the National Baseball Club of Washington was making the most extensive trip of its kind ever undertaken. They were to play the Forest City Club of Rockford and the Excelsiors and Atlantics of Chicago.

Impeachment sentiment was strong, it was reported on July 2. "It may become necessary to impeach Andrew Johnson but that course should not be adopted except in response to the voice of outraged law and on no less grounds than the imperiled safety of the country."

Congress reassembled and was declared the master of the situation. An article was printed on July 9 on a new process of making paper out of straw at Beloit. This was good news to publishers. "The shoddyites may now keep their rags," said the *Tribune*.

A new congressional committee was named to investigate the assassination of Lincoln. "It was a lame and impotent conclusion," said the *Tribune* on July 10, "to hang a woman and a few low-lived ruffians who never originated the crime in which they took so guilty a part."

The Chicago and St. Paul railroad was projected and investors urged to back it. A first-page article told of "trade union atrocities" in England, where a murderer was hired.

Baseball reports began to appear regularly, with scores such as 90 to 10.

A special reporter, "Vigo," was sent south on the political situation. It was reported that Georgia, Alabama and Mississippi would go Republican, as the Negro vote would predominate.

The Radicals in Congress passed a Reconstruction bill which the President vetoed and which was promptly passed over his veto. "Andrew Johnson now stands powerless before Congress," said the *Tribune* on July 21, "trembling in his sleep from apprehension of impeachment."

Settlement of the Gerrit Smith libel suit was announced on July 22. The original article in the *Tribune* was reprinted and it was admitted that Smith had suffered a true, not a feigned insanity, in 1859. The case was settled outside of court.

A *Tribune* reporter, on a junket to New York on the new "silver palace" car line, wrote a few verses about "silver dreams and silver streams and the beauties of sleeping in silver palace cars."

The first Tribune building, erected in 1869, after the newspaper had occupied four earlier homes, all rented. Constructed of Joliet marble, it was destroyed in the Chicago fire of 1871.

A column and a half was given on July 25 to Ralph Waldo Emerson's Phi Beta Kappa address at Harvard.

On July 26 two and a half columns went to the first baseball tournament, an upset when the Rockford team beat the Washington Nationals 29 to 23.

Editor Horace White had a "card" in the paper on July 26 explaining that he had been away when the Smith libel case was settled by a "quasi retraction," implying that while Smith loved John Brown he had no knowledge of the Harpers Ferry raid. White said that if he had been home the settlement would have been different, as he had personal knowledge and proof that Smith did have knowledge of the raid.

Baseball was well under way with 54 clubs organized into a state association. In Chicago the Nationals beat the Excelsiors 59 to 4, with immense interest displayed. The Tribune explained this further "upset" as follows:

"The Nationals are professional athletes. The catcher, Alsted, receives $1,500 a year besides what can be made by gambling. It is like a company of circus riders or Japanese acrobats. The Rockford victory was a confidence game, a defeat to win a pile. It is estimated that $20,000 changed hands on the game here. THE TRIBUNE was the only paper not deceived by this simulated defeat."

Elections in Tennessee were carried out under military protection for Negro voters and the Radicals won, it was reported on August 2. The *Tribune* said this was the first fruits of impartial suffrage in the South, that without the "blacks" Governor Brownlow would not have won.

A strike of coal miners was reported at La Salle. The *Tribune* was against the labor union and its methods, warning that order would be preserved and the union men swept away if they attempted to keep others from working. They looked upon the "honest, free laborer" as surrendering to lazy demagogues.

President Johnson asked for the resignation of Secretary

Stanton, who refused to give up his office. The *Tribune* said Stanton would be sustained by Congress and by the majority of the people.

A "lake monster," some sort of a "sea serpent," appeared among dog day stories in August. A vast monster, part fish and part serpent, was reported lashing the waves off Evanston.

Printers and journalists played ball on a west side lot, with the journalists winning 90 to 80. There were seven home runs. Medill played center field, City Editor Colbert third base, and critic Upton right field. A three-column report of the game on August 9 said that Colbert knocked the cover off one ball and that Upton "went to bat with cool nonchalance, smoking a cigar." Upton went to bed for two days after the game and in a letter to the editor said: "It is a game for Democrats and all your enemies, especially your tailor, and should be played when the snow is ten feet deep."

The miners' strike continued and the *Tribune* on August 11, 1867, said the remedy was in co-operatives rather than in unions.

Secretary Stanton was suspended by the President and Grant was made Secretary of War *ad interim*. Jefferson Davis was interviewed in his home in Montreal. The Sherman House was to extend on two 20-foot lots, it was reported on August 17. Twenty years before F. C. Sherman had sold the lots for $1,000 each and now paid $50,000 for the same property on repurchase.

Agitation began over a Sunday closing law. The Germans at a mass meeting resolved on "personal liberty." This was the cardinal point in their political activity. "We intend to enjoy the Sunday with our families in the usual way, and we intend to partake of that which a God more kind than the fanatic has vouchsafed to us," they resolved.

The *Tribune* said on temperance on August 18: "All the experiments that have been made in prohibition have failed to effect their object, though they have caused injury and riots and general contempt for the law wherever they have been tried."

A report was received from "an undiscovered country," the Black Hills of South Dakota. The Union Pacific railroad was moving west of Omaha at the rate of two or three miles a day.

The President removed General Sheridan from his command. The *Tribune* said on August 21: "The country has endured Andrew Johnson as long as endurance can be counted a virtue. There being reasons now in law as well as in fact, why he should be impeached and ejected from office, and rendered incapable of holding office hereafter, we hope that Congress will resolutely take hold of the work at the coming session and put him out." This was a reference to the Tenure of Office Act, under which it was necessary to get Senate approval before a cabinet officer could be removed.

The Cheyennes and Pawnees were at war in Colorado during August and the national labor convention decided that it was inexpedient to insist on eight hours of labor at present.

A building boom of the year had been injured by "the eight-hour fanaticism," the *Tribune* said on September 15, "but Chicago is now going ahead, trains and fleets crowded with rich products, labor everywhere busy, paved streets extending, miles of new sewerage, with new business blocks and new dwellings in all parts of the city."

Impeachment talk continued and the *Tribune* thought that Grant's sympathy with Congress had been fully shown.

Prison labor in Illinois was advertised for contract, particularly cigar and shoe makers.

"The issue between the President and the people," said the *Tribune* on September 19, "is whether the rebels shall govern the rebel states, to the exclusion of the entire loyal people, or whether the whole people, rebels and loyalists, shall have an equality of privilege at the polls."

Dwight L. Moody, president of the YMCA, appealed for

funds to help the organization, now grown to 2,000. The *Tribune* printed an illustration of the YMCA building at 148 Madison Street.

"The philosophy of the protective tariff is absurd," the *Tribune* said on September 21. The temperance debate continued. The *Tribune* on September 24 commented on "the mysterious purpose of God in putting materials for the making of alcohol into fruits and vegetables. How much better the world would have been if the Maine legislature had been in charge." On the question of wine and the Bible, the *Tribune* found that condemnation of wine was for intoxication and excess, not for the substance.

Questions of "the rights of ladies" began to be heard.

A lake shore avenue from the water works to Lincoln Park was proposed as "a commendable improvement" on October 3. A page-one story on pugilism appeared on October 6. This was a special dispatch covering a fight near Detroit between Davis and Gallagher. No first names were mentioned. The fight went 44 rounds with the stakes $500 a side. Davis won and a purse of $40 was made up for Gallagher. The fight was attended by a "large party of roughs," the story said.

Congressman Washburne started a boom for Grant for President in a speech at Galena in which he identified Grant with the Radicals. Copperhead gains were shown in state elections that month, but the *Tribune* said this would be reversed the next year, "when Grant leads the column."

The armistice between the *Tribune* and the *Times* was over, and the *Tribune* editors probably felt more comfortable in fighting the old Copperhead paper. "Some months ago," said the *Tribune* on October 11, "we received The Times into the Negro suffrage party at its own request and granted it absolution. Events prove we were in too much haste to baptize the new convert. It has backslidden and should have been put on probation for a year."

The Democrats of Chicago held a jubilee meeting in Court House Square on October 13. Among the speakers were S. S. Hayes and Dr. N. S. Davis. Dr. Davis said that during six years past "the hydra-head of intolerance and fanaticism had raised its bloody hand and had lacerated the country to its heart's core. Ten states have been placed under the iron heel of the military and now they aim to break down every vestige of constitutional rule. The Republicans intend to enslave the whites by the Negroes."

The victory of General Thomas O. Osborne, soldier candidate for county treasurer, against the "courthouse ring," was announced in the *Tribune* October 16. The *Tribune* again advocated direct voting against "the corrupt convention system and professional delegates."

An editorial excursion to the Rocky Mountains brought letters describing a buffalo hunt, a Pawnee war dance and a visit to the end of the Union Pacific near Julesburg, Colorado.

Another prize fight was reported on October 18. "One brute pounds another for the benefit of a gang of other brutes," said the *Tribune*. "There seems no way to stop it and the public is inclined to tolerate it." The fight was given 200 words while Unitarian and Presbyterian conventions, and an article on the power of prayer, were given several columns.

Edward P. Weston was to walk from Portland, Maine, to Chicago in a month for a wager of $10,000, "sure that God would guide him," it was reported on October 22, 1867.

Charles Dickens was to leave for the United States on November 9 for an extensive lecture tour.

Grant was reducing expenditures of the War Department at a rate of $5,000,000 a year.

The opera season opened in November. There was a big sale of camel hair shawls at the Ross and Gossage store. Charles Tobey advertised furniture at "immensely reduced prices." A good farm 80 miles southwest of Chicago was for sale at $25 an acre. In the local elections Chicago went

Republican. The Copperheads won in New York. The *Tribune* said this was due to Horace Greeley's "isms" and the liquor question. Court House Square was declared to be county property and the city was asked to move its offices. The *Tribune* on November 9 took up the fight to keep the City Hall on Court House Square.

The *Tribune* objected to the stories of the Associated Press correspondent in Richmond, characterizing them as "malignant inventions of a mourner for the lost cause." The editorial page pounded away against protective tariffs.

"THE TRIBUNE is for justice in national as in individual affairs," it said on November 15. "It wants no kings, nobles, priests, with their affectations of necessity and sanctity, with their robes, crowns, and incense—the protected classes of the old world. It wants no protected classes in our own country to rob all other classes by the operation of a law, of what they have gathered from their toil."

Commenting on the suggestion by the *New York Herald* of Chase for President, the *Tribune* said on November 16: "The people want Chase to remain at the head of the judiciary, while they also intend to obtain the services of General Grant at the head of the executive department of the government. The people know what they want and their will is the supreme law of the land and must be obeyed."

Three columns were devoted to a prize fight in Lake County, Indiana, on November 20. The *Tribune* suggested that the sheriff of the county deputize and arm a body of men and arrest all who came to see the next fight, and fine them. "Let the next legislature make prize fighting punishable as a crime," said the *Tribune*. "Anything is preferable to barbarism growing up among us."

The exploits of Weston, the walker, became first-page news on November 22. His progress from then on was featured day by day.

Susan B. Anthony talked on suffrage at the Opera House.

Boston was excited over the arrival of Dickens. On the temperance question, the *Tribune* said on November 23: "Some would invoke force to compel men to practice total abstinence from all stimulants. They would invoke the arm of the law to crowd ideas on those who reject them. They seem to forget that freedom is as vital to morality as to pure religion."

A Grant Club was formed in Chicago with General T. O. Osborne as president. Medill was one of the vice-presidents.

A true history of Chicago, a *Tribune* writer said on November 25, would include such a story as the death of a Michigan citizen, a wealthy lumber man, in a Wells Street brothel after debauchery with a woman.

A majority of the House Judiciary Committee reported on November 27, 1867 for the impeachment of the President for high crimes and misdemeanors. There were 22 specifications, with the general charge usurpation of power. The *Tribune* said the charges were all inferential and circumstantial, strained and threadbare, and did not necessarily show a legal guilt.

Weston made a triumphal entry into Chicago on November 30. Reporters rode beside him on horses. He had walked 1,326 miles in 26 days. He appeared in the Opera House where the Mayor welcomed him. The *Tribune* had four columns on the event.

In answer to a letter complaining that there was no paper on Thanksgiving and mentioning the *New York Herald*, the *Tribune* said on December 1: "The selfish barbarism of Old Satanic of New York affords no precedent for THE TRIBUNE to follow, nor is Chicago a godless corrupt, Copperhead city like New York."

The *Tribune* objected on December 2 to the inclusion of Latin and Greek in the "Illinois Industrial University" at Champaign, the slighting of mathematics and the non-inclusion of chemistry. This sort of a curriculum "breeds charlatans and fools," it was stated.

New subscriptions, it was reported on December 6, " come pouring in with a rapidity unparalleled in the history of THE TRIBUNE. A dozen years ago the circulation was confined almost to Illinois. Now it goes into every state and some counties take more than the entire edition of the 1855 weekly. We commence the new year with between 40,000 and 50,000 weekly circulation, 8 to 10 thousand tri-weekly and a daily larger than at any period since the abatement of the war excitement. THE CHICAGO TRIBUNE is now recognized as the leading exponent of Republican principles in the United States."

An eleven-column report by an investigating committee on conditions in the state insane asylum, showing much brutality, was printed on December 7, 1867.

Impeachment was defeated in the House by a vote of 108 to 57. The *Tribune* said on December 9 that Congress had done well. "A source of mischief falls to the ground."

Chicago was to get the Republican national convention on May 20, it was reported on December 12. Letters were printed commenting on the fate of Dr. David Livingstone, lost in Africa. Whittier's recently published *Snow-bound*, was printed in the December 13 issue. There were reports of an expedition to "Russian America." An editorial on qualifications for the presidency gave specifications which exactly fitted Grant.

The annual prospectus printed on December 21, stated:

"A most important presidential election approaches, and it must be decided whether the loyal party, which put down the rebellion and saved the Union, shall administer the government or whether the destinies of the Union shall be allowed to pass into the hands of those who openly or covertly sought to destroy it, and who now, with the aid of an apostate executive, seek to elevate Treason above Loyalty. Oligarchy above Liberty, Secession above Union and Repudiation above National Faith.

"By increasing the circulation of THE CHICAGO TRIBUNE, its influence for good will be enlarged and the cause of equal rights and pure administration promoted. It is the only daily paper in Chicago which possesses the honesty and independence to fearlessly attack 'rings' and monopolies and corrupt schemes for robbing taxpayers through the machinery of state or national legislation. THE TRIBUNE advocates strict economy in the expenditures of public money and the lightest taxation which the maintenance of government will permit."

Ralph Waldo Emerson lectured on country life at the YMCA.

The statistics which were printed at the end of the year showed 417 fires during the year, 2,000 liquor licenses, an estimated population of 220,000, 30 suicides, 200 divorces, 9,000 additional buildings, 5 miles of wooden block pavement built.

Chapter Six

JOHNSON IMPEACHMENT FAILS

THE IMPEACHMENT trial of President Johnson and the election of General Grant to succeed him were the big news events of 1868. While demanding the impeachment of Johnson after Secretary Stanton had been removed from office, the *Tribune* decided later that the charges had not been legally proved and anticipated the failure of this partisan effort to get rid of a President. The Republican senators who refused to vote against Johnson were not condemned by the *Tribune*, Senator

Lyman Trumbull, in particular, being praised for his courage.

The Grant and Colfax ticket was backed by the *Tribune* with its customary vigor. The campaign weekly, issued at special rates, went into 100,000 homes of the Northwest, frankly partisan, calling upon the people to rally once more to the old flag and defeat the enemies of the Republic. Democracy and treason were synonomous terms. Irish Republicans were fine people, Irish Democrats unspeakable. Another civil war was pictured if the Democrats won. Horatio Seymour was a traitor to his country. In the opinion of Dr. N. S. Davis, leading Chicago Democrat, Seymour was a great patriot.

Negro suffrage, which had been established by Congressional legislation in eight Southern states, brought "glorious Republican victories," and it also brought the Ku Klux Klan. It was a year of struggle and bitterness, and Grant's simple message, "Let us have peace," probably appealed to the people more than anything else.

During the early part of this year City Editor Elias Colbert was made commercial editor and Samuel Medill, brother of Joseph, was moved to the city desk. Joseph Medill, then in Washington, wrote "Brother Sammy" as follows:

"You will find the head of the City Dept. of THE TRIBUNE a pretty hard post to fill. Your predecessor is a very able man, of varied learning and ripe experience, a fine scholar, quick-witted, and a writer of extraordinary rapidity, to say nothing of his short-hand accomplishments. . . . If you are to undertake to discharge his duties you will have to labor and study a good deal harder than you have ever done before."

The *Tribune* opened the year as follows:

"The year whose commencement is welcomed today will witness the election of a President of the United States, to succeed the miserable ingrate who now fills the chair. In the perils that environ the nation, the threats of repudiation, restoration of rebel rule in the rebel states, and consequent anarchy, disunion and ruin, there never was an occasion when we so much needed a President uniting in his own person an inflexible integrity and a personal courage that will not be deterred from duty by any contingency. The nation possesses but one man who possesses all the requisites of a President fit for the present great emergency. The American people in all sections of the country have but one choice for that office, and all look to the great hero of the war to lead the country as successfully through the civil strife in which it is involved."

Publication of the military history of Grant by General Badeau was begun on January 7, 1868.

The police arrested the spectators at a pugilistic exhibition at Uhlich's Hall. This meant the decline of pugilism to the *Tribune* editor.

The burning of Farwell Hall on Madison Street, housing the YMCA and many stores, was reported on January 8. It had been intended to hold the national convention there in May.

An investigation of the police force on charges of bribery and extortion was begun on January 9. One question was whether a Wells Street den, "Under the Willow," had paid protection money to the police. The *Tribune* gave daily reports of the investigation, with detailed testimony. As reporters had been excluded, it was thought that a reporter for the *Tribune* was secreted in an adjoining room, and a carpenter was called to board the crevices and stuff every aperture through which sound could travel. The reports, however, continued, both the *Tribune* and the *Times* carrying accounts of the investigation.

Carrie Watson, owner of the brothel, denied she had ever given money to the police. She said she had given them information and had helped buy a horse and buggy for one officer. Carrie was asked if any aldermen ever had been in her house.

She laughed and said she would never answer that question, even if confined in the lowest dungeon.

A brilliant charity ball in the Opera House exceeded anything of the kind in the history of the city, according to the *Tribune* of January 21. A band from Boston played and dress, decorations and banquet were described in great detail. Medill was a member of the invitations committee.

It was chronicled on January 23 that 59 firms in the city had done a business of over a million dollars each and 14 firms had exceeded two millions. The business of Field, Leiter & Company totaled $12,365,786. Chicago was the fifth city in business in the country.

A fire on January 29 caused the destruction of three blocks on Lake Street, a $2,000,000 loss. The *Tribune* called for a better system of constructing buildings, said the buildings should be lower with thicker walls.

Although reporters were finally admitted to the police investigation it fizzled out after the manner of such things.

The Alaskan expedition made a report on that country, purchase of which was being considered. "No white man will ever live there," said the *Tribune* on February 5, describing this land of rain and snow with its "miserable population." "All we purchase is the privilege of being responsible for the degradation and bestiality of the native Esquimaux."

In an article on February 6 on why Charles Dickens should extend his American visit to Chicago, the *Tribune* said that his brother, Augustus N. Dickens, lived here for 15 years, died in poverty and his body was in an unmarked grave here.

A four-column description was given of graduating ceremonies of 116 students at Rush Medical School. It was reported that 3,500 persons were on poor relief in the city.

"A new and terrible despotism" had risen in the South, the *Tribune* said on February 12, telling of the cowardly operations of the Ku Klux Klan, when Negro school houses were burned in Tennessee.

Thaddeus Stevens was moving for impeachment in Congress. "Aurora" wrote of a winter in Florida. "Peregrine Pickle" had recovered from an illness and had resumed his column.

The *Tribune* challenged the *Times* on February 19 to say when it had ever charged Grant with drunkenness. Johnson again removed Stanton from office and appointed General Lorenzo Thomas as Secretary of War. The *Tribune* made the point that the commission had been issued to Thomas before the appointment had been confirmed by the Senate. The question of the violation of the Tenure of Office Act arose and Congress had Thomas arrested and barred from his office. An impeachment resolution was carried in the House by a vote of 126 to 47. The President sent the nomination of Thomas Ewing as Secretary of War, explaining that he did not mean any violation of the law in the Thomas case.

"Too late," said the *Tribune* on February 25, "The lion's skin is already off and the animal of long ears stands trembling under the lash. The American people impeach you, Andrew Johnson, as the disturber of the national peace, the violator of national law, the stumbling block of national justice and the organizer of national ruin. He must be cast out. There is no good in him."

The Chicago city council passed an impeachment resolution 20 to 4, declaring: "Let the usurper and traitor be impeached in order that free America shall no longer tolerate a would-be dictator." A public meeting was called to ratify the impeachment. There was a demonstration at Library Hall, on which the *Tribune* printed six columns on February 26. An extra edition of the paper was printed, which was soon exhausted. Impeachment was the talk of the town.

The impeachment must stand or fall, the *Tribune* said on February 28, solely on Johnson's guilt or innocence of a violation of the Constitution in the removal of Stanton and the appointment of Thomas. "It is a party movement. It is a continuation of the struggle against the slaveholders' rebellion.

75

Johnson has taken the place of Jeff Davis. Impeachment is a hopeful sign of the times."

A great snow storm blotted out the impeachment news from the paper for a few days. Alderman Comiskey of the Eighth ward fell into a row with the *Tribune* over the police investigation, which had been a failure. The *Tribune* admitted that the investigation resolution had been drawn in the *Tribune* office and said that the alderman had made a failure of the investigation and that was that.

Japan opened new ports to foreign trade, it was announced on March 7. The state university opened at Champaign. Attorney General Henry Stanberry resigned to take up the defense of the President, William M. Evarts succeeding him. The impeachment trial opened formally on March 14 with Chief Justice Chase in the chair.

A story was printed on March 19 of the widow of Dickens' brother, who had been found in poor circumstances and ill on North Clark Street. Dickens had sent no money to her and declined correspondence, it was stated.

Delay in the impeachment trial brought it late in the month. The *Tribune* said there was no chance for Johnson to escape. The trial was opened on the 30th by Congressman Ben Butler. The *Tribune* suggested at this time that Senator Yates resign his seat because of his intemperate habits. He had taken the pledge but had been unable to live up to it, it was stated. He had been absent for weeks and during the impeachment proceedings.

Twenty-three states elected delegates to the Chicago convention. The *Tribune* said they had all pronounced for Grant, who was certain to be nominated by acclamation.

Chief Justice Chase was criticized in the *Tribune* of April 1 for his assumption of power in deciding questions of law at the opening of the impeachment trial. His "arrogance" as a member of Lincoln's cabinet was spoken of, and how Lincoln forgave him many things.

"The American people," said the *Tribune*, "will not overlook any fractiousness in the Chief Justice having for its end either gratification of spleen or the shielding of the culprit on trial for high crimes and misdemeanors."

Two columns were carried on the trial in the April 2 issue and the *Tribune* took back some of what it had said about Chase's assumption of power. It was admitted that this was an "error," but they were still "watchful" of him.

There had been 147 arrests for fast driving during the year, it was reported on April 3.

At the opening of the impeachment defense on April 6 the *Tribune* said the case had been clearly proved and "Johnson may be en route to Greenville, Tennessee, in a few weeks."

The Republicans opened an organizing campaign in Chicago. Grant Clubs were being formed. "The eyes of the entire Union are now on the Garden City," said the *Tribune*. "As goes Chicago, so goes the nation."

Field, Leiter & Company advertised a spring opening with Paris novelties in silk and cotton garments.

The Vice-Presidential nomination seemed to be narrowing to Schuyler Colfax and Ben Wade. The *Tribune* was for Colfax, "because of his unwavering devotion to anti-slavery." The test of Republican strength in the city was placed in the nomination of General Robert W. Smith for recorder.

Copperheads were in glee, the *Tribune* reported on April 15, over the reports of the Republican senators who were going to vote against impeachment. It was a mistake, the *Tribune* said, to put in any but the first article of impeachment, "but no Republican senator is going to spend the remainder of his days in oblivion."

"Glorious Republican victories" were reported in South Carolina and Louisiana during April, and at the same time Ku Klux outrages were growing.

The impeachment case testimony was closed on April 21 and the next day Republican aldermen were elected in ten of

the 16 wards. The Democratic candidate for Recorder, however, won and the *Tribune* said this was a lesson not to be
lost. "A shiver of this kind will do the Republicans good."
The Democrats, the *Tribune* charged, had stolen 2,000 votes
by the use of illegal naturalization papers.

On April 27 the *Tribune* attacked the aldermanic ring
which dictated the selection of school books and in succeeding days put the Board of Education on the spot for its votes
on this issue.

The *Campaign Tribune*, it was announced, would be issued
from May until election day, and a verbatim report would be
published of convention proceedings.

"The principal issue of the campaign," said the *Tribune*
on April 29, "will relate to the Reconstruction policy of
Congress as opposed to that of Andrew Johnson and the
Democratic party. The Republican party holds that in the
creation of new governments in the seceding states, both
public and private safety require that all citizens enjoy equal
rights. Andrew Johnson and the Democratic party hold that
a monopoly of political rights and privileges should be conferred upon conquered traitors, and that opportunity should
be given them through the instrumentality of local laws, to
wreak vengeance on the loyal portion of the community,
both whites and blacks, and even reduce the latter to slavery
again.

"The policy of Congress has achieved an important triumph by the adoption of constitutions, in six of the seceding
states, based on impartial suffrage. It will be the aim of the
Republican party, under the leadership of Gen. U. S. Grant,
to carry forward the work so auspiciously begun. THE
CHICAGO TRIBUNE is opposed to repudiation in every
form and is in favor of those measures only which shall tend
to lift up the public credit and improve the value and purchasing power of the currency."

A resolution in the school board to abolish corporal punish-

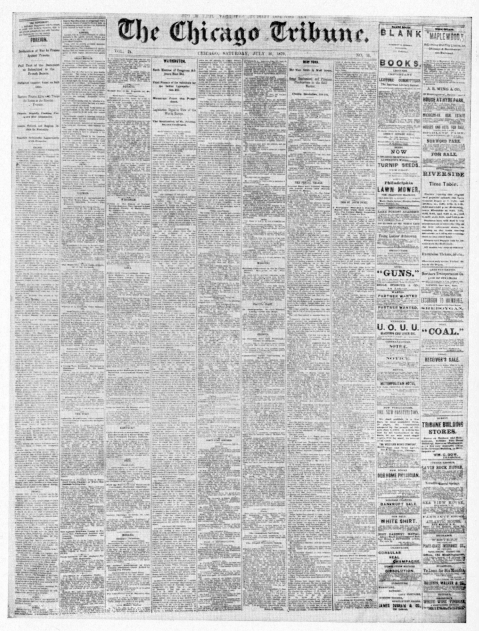

Largest armed struggle following the American Civil War was the conflict between France and Prussia which began in 1870. The Tribune broke the news of this event in a single column in its issue of July 16.

ment for children under 10, and that no punishment could be inflicted except by the principal, was defeated in committee.

The Washington correspondent who signed his articles "Nix," wrote on April 30 that Andrew Johnson's moving day was close at hand as conviction was certain. Johnson was having his residence in Greenville put into repair, it was reported by this correspondent on May 4. On May 6, however, the *Tribune* editors, being apparently better informed, wrote of the probable failure of the impeachment. They blamed in part the efforts of Ben Wade and the "eastern ring" to force a new tariff on Congress.

"No matter what personal antipathy senators may feel toward Wade," said the *Tribune* of May 7, "they have a solemn duty to perform — punish a wilful and malicious violation of law. If the President is not amenable to law he is an emperor, a despot."

General John M. Palmer was nominated for governor at the Republican convention at Peoria. A new correspondent, "Gath," wrote from Washington.

Senator Trumbull was against impeachment, it was reported on May 12 and conviction was improbable. Thirty-six votes were necessary to convict.

"Johnson's legal guilt was not made out according to the satisfaction of a majority of the Senate," said the *Tribune* on May 12. "Far better his acquittal than his conviction upon grounds that might be condemned by the next generation. We do not propose to put the Republican party in liquidation because the Senate votes to leave Andrew Johnson in the White House ten months longer. We have too vivid a recollection of Bull Run to join in a stampede of panic stricken journals and politicians merely because we have lost a battle. Nor shall we join in crucifying any Republican senator of previously good repute who takes upon himself the penalties of martyrdom rather than do violence to his own conscience."

The Grant Club of Chicago at an executive meeting passed a resolution that the Republicans of Chicago without a dissenting voice should demand the conviction of Johnson. This was evidently aimed at Senator Trumbull. The *Tribune* said on May 15, 1868:

"Those who demand that Trumbull should vote for conviction whether he believed Johnson guilty or not, ought rather to thank God that they have a senator who has the high courage and manliness to go through the Red Sea of obloquy and odium for conscience sake. One thing is certain, the Republican party cannot carry the next election on a verdict obtained by coercion and terrorism. It cannot carry any election at any future time on such a record."

Delegates began arriving on May 16 for the national convention which was to be held in the Opera House. A thousand members of the press were expected.

Failure of the Johnson impeachment was reported on May 18. The *Tribune* said it was of no importance and attacked those who would turn aside from the election of Grant to score the Republican senators. "Let the constituents of these senators try them, not the Republican convention." The *Tribune* printed in full the speeches made in secret session by Henry Wilson for conviction and by Senator Trumbull for acquittal.

The Illinois State Republican platform was printed at the top of the editorial page on May 19. Soldiers and sailors were holding a convention at Turner Hall. The *Tribune* on May 20 advised against impeachment action by the convention and against Wade for Vice-President. The soldiers and sailors voted for Grant and denounced those who voted against impeachment.

The opening of the national convention was reported on May 21, 1868. Grant narrowly escaped nomination by acclamation before the committee on credentials reported. Carl Schurz was made temporary chairman. The *Tribune's* first page was nearly filled with advertising and the convention was given the second and third pages.

Grant and Colfax, the ticket backed by the *Tribune*, were reported as nominated on May 22. The platform, too, was along the lines advocated by the *Tribune*, including equal rights, impartial suffrage, national integrity and retrenchment and reduction of taxation. An extra page was printed on the convention news and ratification meetings were held in the city.

"Never since the Republican party was organized has the response of the country to a presidential ticket been so cheering, so enthusiastic, so unanimous," said the *Tribune* on May 25. "Four years ago the Republicans were not waked up until the first of August, when the Copperhead national convention met and declared the war to have been a failure. This year, if we are wise, we shall have our organization perfected and put in thorough working order before our enemies shall have got out of their muddle and selected their candidate. We have only to beat this hide-bound, reactionary, repudiating, rebel-sympathizing party once more to beat the life out of it."

The Republican national platform, a half column of small type, was printed on the editorial page on May 26. Under the head of city improvements the new *Tribune* building at Dearborn and Madison Streets was described. It was to be strictly fireproof, of stone and brick and iron. There were to be four stories above the basement, with stores and a court. The press room in the basement was to have two eight-cylinder presses. It was soon to be ready for occupancy and the cost was $175,000, outside of the two presses ordered.

The *Journal* said that the *Tribune* had demanded the removal of Grant during the siege of Vicksburg and the *Tribune* offered its files to prove this was "one of Joe Forrest's yarns."

The death of former President James Buchanan was reported

on June 2. "Fortunately he is the last of his race," said the unforgiving *Tribune*. "No son or daughter is doomed to acknowledge an ancestry from him."

In comment on New York speculation as to Chase for presidential candidate, the *Tribune* said he would be the poorest candidate they could take. They spoke of his consuming passion to be President and said he was most unpopular with the masses.

Three columns of names of leading income taxpayers and amounts were printed on June 9. These included William Bross, $35,710; Alfred Cowles, $45,996; Medill, $41,871. The incomes were chiefly under $5,000. Dwight L. Moody reported $1,500. Fred Lehmann's was $116,212.

The gravel toll road between Rosehill and Evanston was so poor that the supervisors recommended that it be free.

Negro suffrage had been established in eight of the rebel states, the *Tribune* reported on June 12 and was soon to be established in three more, "making eleven states in which freedom and manhood have been made the standard of political right instead of complexion. It has been accepted by the democracy. The political cry of white man's government is now an absurdity."

The North American Sængerbund held a great songfest in Chicago that month. The Old Settlers in Libertyville had a celebration. Rockford and Philadelphia played baseball, with the result 94 to 13 in favor of the Phillies. The life boat *Little Western*, capsized with reporters for the *Tribune* and other newspapers on board. Henry Chisholm of the *Times* was drowned. The American Association for the Advancement of Science was to meet in Chicago on August 5.

The *Madison Journal* attacked the *Tribune* for its tariff stand. The *Tribune* replied: "We have been informed by the high tariff gentry themselves, that but for the opposition of THE CHICAGO TRIBUNE they would have passed the bill that was defeated in March 1867 — a bill which would

have done the Republican party more harm than all the newspapers could have repaired."

The Democratic national convention got under way at the
new Tammany Hall in New York on July 6, with Horatio
Seymour the chairman. Thirty-six planks were submitted.
The *Tribune* on July 7 carried six columns on the convention
on the first page. The Democrats declared in favor of paying
bonds with greenbacks. "The George H. Pendleton crowd,"
said the *Tribune* reporter, seemed to have things their own
way in "betting, swearing, and drinking to their favorite,"
but there was no leader for the nomination. Chase approved
the platform adopted and his name came up for the balloting.
Seymour was finally chosen on the 22nd ballot, with Frank
P. Blair for Vice-President. The *Tribune* found the only
consolation in this that it meant the end of "Pendletonism."
Chase got four votes.

"Seymour has been a traducer of this government even
while the enemy's cannon could almost be heard in the borders
of his own state," said the *Tribune* on July 9. "He was for
dissolution of the Union and reorganization under the Democratic auspices with slavery included. He called the New
York draft rioters 'my friends.' Blair has been against the
reconstruction act of Congress."

The platforms of both parties were printed in one column
of small type on July 11. The national convention of plasterers
in Chicago asked support for an eight-hour day.

"The power of the nation," said the *Tribune* on July 16,
"the existence and authority of the nation, underlies all the
issues. The restoration of the Democrats to power in Washington means a total surrender of the principles for which the
war was fought. Unless the people intend to fight the war
over again within a generation they will take good care to
keep the Democratic party as helpless as the confederacy."

In Chicago the Democrats held a ratification meeting. S. S.
Hayes and Dr. N. S. Davis were among the speakers. "We

have come to ratify the nomination of one whose record was pure," said Dr. Davis, "one who was truly loyal during the war and whose name will ever live as one of the noblest patriots in the country." The Radical policy of "keeping the military in the South and supporting lazy niggers" was condemned.

"Gath" went to Utica to write a story of Seymour at home. "Familiar glimpses of the little joker and his game," was the heading.

The *Chicago Weekly Tribune* was offered for 25 cents until the end of the campaign. The question arose on July 24 as to whether Seymour would accept the greenback interpretation of the platform.

On July 27 the *Tribune* described a Lake View picnic of the Democrats. Included, it was said, were ten reporters, 75 bartenders, and 150 prostitutes. "It was a scene of debauchery. The devil loves his disciples. The girls danced the can-can, howled and rolled on the floor." The moral of the story was that a Democratic picnic without Germans ran to riot, that Germans did not attend Democratic picnics.

Schuyler Colfax visited Chicago and was welcomed at a reception at the home of Lieutenant Governor Bross on July 30, 1868.

Seymour was reported to be willing to pay the 5–20 government bonds in gold, through taxation. A *Tribune* reporter visited Blair's home in St. Louis and concluded that Blair had made Missouri safe for Grant. "Let us have peace," an expression in Grant's brief letter of acceptance became the Republican watchword of the campaign.

The *Tribune* in August announced that in its opinion the voters were presented with a choice between peace and prosperity under General Grant or civil war and national dishonor under Seymour. The Democrats played up "military dictatorship" under Grant and the Republicans played up Southern outrages.

Chicago sought the mechanical branch of the state industrial college, and offered $550,000 to help build it.

The national gathering of scientists took place at Library Hall, with Professor B. A. Gould of Cambridge observatory presiding. The *Tribune* printed four columns of the proceedings. A convention of women, described as "strongminded," met at Crosby Hall at the same time, resolving against the press publishing accounts of prize fights, and for a dual presidency of a man and a woman. These were "progressive nuts" to the *Tribune* reporter.

Grant was given a first-page story on the occasion of a visit to his Galena home, where he made a ten-line speech.

Daily editorials on the campaign kept it boiling. Tanner Clubs, as the Grant Clubs were called, were organized. A ratification meeting for Grant and Colfax was called for the night of August 12 in Court House Square. "Chicago sends assurance," said the *Tribune* after this meeting, "that this city will give Grant and Colfax in November a majority such as no candidate has received in a previous election. The shout will be heard in every rebel camp from Utica to the Rio Grande."

The last hours of Thaddeus Stevens were recorded in this issue. He was praised for his honesty and fidelity. Ten columns on the back page were necessary to describe the Grant meeting, attended, it was said, by not less than 60,000. There was a torchlight procession of Tanner Clubs, tanners dressed in blue, tanners stepping on Copperhead snakes, etc. The Tanners' Corps took the place of the Wide Awakes of 1860.

A survey of new buildings on August 18 showed 8,000 in the course of erection, including The First National Bank, Potter Palmer's "palace" and Trinity Methodist Episcopal Church.

The Board of Health reported on the mortality among milch cows in the 5th ward. A report was published from an English journal on August 24 that Alfred Nobel, a manufacturer of nitro-glycerine, had introduced to the public a modified form of that explosive to which the name of dynamite had been given.

The Paris velocipede was introduced to the "fashionable denizens" of Wabash and Michigan Avenues.

On August 29 the Tanner organizations serenaded Grant at the home of his brother, O. L. Grant, at 923 Wabash Avenue. Grant appeared before a crowd of 15,000, abashed. N. B. Judd and J. Y. Scammon talked for him.

"Annihilation of time and space" was hailed on September 1 with the dispatch of a letter from San Francisco to Chicago in ten days.

Thomas Hoyne complained, according to the *Tribune*, that he had "the heel of a Negro at his throat." "It would be a rash darkey," the paper commented, "who attempted to shut off all Tom's wind."

The *Weekly Tribune* was going at a rapid rate, it was reported, with an estimated circulation of 80,000 to 100,000.

A twenty-page campaign document on the financial issue of the campaign was issued by the *Tribune* on September 5, The Republican Tanners, "Grant's Boys," marched 7,000 strong in parade. "They were all young and able bodied voters," said the *Tribune* report of the parade. "No children, drunkards, vagrants, fraudulent voters," as in Democratic parades.

Major W. H. Powell's expedition to the Colorado River was given special attention this month. On September 15 a 23,000 Republican majority in Maine gave joy to the *Tribune*. This was considered assurance that Grant would carry every state that Lincoln carried four years before. "Grant, Colfax and Peace," was the slogan.

An Irish Republican mass meeting was held in the city. The Irish Republicans were highly respectable, according to the campaign views of the *Tribune*. Not so with the Irish Democrats.

A torchlight rally was held on the night of September 23. The *Tribune* broke into verse, quoting:

> *Come, boys in blue, ye brave and true,*
> *In Freedom's periled hour,*
> *To vote or fight for truth and right,*
> *Let traitors feel your power.*

"Higher and higher rises the swelling tide of Republican success. It was the greatest demonstration in political history. Adjectives fail."

A Democratic meeting was referred to as "the inconsistency of the unwashed." On September 28 the *Tribune* asserted: "Treason and Democracy — one and indivisible." And on September 30 it stated: "The issue of this campaign is whether the Negro would have pay for his work or not — greenbacks or the lash."

The *Tribune* became more and more confident of the election of Grant. "The financial policy of the Democratic party," it said on October 6, "would ruin the United States government just as it ruined the Confederate government and those who are clamoring for it are rebels at heart and desire the overthrow of the Union, the restoration of the Confederacy and the establishment of slavery."

"This is the continuation of a struggle as old as the world, between power and privilege on the one hand and humanity on the other. The central idea of the Republican party is equality of rights and privileges," commented the *Tribune* on October 10, 1868.

In a Democratic torchlight procession, reported October 12, the *Tribune* said 4,500 were in line, a "pro-slavery procession, non-American." The opposition referred to as "the Democratic Ku-Klux organ," said 15,000 were in line. "Down with the bloated bond holders," said the Democratic banners.

The opening of Potter Palmer's "new marble palace" at

State and Washington Streets was described on October 13. "It was an assemblage of wealth, beauty and fashion. Long lines of carriages were filled with the cream of the avenue," the *Tribune* said. Palmer's life was reviewed and he was praised for his work in building Chicago. There was a column on the retail goods displayed by Field, Leiter & Company.

Republican victories were reported on October 14 in Pennsylvania, Ohio, and Indiana. The election of Grant was settled, according to the *Tribune*, which said in response to the *Times*, still talking of a Democratic victory: "Nothing but a blow on the head from a pile driver will knock the absurd conceit out of these thick headed dolts, and that blow they will get on the third of November."

The Democrats, in a flurry, talked of substituting Chase for Seymour. Chase would not run, however, except as an independent. A Frank Blair meeting in Chicago on October 22 was called a "humiliating fizzle." "Seymour on the stump, deserts Democratic platform," was the political heading of October 23. In an article on the Chicago Democracy on October 30, the *Tribune* said:

"A true Democrat is never so delighted as when he has one hand upon your throat and the other in your pocket. Brought forth in sin, baptized in ignorance, cradled in dirt and swathed in rags, the great majority of the self-styled Democrats of Chicago come forth from their foul abodes full fledged to prey upon the better portion of society, sometimes to do a little honest work in our tunnels and canals, to vote, to nominate themselves by universal acclamation as candidates for the Bridewell and state prison, and to give our good natured police functionaries all the trouble they can. That is Chicago Democracy! "

Twenty thousand Tanners were in line of march on October 30. Grant's letters and speeches were printed. He had not taken the stump.

"Let every man who values the blood already shed for

the Union be at his post next Tuesday," said the *Tribune* of November 2. "The fate of the Republic is in issue. Whether the country shall go on in the paths of equal rights traced in the Declaration of Independence to the pinnacle of human glory or turn back into the thorny ways of caste, privilege, aristocracy, monopoly, slavery, civil war, must be decided now. Once more into the breach, dear friends."

"The great victory" was announced November 4. Grant and Colfax had carried 202 electoral votes out of 294. Chicago's Republican majority was 5,170. "The end of the rebellion has been reached at last," said the *Tribune*. "The Klan can now cease their infernal work or expect a sudden visitation of the halter. The reconstruction law of Congress will not be tramped in the dust at present. All is well. Thanks be to God who giveth the victory."

The *Tribune* during the year 1868 was partly responsible for changes in the new federal naturalization law. Chicago had become a great center for the foreign born. After 1850 one half of its population was made up of these naturalized immigrants, chiefly Irish and German. In 1860 the German immigrants comprised 20 per cent of the population. A bill before Congress in 1868 was objected to by the *Tribune*, and its passage blocked, because it did not provide protection for naturalized American citizens abroad. The *Tribune* insisted that a naturalized American citizen had all the rights of any American citizen and could not be held for military service to a foreign monarch. An amended bill was passed giving these citizens the same rights as the native born.

Chapter Seven

MEDILL'S ADVICE TO NEWSPAPERS

THE OPENING of the Grant administration in 1869 did not bring the promised peace, although all talk of civil war was ended. National prohibition, woman suffrage, the extension of suffrage to Negroes under the Fifteenth Amendment, gold scandals, and a controversy between religion and science, enlivened the columns of the *Tribune* during this period.

New discoveries in geology led to the abandonment of the old theological view of the age of the earth and precipitated a general airing of religious beliefs which could not be supported by science. At this time and later the *Tribune*, which was accused of having a Unitarian cast, gave comfort to the scientific outlook, leading toward modernism or liberalism in religion. The new truths of science, it was held, must be squared with religion. William Bross had spent years in trying to reconcile scientific and religious truths, and the *Tribune* was well prepared to lead the thought of the people in this great controversy.

The *Tribune* moved to its new quarters at Madison and Dearborn Streets during the year, and proudly told the world the wonders of its first home built by itself. The Union Pacific railroad was completed, the golden spike driven and a new era of prosperity was predicted for Chicago.

Leaders of the woman suffrage movement descended upon Chicago. If Negroes could vote, why not the women? The *Tribune* said that when women really wanted suffrage they would get it, but that time had not yet come. They advised women to be happy in their own "sphere," where they held the greatest power on earth.

The *Tribune* criticized President Grant freely but on the whole found the early part of his administration satisfactory. They were slow to blame him for the scandals following the gold conspiracy in Wall Street, and always held that he was more sinned against than sinning in this and other scandals growing out of his appointments and associations.

The *Tribune* sales of November 4, 1868, were reported at 42,240. The Grant victory grew as the returns piled up, with Illinois going Republican by 60,000.

Grant at Washington was taking things quietly and coolly, it was reported on November 10, with office seekers already swarming into town.

The *Tribune* welcomed the Western Social Science Association, a new organization. The eight-hour system of labor was reported not a huge success, as the extra hours of labor were not used in reading but in whisky drinking. The Relief and Aid Society had spent $30,791 during the year in aiding 1,363 families.

"The election of Grant means peace," said the *Tribune* on November 11. "And that peace means the finality of the reconstruction measures and the establishment in the recently rebellious states of the civil and political equality of all freemen." The Democrats in the meantime were building on Grant's supposed conservatism.

Pugilism and billiards made page one on November 13.

The *Tribune* urged an amendment to the Constitution on political equality of all American citizens, one that should be irrepealable by the states.

The new building of the Chicago Historical Society at Dearborn and Ontario Streets was dedicated on November 20. There was much activity in theater and opera circles.

The Washington "vultures" intended to make a raid on the

treasury this winter, it was reported on November 23. "This winter furnishes the last chance of the ring and the rascals to plunder the treasury for at least four years to come."

Grant maintained his silence on all political questions.

On December 7 the *Tribune* said in a first-page advertisment that it was the best paper published in the United States. It was among the first papers, it was recalled, to hoist the names of Grant and Colfax. "It was the first in the West to confront and denounce schemes for repudiating the national debt recently put forward under various disguises. It challenges any journal in the accuracy of our predictions and the truthfulness of our conclusions on questions of public interest. It challenges comparison in the character and quality of the original matter in its columns.

"It advocates the cause of the people as opposed to monopolies, rings and swindling combinations of all kinds. It has no alliance apart from those of the great public."

President Johnson's message was printed in full on December 10, although it was declared to be "the worst ever given to Congress by anybody."

A description of the pork packing industry, in which it was said that Chicago now led the world, was given on December 11, 1868.

The religious world was shaken by new discoveries in geology, relating to the age of the earth. A national prohibition party was organized.

The Rev. T. M. Eddy of the Indiana Avenue Methodist Episcopal Church, preaching on the religious tone of the *Tribune*, found it of Unitarian cast, according to a report of December 14. The *Tribune* said it "does not know what this is and does not care. It treats all isms alike and thinks of each with respect."

Of the *Tribune*, Eddy said: "It is strong, both financially and in editorial brain, bold, daring to audacity, radical, saying what it has to say in unmistakable Saxon. It moulds the sentiment of the Northwest to an extent scarcely equalled by any other single power."

The ministerial union discussed the *Tribune* and the controversy it had started over science and theology. Christianity was the great fact, it was stated, geology only a hypothesis.

The Boston correspondent reviewed Browning's new work, *The Ring and the Book.*

The Western armies held a grand reunion in Chicago, with Grant, Sherman and other generals present. "With the rising of the sun today," said a *Tribune* writer on December 15, "an event is inaugurated that will transcend in eclat and glory any meeting of men in the world's history."

Lieutenant Governor Bross gave a reception to the generals and their staffs at his home at 202 Michigan Avenue. Medill and White were among the guests, also Dr. Ray, now of the *Evening Post.* A grand banquet was given on December 16 by the Chamber of Commerce. A general consolidation of the army societies was said to be in the making. Two pages of the *Tribune* were devoted to this affair, at which 18 toasts were given.

On December 18 the *Tribune* printed three columns on a fight between Fred Bussey and Tom McAlpine, 75 rounds for a $200 stake, just across the Indiana line. McAlpine won on a foul. The reporter spoke of the whisky bottles in the respective corners.

A libel suit brought by Mrs. Frances M. Wilkinson against the *Tribune* was given five columns on December 23. This was based on a story printed on October 3, 1867, headed "Scandal and Turmoil," which told of a wife "breaking in on her husband's devotions." The scene was 277 Randolph Street. Mrs. Wilkinson's name was mentioned, also that of Albert C. Ellithorpe, a real estate man. The case was heard in police court and the *Tribune* sought to make amends for its article the next day, and had thought it forgotten. Medill was called to the stand on the first day of the libel suit trial by the plaintiff, but his testimony was dispensed with. On the second day of the trial, with a crowded courtroom, much more was brought out concerning the relations of this couple. The alleged libel was inserted in the *Tribune* by mistake, it was pleaded.

Medill, on the witness stand again, said he heard of the row when it happened and told White, the managing editor, that he did not want it printed, whether true or false, as Ellithorpe was a neighbor of his and it was a " woman row."

Nothing appeared in the paper at the time but later when the case got into police court the article got into the paper. White said that orders had been given to Elias Colbert, the city editor, and C. B. Langley, the foreman of the composing room, that nothing should appear about the case. Colbert, now commercial editor, was on the stand, said he had ordered the story out. Langley testified that he had forgotten these instructions.

In the course of the trial Mrs. Wilkinson admitted visiting Ellithorpe in his room. The jury on December 31 awarded damages of $7,500. The *Tribune* said it was a malicious verdict, in defiance of common sense, law and public decency.

"This verdict will not arrest the publication of THE TRIBUNE," it was stated on January 1, 1869. "It is in behalf of freedom of the press, in behalf of every other paper published in this city and country, and in behalf of the liberty of the people themselves, that we arraign this verdict as the embodiment of an ignorance whose stolidity is only equalled by its personal malignity." If the case stood, the *Tribune* pointed out, it would hardly be safe to publish police court news any longer.

On January 12, the *Tribune* won judgment of the court in the libel cases of Samuel Carson, John T. Pirie, George Scott and Robert Scott, on an article published in January, 1868 regarding a fire on Lake Street. The question was whether the article charged arson. The court said it did not.

The Tribune building as it looked after the fire which destroyed it and most of Chicago in October, 1871. It survived through the first day of the fire, not succumbing until the night of October 9.

A motion for a new trial in the Wilkinson suit was made on January 20. This was granted on February 16.

Agitation for the rights of women and for the new suffrage amendment to the constitution ushered in the early part of the year. Mrs. D. P. Livermore said women were "tired of chignons and husband-catching and wanted to have equal right with men to vote and hold office."

The new First National bank, at State and Washington Streets, was opened on February 1, with Lyman J. Gage as cashier. The cry that a high tariff was necessary to the protection of pauper labor was called humbug in the *Tribune* of February 4. The Walter L. Newberry estate was estimated at $2,500,000.

A revolution was near in car wheels, with perfect steel castings produced. "This is the age of steel," said the *Tribune*.

Real estate advertisers were advised by the *Tribune* to be more explicit in their advertising. It was suggested that advertising rates should go up. Skaters in Lincoln park were enlivened by a band.

The Senate debated long over the suffrage amendment. "It is a simple thing," said the *Tribune* on February 11, "that at all elections the right of voting shall not be denied by color, race or former condition of slavery. The people will approve that."

It was a logical step from this to give women the right to vote, but the *Tribune* was not ready for that. Women's suffrage conventions were at hand. Women had a "sphere," according to the *Tribune* on February 12. "She must not come down to the lower level where men wrangle. Her kingdom and power is simple faith and goodness, the greatest power on earth."

The murder of former Senator Murray McConnell, 75 years old, at Jacksonville, Illinois, provided a major mystery at this time and for several weeks. The *Tribune* compared it with the famous Parkman-Webster case in Boston, where

95

the motive for the murder was a desire to get rid of a debt. The old Senator, something of a miser and strict in his business dealings, had been killed in his office as he mulled over his account books, and the suspicion of guilt fastened on a young man who owed money to the Senator.

Resolutions for universal suffrage, including women, were passed at the Chicago Sorosis convention, a meeting to which the *Tribune* gave a page report.

Grant's acceptance speech was approved by the *Tribune*.

A mass meeting was called to keep the lake front free of commerce, to retain it for beauty and as a breathing place for the poor. Bross was one of the speakers. A committee was appointed to go to Springfield to oppose legislation affecting the lake front and the Illinois Central railroad.

The *Tribune* on February 23 opposed the return to the system of leasing out convicts to labor contractors. "The old system, based on the theory that the sole aim of imprisonment is punishment, without any reference to the improvement or reformation of the convict, is unworthy of our age and country."

The Fifteenth Amendment passed both Houses of Congress. "Ratify and put an end to the Negro question," said the *Tribune* on February 27, 1869.

Six columns were printed on Grant's inauguration on March 5. President Johnson's departure was described as "a terrible death bed scene." The *Tribune* consigned him to a place with Benedict Arnold and Jeff Davis.

The cabinet, which included Elihu B. Washburne of Galena as Secretary of State, was announced. The list was received with satisfaction in Chicago, the *Tribune* said, and with much dissatisfaction in Washington. A few days later Washburne resigned and Hamilton Fish of New York was put in his place. John Rawlins of Illinois was named Secretary of War at this time. The *Tribune* approved this change.

The *Tribune* correspondent at Springfield wrote on March

11 that he had but one prayer — that the legislature would adjourn. He was lost in amazement at legislative incompetency and dishonesty. "It is not a pleasant thing," he wrote, "to have the fact forced upon your attention that man is venal, nor is it agreeable to see a member behave like a ninny. Men of doubtful character sit upon the floor and are tutored by the representatives of monopolies. Women of doubtful character sit in galleries and throw notes to senators. If she is not expert with the pencil she besieges with smiles, and he capitulates with a nod. He bargains with the lobby and he bargains with the gallery, and one is not expected to mention this because it will hurt the feelings of the members."

Offices in the new, fire-proof *Tribune* building were advertised for rental on March 15. The city was expanding and planning at this time and the *Tribune* fought for boulevards and south and west side parks, as well as for the lake front.

"J. M.," probably Medill, wrote from New Orleans on April 9, describing political and social conditions. "The hardest heart could not wish more punishment to the people of the South," he wrote. On April 13 he wrote on the South as a great new field for investment and enterprise. "The South is now ready to travel the same path of progress as the North, rebuild her broken fortunes and found her future on the enduring rocks of Freedom and Equal Rights."

The tone of the Grant administration was progressive, yet conciliatory, the *Tribune* said on April 15. "All men respect his motives and the country generally is willing to await, in confidence and hope, the full result of his actions. We believe his civil administration, like his military career, may meet with a Belmont or a Shiloh at first, but will come to a Vicksburg, a Chattanooga and an Appomatox at the end."

The offices of the *Tribune* had been moved from 50 Clark Street to the new building at Dearborn and Madison Streets, it was announced on May 7. Advertisements were piling up and most of the first page was covered with them. The Sunday issue of May 9 carried a supplement of 20 columns.

The *Tribune* became critical of Grant's cabinet and new office holders in May. This caused some astonishment.

The cost of foreign news at this time was high. The cable rate from London to New York was $1.67 a word, 84 cents a word to the New York Associated Press on contract.

A great parade was held on May 10 to celebrate the completion of the Union Pacific railroad, which was to mean much to Chicago. The *Tribune* carried ten columns on the celebration and a special dispatch from Promontory Point, Utah, where the last rails were laid and the Atlantic and the Pacific "saluted each other." Leland Stanford reported to President Grant that the last spike had been driven. "This cements the social and commercial interest of the eastward and westward extremes of the American continent," said the *Tribune*. "It is the dawn of a new era for Chicago." The building of the railroad, it pointed out, was a Republican party policy.

On May 24, in an address to editors and publishers at Indianapolis, Medill said on the making of newspapers:

"Be very particular with the mechanical execution, charge fair living prices for your work and stand by them; do a cash business, as nearly as practicable, refuse long credits, 'short settlements make long friends;' devote your main editorial efforts to discussion of home topics and furtherance of home interests. Let each issue be a photograph of the doings of your county of the previous week and a foreshadowing of the week to come. Preserve your independence of all demagogues and place hunters and never submit to their dictation; write boldly, and tell the truth fearlessly; criticize whatever is wrong, and denounce whatever is rotten in the administration of local and state affairs, no matter how much it may offend the guilty or wound the would-be leaders of your party. Depend little on professional politicians for patronage, and less on their promises, for you will surely be deceived and disappointed — after the election is over — and despised for your subserviency to them. Make an earnest and conscientious journal; establish its reputation for truth and reliability, frankness and independence. Never wilfully deceive the people or trifle with their confidence. See that your journal is devoted to the advocacy and promotion of their temporal interest and moral welfare and they will repay your favors with their esteem, friendship and patronage, rendering you influential and respected in the community, and prosperous in your pecuniary affairs."

The trial of William A. Robinson, young business man of Jacksonville, Illinois, for the murder of aged Senator McConnell, opened May 26. The *Tribune* carried several columns daily on the progress of this case.

The *Tribune* announced on June 5 that it was now permanently at home to its friends at its new address. "It is better prepared than ever for the transaction of business and with facilities to meet the inevitable increase of business which must follow upon completion of the great highways of commerce and the consequent development of the West." There was a two-column description of the new four-story building, described as being "classic Roman adapted to business."

There was agitation for a gravel road to Hyde Park, a suburb six miles south of Chicago. A horse thief was caught on Madison Street and nearly lynched. The old one-horse and conductor street cars disappeared. A temperance picnic was held on June 11 at Evanston, "a little town famous for its cold water principles."

The death of Henry J. Raymond, editor of the *New York Times*, was announced on June 19. "Peregrine Pickle" wrote from Boston on the peace jubilee and music festival there. "Deacon" Bross went west and wrote of a trip of four and a half days from Chicago to Sacramento. Ladies were to be admitted to Northwestern University, it was announced June 24. The *Tribune* carried an article on the burlesque of justice in Chicago's justice of the peace courts.

On the subject of "Four months of Grant," the *Tribune* said on July 1: "While commending the general aim and policy of the administration, we have criticized features freely. That is our view of conducting a newspaper. The results of the administration thus far justify the most ardent hopes of those who elected him. His platform is retrenchment, economy, reform. So we thank God for President Grant, as we used to thank him in the old, trying days, for General Grant. Reconstruction is advancing with silent rapidity. The Democratic party is gone and meaningless."

The salutatory address at the University of Chicago was delivered in Latin and loudly applauded.

The Powell expedition to the Colorado River was reported lost on July 3. The Prohibition party was to be organized in Chicago on September 1. "The national prohibition party can never achieve its purpose by physical force," said the *Tribune.* "Its one idea is the subjugation of the many because of the misfortunes of the few."

Removal of the national capital from Washington to St. Louis was spoken of favorably by the *Tribune* on July 5. "H. W." wrote on July 16 of Utah under the Mormons. Brigham Young was defying the law against polygamy at that time. "H. W.," probably Horace White, wrote that the opening of the western railroads spelt the doom of "Youngism."

The *Tribune* boasted on July 19 that it had beaten the *Times* in two stories, a suicide and an elopement.

The Powell expedition was finally discovered as safe. "J. M." wrote as a member of a commercial excursion party to the West. He had arrived at Salt Lake City by stagecoach. "A good square dinner, washed down with champagne and claret, a fragrant Havana, a plunge bath in a warm sulphur pool, a stroll about town, shaking hands with old and new friends, a visit to the theater, closed the labors of the day and made us forget our rough ride from Deseret to Salt Lake City."

Hundreds of buildings were under construction, at a cost of ten million dollars, the *Tribune* reported on July 19. The Stock Exchange, to cost $800,000, was being built. The cornerstone of the Hyde Park Presbyterian Church was laid. "The days of tenements are gone," said the *Tribune*.

The trial of the Rev. C. E. Cheney for violations of the canonical law was opened in the chapel of the Cathedral of Saints Peter and Paul on July 22 and was followed with great detail. Medill wrote from California. "Revere," the Boston correspondent, wrote from the Maine wilderness. "Gath" described the Long Island resorts.

"Protection," said the *Tribune* on August 3, "is the great American blunder, the evil of the day."

The great astronomical event of the age, a total eclipse of the sun to take place August 7, was described in advance, with illustrative maps, in an article written by Elias Colbert, *Tribune* city editor. "H. W." wrote about a trip to the Sierras and the Yosemite valley. Four columns were carried on the eclipse, which lasted one hour, 58 minutes and two seconds in Chicago.

Grant was being criticized for his social activities at Long Branch. The *Tribune* defended him. "Wait and see if any evil comes from it."

A letter from Major J. W. Powell was printed on August 19 telling of his success in running the rapids of the Colorado River. "Peregrine Pickle" in his column told of a notable gathering at the home of Colonel J. H. Bowen on August 22. Carl Schurz, William B. Ogden, several Senators and Congressmen, and citizens including Joseph Medill and Alfred Cowles were there.

A suggestion was made in the *Tribune* on September 2 that the baseball clubs of Chicago consolidate and make a good team. "It is a noble game and has a great future."

Advocates of the new temperance political party met in Chicago. This sort of action did not suit the *Tribune* which said on September 2: "Let the prohibition party organize. It is a small pot and soon hot. It is as practicable to enforce universal non-intercourse between the sexes as universal abstinence from spiritous liquors." The temperance convention speakers flailed the *Tribune* for its stand.

Columns of speeches were printed on the dedication exercises of Northwestern University held in an Evanston grove on September 8, 1869.

The Western Female Suffrage Association met in Chicago. Lucy Stone, Susan B. Anthony, Mary Livermore, were there. The *Tribune* attempted to state its position on this question and the women attempted to say what they thought of the *Tribune*. It was agreed that the *Tribune* had given a full and fair report of the proceedings.

Miss Livermore said she was surprised that the editors of the *Tribune* were not entirely on the side of the women, as she had taken a bouquet to the *Tribune* office and had friends there. The *Tribune* said that women should be aided in their natural sphere, nursery, kitchen, schoolroom, church, but "we should not point to the plow, the steamboat, the army, the navy or the legislature. . . . When the sex generally demand the right of suffrage they will obtain it," was the sage conclusion of the editorial writer. "That demand is not general now."

There was a great gale in New England, a coal mine disaster in Pennsylvania, a meeting at the Plymouth Congregational Church to speed seven missionaries to China, and reports from the West where Governor Bross was spearing salmon in the Columbia River. Indians were on the warpath in Wyoming as were the Ku Klux Klan in Tennessee. Wall Street was excited over gold.

Chicago had a citizens' ticket, a coalition with eight Republicans and seven Democrats offered for office, headed by R. B. Mason for Mayor. The *Tribune* said it would labor for this ticket. A six-story building was to go up at Wabash

As downtown Chicago looked following the great fire of October 8 and 9, 1871. The ruins at upper right are what were left of the Tribune building erected two years before.

and Washington Streets, at a cost of $600,000. Twenty-one new churches had been built during the year at a cost of a million dollars.

The gold speculation in New York was referred to by the *Tribune* as licensed gambling, and the excitement in New York was called a "South Sea Bubble." Foreign news headings took the place of editorial comment on the first page.

Medill and S. S. Hayes were made nominees of the 59th district convention as delegates to the Constitutional Convention. "As the name of Medill is on both tickets and as he will probably receive the unanimous vote of his district, it is scarcely necessary to allude to him," said the *Tribune* on September 30. "So emphatic an expression of the confidence of the public is seldom accorded to any person in political life."

Intimations of a scandal involving the Grant administration came in the Washington correspondence of October 2. Jim Fisk, in an interview, had said that he had had assurances from Washington that the government would not interfere in the gold situation. These assurances, apparently, emanated from A. B. Corbin, the President's brother-in-law.

Heavy advertising demand called for a Sunday supplement, the *Tribune* announced, adding that it might have to print a supplement every day. In an editorial on consistency, evidently in reply to critics, the *Tribune* said on October 6: "THE TRIBUNE was in favor of the maintenance of the Republican organization intact in 1865, and is in favor of overthrowing all Republican rings, formed for plundering tax payers, today."

The money scandal simmered in the news dispatches, Fisk declaring that he had talked finances with Grant while the President was a guest on his boat the previous summer. Corbin was called a liar.

A Chicago press club was organized with 74 members, it was announced on October 14. It was to allow no political discussions or questions of relations between employer and employe.

A 6,000-word stenographic report of what went on in the justice of the peace courts was printed on October 18. Local Republicans were referred to as "barnacles" or "the ring," in the *Tribune*. The *Staats Zeitung* said the *Tribune* was trying to break down the Republican party and establish a free trade party on its ruins. J. Y. Scammon, a candidate for delegate to the Constitutional Convention, mourned over the *Tribune* attitude. He said he had once owned the paper and had nursed it in its infancy. The *Tribune* said this was not true. The campaign grew hot for the "peoples' ticket." John Wentworth and Thomas Hoyne were with the *Tribune* in this campaign. Norman B. Judd, old *Tribune* ally, was now on the other side, complaining about editors. The *Tribune* said that its editors had made all there was of Judd in a political sense. The Republicans, refused space for their speeches, took a first-page advertisement in the *Tribune* on November 1. George W. Gage was their candidate for Mayor. Registration day was said by the *Tribune* to be one of the most important days in the city's history.

On election day, November 2, 1869, the *Tribune* said: "The great question of this election is whether the city of Chicago, after having contributed her great strength to the emancipation of the slaves, has strength enough left to emancipate herself."

The results next day were announced as a victory for the people. A majority had voted for the coalition ticket. "They have shown," said the *Tribune*, "that the great cities of America are capable of self government. THE TRIBUNE promises to see that every official carries out the promises he made to the people." The majority for the ticket was over ten thousand. Medill and Hayes were elected as convention delegates.

In the meantime the national money scandal was simmering. It was called the "gold conspiracy" and was concerned with the President's brother-in-law. The *Tribune* was slow to blame the President, contenting itself with printing letters from Grant that he had nothing to do with it except to destroy the gold ring. "Gath" in Washington said after eight months of the Grant administration that it had been a success on the whole, that the financial condition of the country had improved.

"Grant has not always been fortunate in his nominations to office," the correspondent said. "He has not proved a perfect judge of character. There have been too many young men, a premium on obscurity. The worst that can be said is that he is somewhat of coarse fibre and too fond of his reputation for stolidity. Still we have a responsible government with a patriotic head."

The trial of the Rev. Isaac B. Smith for murdering his wife opened at Geneva on November 5 and on this and succeeding days occupied much attention in the *Tribune*. The death was by drowning in a small creek at the boundary of Cook and Kane Counties, and the question was, as in Dreiser's *American Tragedy* many years later, whether she might have been saved. The minister was acquitted on November 14. The *Tribune* said the charge had not been proved.

A free trade meeting in Farwell Hall was given 15,000 words in the *Tribune* of November 6. On November 9 the prospectus of 1870 was published, recalling the events of the preceding year, the election of Grant, the acceptance of Reconstruction on a Republican basis, the ratification of the Fifteenth Amendment by 21 states, in which suffrage was given to freedmen.

"For these results THE TRIBUNE has been second to none in vigilance," said the prospectus. "THE TRIBUNE was the first journal to point out and characterize in proper terms the fatal policy of Andrew Johnson which sought to confer a monopoly of political power upon those who had sought to destroy the Union. THE TRIBUNE was ever on the side of impartial suffrage and equal rights.

"With the extinction of slavery, the public debt, taxation and currency are the ruling questions. We hold that an irredeemable and fluctuating currency is the most expensive, injurious and oppressive form of circulating medium, for all classes except speculators and stock gamblers, that the credit of a nation is its most valuable possession and the efforts of government should be directed to the improvement of credit and the refunding of the bonded debt. The government should pay its demand notes or greenbacks by redemption or funding. All taxes should be adjusted to the point of revenue for the government and should be reduced in internal revenue and tariff taxes."

The *Tribune* said it spent more money for news than any other paper west of New York and had a corps of reporters and correspondents equal in intelligence to those in New York. A special corps of reporters, it was stated, would cover the Constitutional Convention opening in December. It told of changes in the weekly paper, its original matter and condensation of news.

The case of Willie Atkins, who was punished in school by a teacher, Miss Adelaide Herrick, rocked the school board and got 5,000 words in the *Tribune* of November 13. A resolution in the board to abolish corporal punishment was lost by a tie vote.

A hotel column was begun in the *Tribune* on November 25, listing important arrivals. Attention was called to the overloading of horses in the streets and an anti-cruelty society was suggested. The Theodore Thomas concert orchestra attracted attention at Farwell Hall. The music critic, George P. Upton, wrote of Thomas' career from viola player to orchestra leader.

The murder of Albert D. Richardson, New York journalist, by Daniel McFarland, was given prominence in the paper for several days. A mastodon's remains were found on a farm near Wheaton. It was reported on December 5 that 20,000 men were out of work in Chicago.

President Grant's first message to Congress was printed on December 7, 1869. It was only half as long as Johnson's, a relief to editors.

Medill was named presiding officer of the Constitutional Convention on December 2 but declined the honor, largely on account of his defective hearing. Charles Hitchcock was made president.

A holiday edition of the articles of "Peregrine Pickle" was printed by the *Tribune*. This was a 500-page volume called *This and That*, forerunner of today's annual "Line" and "Wake" books.

The cost of the war was estimated at 4 billions, 171 millions for the Union, with about two billions more for the Confederate states.

Chapter Eight

HORSE AND BUGGY DAYS

THE RATIFICATION of the Fifteenth Amendment in 1870 was regarded by the *Tribune* as marking the end of the rebellion. The editors turned their attention to other matters, such as polygamy, a new constitution for Illinois, the tariff, the struggle of the people against great corporations, and the growing tendency toward paternalism in government.

Several disastrous fires occurred during this year and the Tribune started a campaign against man-trap structures and faulty construction in the new buildings rising all over Chicago. It was pointed out that fire was not a "visitation from God" but a man-controlled event.

The *Tribune's* tariff policy brought opposition from Republican party journals and the paper's criticism of President Grant, particularly his assumption of authority over legislation, caused some astonishment. The *Tribune* again called attention to the fact that it was an independent newspaper, and would speak out against corruption in its own party as well as against the evils of the opposition policy.

The new year brought gambling raids by the police in Chicago. Faro games had been closed and now poker parties were the object of police attention.

Negro citizens celebrated the sixth anniversary of the Emancipation Proclamation with parades and song. Mark Twain's articles, taken from the *Buffalo Express*, where the author then worked, were reprinted in the *Tribune*.

It was suggested by the *Tribune* at this time that a citizen's committee be appointed to inquire into law enforcement. Particular objection was taken to twenty-eight pardons granted by Governor Palmer during the previous year. The continued agitation over woman suffrage led to the suggestion that the question be submitted to a vote of the people.

Willie Atkins, who had been whipped in school, died. The medical examiners said the cause was inflammation of the brain and not the whipping injuries, but the people were aroused and an anti-corporal punishment society was organized.

Efforts to hold President Grant responsible for the sins of his brother-in-law had failed, the *Tribune* said on February 1. It jibed at the *Chicago Times* for copying *Tribune* stories and said that paper was in a state of chronic somnambulism. Medill was active in the Constitutional Convention on the question of the improvement of the Illinois River and canal connections to hold down the railroad monopolies. A

new tariff bill was reported in Washington. The death of
Dr. David Livingstone in Africa was reported.

The Fifteenth Amendment was ratified, it was announced
on February 4. "It is now a part of the Constitution," said
the *Tribune*. "The right of citizens to vote shall not be
abridged by race, color or previous condition of servitude.
The rebellion may now be regarded as over and the great
war finished."

A full report of a cock fight at Michigan City, Indiana,
was printed on February 4. The new tariff bill was printed
in full. The Washington correspondent, "Gath," described
Congress as craven and pliable. Bross, still in the West, wrote
of trout fishing in the Yosemite Valley. He used worms.
The Chicago Dental Society adopted a code of ethics and
decided that advertising was vulgar. The city got a new steam
fire-engine. A committee of which Medill was chairman
reported on electoral and representative reform. The police
raided a ten-cent poker game on Halsted Street.

"Peregrine Pickle" started a controversy on February 20 as
to whether blondes have any dramatic ability. Not one of
them displayed a spark, he maintained. A special article was
printed on working women in Chicago, particularly seam-
stresses. It was suggested that if women wanted to reform
something or work for "rights," here was a good field. The
night police reporter wrote a two-column story on how he
covered his beat.

A mass meeting against liquor selling on Sunday was held
at Farwell Hall on February 23. Editor Storey of the *Times*
was attacked on the street by two members of the "Blonde
Burlesque Troupe" appearing at the Opera House. He was
whipped with rawhide and got a column in the *Tribune*.
The *Times* on the previous Sunday had devoted a page to a
discussion of the prostitutes of Chicago and in this connection had discussed the moral reputation of "the blondes."
The *Tribune* said this was a case of the pot calling the kettle

black, that it was no defense of virtue to horsewhip a man. "Pickle" said the war of the blondes was now over and he hoped the Opera House people had learned a lesson. The case of assault against Storey came to trial and the *Tribune* printed six columns about it. The blondes were fined but they got an ovation and 3,000 persons flocked to the Opera House to see their next performance.

The gold investigation in Congress was printed verbatim by the *Tribune* during March. In Chicago conferences were called on how to combat the fire menace. It was proposed to expand the department and build four great water towers. A mass meeting was called by a group of citizens headed by John V. Farwell to demand reduction of taxation. The *Tribune* said that this demand was general throughout the county and the need was great.

The wings of the new court house under construction collapsed on March 12, leading to a long investigation.

"Chicago now has a first class baseball club," the *Tribune* declared on March 13. The members were James Wood, W. C. Fisher, Michael McAtee, Charles Hodes, Marshall King, James White, William Flynn, Edgar A. Cuthbert, Frederic Treacy and Levi Myerle. Alderman W. S. Powell was president of the Garden City Club which owned the team.

The city was snowbound during the middle of March and grand sleighing was reported. William Cullen Bryant's translation of the Iliad was printed in part. The *Tribune* of this period published many articles of philosophical, scientific and literary note, and its editorials followed closely the latest trends in philosophical as well as political thought. Its weather reports came from J. G. Langgath, optician at 117 Randolph Street, correspondent for the Smithsonian Institution.

What the *Tribune* called "astounding courage" was shown in the indictment of public officials and architects for the collapse of the wings of the new court house.

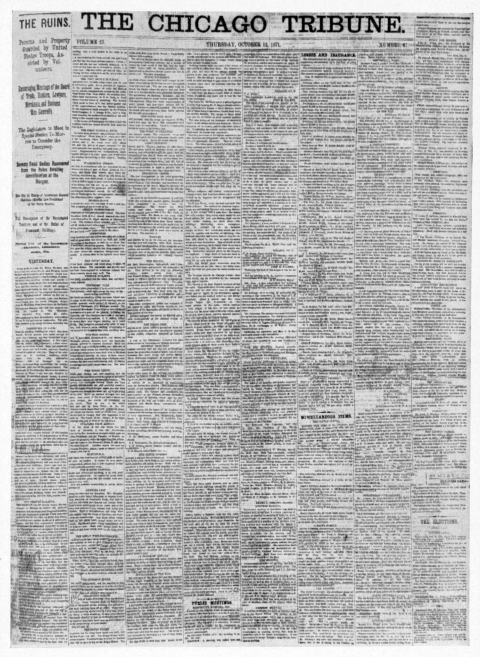

Page one of the first issue of the Tribune *following the destruction of its building in the Chicago fire of 1871. The* Tribune *suspended publication for two days while hunting a new home and plant.*

A suit in the United States Circuit Court on March 30, 1870, recalled to the *Tribune* the experience of Charles A. Dana, then editor of the *New York Sun*, in Chicago journalism. This was as editor of the *Chicago Republican*, a paper which the *Tribune* had practically ignored during Dana's time here. The suit related that on June 1, 1865, Dana entered into an agreement with the *Republican* to act as chief editor for five years, selecting his own assistants and controlling the political character of the paper. No article or advertisment was to be inserted of which he disapproved. He was to be given one-fifth of the capital stock, and a salary of $7,500 a year. The stock was assessed in January, 1866, and Dana gave a note for $5,000. In May, 1866, Dana and the company agreed to terminate their contract. The company was to pay off his note and give him $10,000. The *Republican* had not paid the note, the suit stated, and the court was asked to reform the contract and compel payment.

A story was printed on April 11 of the origin of the Republican party in Chicago, with the names of those who attended the first meeting in February, 1854. The name Republican for the party was first proposed in Cleveland, it was stated. Its great achievements in 16 years were the ratification of the Thirteenth, Fourteenth and Fifteenth Amendments.

The entire first page of the Sunday edition of April 3 was given to advertising. The McFarland murder trial in New York was reported in detail. Tariff debate opened in Congress on April 8. The *Tribune* printed frequent editorials upholding free trade. Five thousand Negroes paraded Chicago streets in celebration of the Fifteenth Amendment. A letter from William Herndon on Lincoln's religious beliefs was printed on April 10, 1870.

Chicago was paying ten millions a year taxes on an assessed valuation of $266,000,000. The *Tribune* said the American people were "on the rack" and it was time to revolt. There had been 600 fires in the city during the year, with a loss of $871,905. On April 14 the *Tribune* printed a special article describing polygamy in Salt Lake City and an editorial advocating its abolition. "Let its pitiless despots bend under the lash of power. Let them be made to feel that the country and the world look upon them with contempt and abhorrence."

Spring fashions at Field, Leiter & Company were illustrated by woodcuts on page one. The baseball teams began to travel. The Chicago White Stockings beat the St. Louis Unions 47 to 1 on April 30.

A speech by Medill in the Constitutional Convention on the question of reducing compensation for Cook County fee offices was printed on May 2. The McFarland case, with its insanity defense, led the *Tribune* to comment on this growing feature of murder trials. The trial was called a rich mine for future research in this question. McFarland was found not guilty.

Two columns were printed on May 11 on a world championship fight between Jem Mace and Tom Allen at New Orleans.

The new state constitution as adopted at the convention was published on May 13. The *Tribune* said it was a great improvement over the old one and they saw no reason why it should not be adopted by the people. Woman suffrage was also to be submitted to the people. "Whether we like it or not," said the *Tribune* on May 15, "whether anybody likes it or not, it may be accepted as very nearly a foregone conclusion that the right of suffrage is eventually to be extended to women."

News dealers were notified that on Saturdays readers of the *Tribune* would receive a 20-column supplement, the same as the Sunday readers.

On the subject of paternalism in government the *Tribune* said on May 25: "The time for many government actions during the war has passed, yet it still clings to power. There is hardly a case in history where any body of men in government ever voluntarily laid aside powers once assumed. Republican government means limitation by law to general objects which the people cannot perform for themselves. Now the theory of paternal government is being revived. Almost everybody who is not prosperous rushes to Washington for relief. Congress rushes to meet the millennium. Its only power is to tax."

A horse and buggy auction was advertised on May 28. The *Sunday Democrat*, published by George W. Rust, advertised in the *Tribune*. The "personals" of those days contained many spicy items, such as this:

"Will the little young lady with light dress and dark eyes who noticed two gentlemen on Lake street and afterwards as she was going out of a drug store on Clark Street on Friday noon, please send her address to Sojourner, Box 22."

Whether the sunspots caused the cool weather of the month was the subject of a two-column article. A baseball match between the Athletics and the Aetnas for the championship of Chicago was held on June 3 before 700 spectators.

The *Tribune* undertook to reform Chicago building practices. It talked of sham architecture and said the system "calls imperatively for reform."

"Retrogression [toward solid buildings] is impossible until we are overtaken by some terrible calamity," it was stated on June 5. "Even then we may excuse ourselves and invite new destruction by declaring it to be a visitation of God instead of recognizing our own criminal carelessness."

The death of Charles Dickens was reported on June 11. He had "taught the world many lessons of love, mirth and charity," the *Tribune* said in a long editorial. Potter Palmer projected a hotel at State and Monroe Streets. A letter was printed from Medill on June 16 advocating the minority representation section of the new state constitution, a measure in which he had been active. On June 20 a first-page article appeared on this subject, submitted by a committee of which Medill was chairman.

Visitors were coming to look upon Chicago as one of the wonders of the world, said the *Tribune* on June 21, mentioning "our tunnels, our cribs, our water works, our Board of Trade, White Stockings, and Court House, marble palaces, lovely women, energetic men, suicides, murders, divorces, pig killing, Historical Society, one-horse cars, etc."

A campaign was carried on until July 2 to get the people to vote for the new constitution, particularly the sections on railroads, warehouses, the Illinois Central railroad, minority representation and the canal.

Six reasons were given the people on July 1 why they should vote for the constitution. The *Tribune* called attention to Chicago's "fashionable airings" in the parks and boulevards between 5 and 6 p.m. daily, where one or two thousand people might be seen, "nearly all capitalists."

"How many will neglect to vote on election day," asked the *Tribune* in a warning to "sluggards." It was declared that the new constitution would save the state five and a half millions annually.

Cook County gave a heavy majority for the constitution, it was reported on July 3. Minority representation was carried and would go into effect in 1872. The majority in the state was around 100,000. There were "a few benighted Bourbon spots in Egypt. . . . The colored troops all voted and the world did not come to an end."

On the question of Grant for President in 1872, the *Tribune* said that Grant must appoint a good cabinet to save the Republican party from defeat.

In an article on flying it was suggested that gliders might come some day but no way had been suggested "to teach man the office of fowl."

The Franco-Prussian war was impending and Wall Street was hit by a flurry. "It is an unprovoked war of conquest, wholly foreign to the spirit of modern times," said the *Tribune* on July 16. Grant had a plan for the United States to gain trade as a neutral.

The new city directory showed 1,481 saloons in Chicago and 1,056 groceries. A three-column map of the war area in Europe was printed on the first page on July 18. A column of cable news was carried.

An agreement had been entered into between the newspaper publishers in Chicago not to publish income tax returns, as "offensive and impertinent." The *Tribune* complained on July 19 that the *Post* had violated the agreement.

In an article on the crime of war on July 20, the *Tribune* said that America sympathized with Prussia in the current conflict because there were more Germans than French in this country and they believed in Prussian institutions rather than French despotism. Many Germans who had seen service in the Civil War went back to fight in Germany.

Medill, vacationing on the Nantucket coast, sent back a letter on shark catching. The Chicago White Stockings were whitewashed nine times in succession. Grant went to Long Branch, with "Gath" on his trail. "Jim Fisk with sublime impudence drives his six-in-hand drag by the presidential door every evening," wrote "Gath," . . . the president whom he failed to entrap in his gold panic job. Jay Gould will not ride with him. Jay will steal but will not allow himself to blush."

The wedding of Potter Palmer and Bertha Honore at the Christian Church was chronicled on July 29. It was described as a simple, dignified ceremony. It was rumored that Potter had settled a million dollars on his bride.

The rights of neutrals were the subject of comment on the war in Europe. There was agitation over England's position. Prussian victories were celebrated in Chicago by local Germans early in August. Chicagoans were advised to buy flour before the price advanced.

Rents were low in Chicago and the wages of a cook were $4

a week. A ten-acre tract with residence on Ridge Road near Evanston sold for $16,500. The murder case of Benjamin Nathan, who was killed in his home on West 23rd Street, New York, on July 29, began to receive much news attention. A son was suspected and a reward of $30,000 was offered.

The Republican party was losing ground in the South, the *Tribune* said on August 18. "They cannot make New Englanders out of the Carolinas and Virginia," it continued. "The carpetbaggers and their supporters in the North, in their endeavor to crush out every speck of manliness and every memory of the past among the Southern people, have done more to defeat Republicanism in those states than the Democratic party could have done in a generation."

Debates on the *Tribune's* tariff policy, which had evidently aroused a widespread opposition, were given space in the paper during August. Also the question of whether the Bible sanctioned polygamy was a subject of controversy. Grant issued a neutrality proclamation on August 23, 1870. "We are opposed," said the *Tribune*, "to any officious meddling with a war whose course we have no right to control and whose results thus far are as just and wholesome as sanguinary wars can ever be."

Paris was preparing for siege and a map of the city and its environs was printed on August 24. The Germans of Chicago held a picnic at Ogden's Grove and raised $50,000 to send to Berlin. The war news was covered by press association reports from Europe and by the special service of the New York papers, particularly the *New York Herald*, which advertised its cables in the *Tribune*.

Medill addressed a ward meeting on August 25 on the necessity of sending able men to Springfield to frame laws to fit the new constitution.

The Illinois Republican platform, printed on September 3, stated: "While adhering to the traditional policy of avoiding entangling alliances and complications with foreign powers, we hereby sympathize with the brave efforts of the German people to protect themselves against invasion and spoliation by the imperial despot who has suppressed the freedom of the press in his own country." [Napoleon III had refused to permit correspondents to go to the front.]

The state Republicans endorsed the administration of Grant as honest, economical and efficient. His great achievement, it was stated, was the reduction of the national debt. John A. Logan was made candidate for Congressman-at-large.

Much excitement was reported in Chicago over the battle of Sedan and the surrender of the French army. King William of Prussia emerged as Kaiser Wilhelm I.

Fire on Wabash Avenue on September 5 destroyed a block of stores, with a loss of $3,000,000 and several men killed. "This is the third time," said the *Tribune*, "that Chicago has been visited with such a calamity. Shall it be the last? The walls of one building had been condemned. Economy of construction was pushed to penuriousness. Mansard roofs, high buildings, weak walls, are not dispensations of Providence. The community will find it has new reasons to demand the enactment of a more rigid system of public supervision over architects and builders."

John V. Farwell and Lyon & Healy were among the concerns which suffered from the fire. The *Tribune* advertised its own building as fireproof. The City Council began an inquiry into defective hose and weak engines.

Paris was under siege and the French republic was recognized by the United States in September. London began to sympathize with the French. A three-column account of the battle of Sedan by William H. Russell in the *London Times* was printed on September 22. This was the same "Bull Run" Russell who had excited the ire of the *Tribune* in Civil War days. A mass meeting on behalf of France was held at Farwell Hall.

The death of Dr. Charles H. Ray was reported on September 24. He had sold his stock in the *Tribune* and severed his connection in 1863, returning to his editorial chair for ten weeks in 1865. At the time of his death he was on the *Chicago Evening Post*. He was survived by a daughter and three sons. A full account of his life and services on the *Tribune* was printed. The funeral was reported on September 28, 1870.

An article was printed telling of a revised version of the Bible that was being prepared in England.

Medill and William B. Ogden addressed a north side improvement committee on the purification of the north branch of the river. The opening of the Palmer House was reported on October 1. Ten thousand visitors were attracted.

"Baseball has now become a profession," the *Tribune* said on October 2. A national tournament was proposed. North side citizens considered putting stray cows in a pound.

The siege of Paris took the first page early in October. Count Bismarck accused Russell of the *London Times* of falsehood. The *Tribune* recalled Russell's "romance" on the battle of Bull Run, exposed by the late Dr. Ray.

The *Tribune* continued its campaign against "man-traps" and shoddy building in Chicago and joined the *Journal* in advocating a good public library. An editorial of October 12 against federal interference in state politics might be interpreted in the light of later developments as a warning to Grant. Medill's name came up at Republican meetings as a possible candidate for Congress. N. B. Judd was not to run again. The printers of Chicago in a resolution printed on October 20 recognized Medill as their "good friend" and recommended him for Congress in the First district. On October 21 a "card" from Medill was printed in which he withdrew from the race. He had entered the contest, he wrote, with the understanding that there would be no pledges and that he would be left free to follow his convictions, as he had done in the Constitutional Convention.

"I had nothing to offer but the honest efforts of a plain, unpretentious man who would be guided by conscience, common sense and patriotic purpose. . . . It is now apparent that the nomination is being resisted by the employment of means and influences which I cannot consent to combat. From the standpoint of self respect and propriety I am compelled to withdraw."

C. B. Farwell was chosen Republican candidate for the district and Thomas Hoyne was nominated by the Democrats. The *Tribune* recalled that Farwell had supported Cyrus H. McCormick in 1864 and expressed the opinion that he could not be elected. Farwell was referred to as "deadwood" on the Republican ticket. "Long John" Wentworth then entered the race as an independent and received the support of the Tribune. This aroused criticism and the *Tribune* said on November 1:

"THE CHICAGO TRIBUNE has too much at stake, to put it on no higher plane, than to confederate with tax thieves and men who make money out of politics. If it should do so, we might see the same state of corruption here as has already culminated in New York. We have men as determined to use the Republican party as a means of swindling as any in New York are to use the Democratic party. A convention of bummers has just nominated the captain of their gang to Congress. . . ."

The *Tribune* was reminded by its political foes that it had once said some derogatory things about Wentworth. "The editor of 1870," said the *Tribune*, "is not responsible for what the editor of 1860 said. The only consistency in a newspaper that the public cares anything about, and the only consistency about which any newspaper need concern itself, is whether its course today is a wise and just one. The main thing is to be right now under existing circumstances."

Wentworth's speeches were played up during the campaign and Farwell was strongly attacked. Despite this Farwell won a seat in Congress by a majority of 5,000, it was reported on November 9. The *Tribune* explained that the Irish vote in Chicago had been cast for him. They still thought him a bad selection but would be fair to him in office. It was explained on November 10 that this was not a personal crusade and that Medill's candidacy had resulted from no efforts on behalf of the *Tribune*. "The election is a symptom of what can be accomplished in a large city by the use of money."

On the subject of possible war with Great Britain over the *Alabama* claims, an action being whipped up by Ben Butler and others, the *Tribune* said on November 13, 1870: "We are opposed to plunging the country into a foreign war to furnish a political issue to men who have not the wit to comprehend, or the honesty to apply to public affairs the principles necessary to a successful and peaceful administration of the government."

The prospectus for 1871 said in part: "THE TRIBUNE enters on its twenty-fourth year stronger than ever in the confidence of the people. We are in favor of a tariff levied for the sole and express purpose of raising revenue for the government. Every man has the right to his own earnings and all laws which seek to deprive him of a portion of the fruits of his labor, for the benefit of any other person or class, are an infringement on his liberty and akin to slavery and robbery in their operations.

"THE TRIBUNE platform includes civil service reform, a return to specie payment by the retirement of greenbacks and the substitution of national bank notes, opposition to every project leading into a foreign war to promote partisan ends.

"THE TRIBUNE is the enemy of monopoly and tax thieves in national and state politics and always the champion of the people."

The first annual meeting of the new Press Club was announced on December 2, 1870. Members were instructed to provide their own liquor and informed that between courses they would be required to shoot at a mark. Elias Colbert, city editor of the *Tribune*, was president.

The great political issue of the future, the *Tribune* said on December 5, lay in the struggle between corporations and the people in matters of special privilege. "Shall the toiling millions possess and enjoy the fruits of their own labor or shall they have only just enough of their earnings to keep them from revolution while monopolists and speculators take the rest?"

The Tribune objected to the President's views on protective tariff as given in his annual message, but thought the rest of it good.

A review of building showed that rapid progress had been made in 1870 and it was predicted that building would be greater in 1871, the most active year in the city's history.

President Grant was criticized on December 10 for his assumption of authority over legislation. "A Senator is not bound to take opinions from the President," said the *Tribune*. "He is part of a body whose function it is to command the executive, not obey."

The Washington correspondent followed this with an article on the relations between the President and the legislative branch, with much historical reference.

Albert Crosby began a libel suit against Wilbur F. Storey, for $50,000 based on "the war of the blondes." Storey's *Times* had said the Opera House was like "a Wells street bagnio." Hooley's Opera House on Clark Street was to open in splendor before the new year.

The War Department began to send out weather reports, without forecasts.

The *Tribune* quarreled with Horace Greeley over his attitude on the tariff, and hoped the President would not "varnish" the reputation of Senator Simon Cameron of Pennsylvania by appointing him to the cabinet.

Jefferson Davis was making speeches to Sunday schools in the South and the German Reichstag was discussing the annexation of Alsace and Lorraine.

A report on the Press Club banquet at the Briggs House stated that more than 90 members were present. A speaker told of the early days when Editor Tom Stewart of the *Tribune* made up his own paper, put it on the press and when the edition was run off carried it on his back to the postoffice.

Chapter Nine

CHICAGO FALLS AND RISES AGAIN

THE TRIBUNE's prediction that Chicago's hasty and flimsy construction would result in a major disaster some day came true in October of 1871, when a great fire destroyed the business section of the city, including the new "fire-proof" *Tribune* building, and made 92,000 people homeless.

In this emergency all questions were submerged into one of survival and re-establishment. Joseph Medill emerged as a natural leader of the people. His indomitable courage and resourcefulness, his high vision for Chicago and for the *Tribune* formed a creative spark that set the human engine going again and turned despair into hope. The world rushed in to help and within a month the new city had begun to take form.

"Chicago Shall Rise Again" was the watchword raised by the *Tribune* in a famous editorial written by Medill. He took the lead of a citizen's committee and was elected mayor of Chicago on a "Union-Fireproof" ticket, serving until the city was set firmly in its new growth. The *Tribune* was also rapidly re-established and by December 1, had ceased to put news of the fire on page one.

During this year the *Tribune* under Horace White went over to the liberal wing of the Republican party and came into stronger and stronger opposition to the administration Republicans. Horace Greeley arose as a presidential candidate, and the *Tribune* came out for a new policy toward the South, opposing "military government from the White House."

The old year, according to the *Tribune* of January 1, 1871, had seen great progress in culture, religion, art and science. "Our own city of Chicago is striding forward 'to her throne amid the marts' with a rapidity unexcelled in the history of cities. Republican palaces are rising around us on every street — palaces where the people resort. These are our palaces and none in the world are vaster or more permanent." Five millons had been spent by the city during the year on permanent improvements.

In Paris the government was feeding half a million people a week. Rats were 25 cents each, cats one dollar and cabbage leaves the same price. An organization called the "Internationalist" was spreading to the United States with the object of uniting the non-capitalist class in a world revolution.

An article from Japan said that the princes of Japan who had put the emperor on the throne were in close league with the British. American diplomacy, it was stated, was with the Tycoon, but could not combat "the tricks of the British."

Bayard Taylor's translation of Goethe's *Faust* was reviewed in two and a half columns on January 9. Bret Harte had a story in the paper. At the residence of H. M. Wilmarth, 222 Michigan Avenue, a "conversazione" was held with Bronson Alcott as the star. Tennyson's new poem *The Window* was printed later in the month. There was a great storm in Chicago. Paris fell to the besieging Prussians.

It was stated in an editorial on February 1, 1871, that the "high tariff ring" had proposed in writing to buy the *Tribune* "to support their scheme of plunder," and they had received an answer in the negative, also in writing. No names were given.

A mass meeting was held in Chicago in aid of the French. Medill was a vice-president of this meeting. New water works and artesian wells were considered. The *Tribune* argued for a new lake tunnel.

The Associated Press in Washington was unfair in its reports, the *Tribune* said on February 10. The *New York Tribune* quoted Medill as having said that an election on the issue of free trade in Chicago would give 50,000 majority for protection. "There are not 50,000 votes here," said the *Tribune*, "so Medill could not have said it."

A letter on free trade in America by John Stuart Mill was printed on February 14. A provisional republic was launched in France with Louis Thiers as president.

A lease of the lake front for a baseball grounds was proposed in Council on February 21. The terms of peace in Europe held the germ of another war, the *Tribune* stated on February 25.

A controversy was aired in the *Sunday Tribune* of February 25, over Charles Darwin's new book, *The Descent of Man.*

A hoop skirt was at last found to have a value. It saved a man from drowning in the Chicago River.

The grand entry of the Germans into Paris was reported on March 2.

The removal of Charles Sumner as chairman of the Foreign Relations Committee of the Senate and the appointment of Senator Cameron aroused the ire of the *Tribune*. Cameron was called the "embodiment of corruption." The President had disappointed the people in many ways, it was stated. "This action has caused a widespread anxiety, a suspicious watchfulness which it will be by no means easy to do away with."

A Republican caucus in Congress agreed upon a Ku Klux suppression bill. "The heathen rage and the Ku Klux is rampant in the South," said the *Tribune* on March 16. "What she needs is a republican form of government created and maintained by herself and not a military government with headquarters in the White House."

The *Tribune* noted in other papers a growing sentiment against making the legislative branch subservient to the executive. It commented on March 17: "It takes a good deal to cloud the popularity of a President chosen as Grant was, almost by acclamation, so when the reaction comes it is all the stronger."

The Commune was master in Paris. The governor of South Carolina called for troops to support his rule. The *Tribune* insisted that Grant was departing from Republican principles. It said on March 24: "There is a feeling of depression among those who desire the success of the Republican party in the next campaign. The hope that such success can be obtained through the nomination of Grant is well nigh abandoned."

Among the reasons for this feeling, over-taxation and a long dullness of business were named. The *Tribune* opposed the President's proposal to march troops into Southern states unless state authorities asked for it. A reform movement within the Republican party started in Ohio. It was against the "violent policy of holding the South in subjection." This received the support of the *Tribune*.

The La Salle Street tunnel was nearing completion and the city council debated in the closing days of March on the installation of fire alarm boxes. The Chicago Library Association held an election on the basis of no entangling alliances with any other association. William Bross led the ticket and was elected. Jeff Davis became president of a Memphis life insurance company. A sensation was caused in Chicago by the murder of Dr. E. S. Scanland by his brother-in-law, P. A. Leonard.

A three-column first-page advertisment, with a wood cut picturing "the greatest soda fountain in the world," was an innovation of April 12. A national music festival, with prizes given on tickets sold, the proceeds to go to an industrial college and home for "unfortunate females," was proposed in April. The *Tribune* said this was a violation of the lottery laws and called the attention of the states attorney to it.

"Gath" exposed a "ten million dollar carpet bag railroad grab" in Florida.

The rise of William Tweed in New York and the decline of Jim Fisk were related in a New York letter. The German Reichstag opened. The Ku Klux or "force bill" was debated in Washington. An editorial from the *Tribune* "Shall the Sword Supersede the Law?" was read in the House by Representative Kerr of Indiana. The *Tribune* hoped it would benefit the members.

Chicago's population at this time was 298,977, of whom 154,420 were American born. Every language was spoken here and every religion had its believers. A map of the proposed Northern Pacific railroad was published on April 28.

Fourteen extra pages were run on May 2 on tax sales. David A. Wells, former special commissioner of revenue, was given seven columns on May 5 in an address in Chicago on the ruinous effect of high tariffs.

The *Tribune* called attention to "advertising bummers, who call on subscribers and seek ads for their sheets." It renewed its attacks on gambling, publishing a list of eighteen downtown gambling places where poker games might be found. Mayor Mason ordered a cleanup.

The *Chicago Times* on May 7 called the *Tribune* a liar for its article on "advertising bummers" or salesmen. The *Tribune* returned the compliment by calling the *Times* a

Said to have cost $600,000, Crosby's Opera House opened in April, 1865. On October 9, 1871, the opening day of its new fall and winter season, it was destroyed in the great Chicago fire.
(Courtesy Chicago Historical Society)

blackmailing institution. This interchange continued a few days. The *Tribune* on May 10 said its employes were "no bummers," and continued, "It takes no means to influence public opinion as to its own advantages as an advertising medium. Its business, like that of a railway, advertises itself."

A reader wrote movingly on May 15 on "Give me work. One more man, skilled, unable to get a job. God help the unemployed strangers in our city."

The one-term rule should be adopted for President of the United States, said the *Tribune*, on May 17. A reign of terror was reported in Paris late in May.

In a Senate investigation into a "leak" concerning the publication of the treaty with England on the *Alabama* claims, two *New York Tribune* correspondents were ordered to jail. They refused to tell where they got it. The treaty was also printed in the *Chicago Tribune*. The two reporters were "jailed" in a private office and then discharged.

Horace Greeley became a presidential candidate. The *Tribune* said that there was little expectation that he would be nominated, but "the politicians cannot whistle him down the wind."

Germans in Chicago celebrated the establishment of the German empire and the overthrow of France. Communists were being shot in Paris early in June. The *Tribune* sent its Washington correspondent to Salt Lake City to write about the Mormons. The warm weather was making the Chicago River "unendurable," the *Tribune* said. The water supply of the city was declared to be insufficient and a new tunnel was proposed.

General Sherman declined to run for the presidency. Greeley toured the South on a political fishing trip. The French republic was launched. Indian policy was discussed at a meeting in Farwell Hall at which Indian chiefs were present.

Enforcement of the Sunday saloon closing law became an issue in the city. The *Tribune* was for mild methods of enforcement. The Democrats resolved that beer and religious liberty were inalienable rights.

The death of C. L. Vallandigham was reported on June 18. The *Tribune*, which had fought him all of his political life, gave him a kindly notice.

A letter from Joseph Medill was published on June 20 in which he denied that he had bought a $450,000 plantation in Louisiana, as alleged in the *New York Sun*. An article was printed on the wonders of violet rays. The work of deepening the Illinois-Michigan Canal which had been going on for six years was reported near completion on July 1, 1871.

Everyone was going to Evanston for the Fourth, it was reported. Excursions by train and steamer had been arranged. " All the beauty, intelligence, brilliancy, wealth, respectability, learning, toilette, fashion, will be there." The celebration was in charge of the Evanston College for Ladies. Bross went to Waukegan for the Fourth and said he was about to start on a trip to the Red River of the North.

"Hound the professional gamblers out of town," the *Tribune* called on July 6, in an article on "the faro hells" of the city. Irish riots in New York were given a first page spread on July 13. Two hundred were said to be dead. The *Tribune* said the Irish were trying to run the New York government.

City detectives were commended in their job of tracking Alfred Zeigenmeyer to Germany and bringing him back for the murder of M. W. Gumbleton. The bones of Gumbleton's arm were offered in evidence in a notable trial which resulted in the conviction of Zeigenmeyer.

The *Tribune* suggested the building of a canal across the isthmus of Panama.

The *New York Times* exposure of the Tammany Hall ring was printed on the first page on July 25. The *Tribune* told of Chicago stealings in which Democratic politicians got big spoils. The net ordinary expenses of the national government during the year were reported at 132 millions on August 16. The war debt and pensions amounted to 160 millions more.

Japan came into telegraphic communication with the outer world, it was related on August 17. Editor White took a trip down the St. Lawrence River and wrote about it. Bross was sending in letters from the West. The postoffice brought five millions in gold from California. The *Tribune* said they could also bring wheat and corn as a way of breaking monopolies.

Speaker Blaine was serenaded at Saratoga and was more in the spotlight as a presidential candidate. Horace Greeley called the editor of the *Tribune* "a sublime liar." The *Tribune* had a light editorial on the subject of lies and forgave him.

Stage robberies and Indian battles were reported from the Far West in September. The city council wrestled with the water pipe question. Science was beginning to forecast weather. South Carolina reported Klan outrages.

Karl Marx, who was referred to as a leading spirit of the "International Society," died in his 53rd year in London.

Greeley called on "Long John" Wentworth in Chicago on September 9 and was told that Grant did not have a chance for the nomination. General J. L. Beveridge was nominated for Congressman-at-large at the state Republican convention.

Five thousand swine were exhibited at Dexter Park. Fall openings of new hats and dresses were announced in the stores.

The *Tribune* on October 8 called for contributions of $3,000 each from one hundred men to buy a public library site at Dearborn and Adams Streets.

On October 8, 1871, a page-one advertisement screamed: "Fire—fire, prepare for fall and winter fires." This was merely the injunction of the Mutual Security Insurance company, which called attention to a disastrous conflagration on the west side of the city the previous night.

The next issue of the *Tribune* on file, that of October 12, turned the clock back to the early days. It was a four-page paper, poorly printed, carrying "cards" of advertising with its big news story. "The Ruins," and long lists of the missing. It was an intimation of what happened on the night of October 8-9 and the next morning. The city was under martial law, with General Sheridan in charge. The *Tribune* "fireproof" building had been destroyed, along with the rest of the main part of the city, and new offices had been opened at 15 South Canal Street.

The *Tribune* said it was by several hours the last newspaper in Chicago to survive the general destruction. "Surrounded by fire on two sides for four hours, it was the last to succumb." The building had cost $225,000 and its contents were valued at $100,000. There was no insurance. The building had lasted until 10 o'clock on the morning of October 10.

The story of what happened to Chicago and the *Tribune* may be found in a general way in the edition of February 15, 1873, when the *Tribune* was housed in a fine new home and had invited its friends to call. "The fire had swept north of Van Buren Street from the east side of Dearborn Street west to the river. The courthouse was gone. The great hotels were in ashes. North of THE TRIBUNE building flames had swept eastward, laying in ruins the massive buildings closest the business heart of the city, Field and Leiter's store and all the section south and east to the river.

"THE TRIBUNE building stood like a mailed warrior, lightly scathed by rolling flames of heat and flames that swept over it. All night long the usual functions of a great journal had gone forward. The whole office force reported, and column after column was put in type long after every other printing establishment in the city had gone down in the tornado of fire. When the gas gave out candles were procured and the work went on.

"The staunch building was fireproof and so seemed THE TRIBUNE workers, who came and went among the streets choked with the fearful melee of the appalling night, and from the top of the building sheltered themselves from the furnace blasts of heat and noted the progress of the devastation.

"Here is the last take set in the old TRIBUNE composing room by the light of the burning city, by John Tippett, who clung to his composing stick:

"'. . . and the wind raging, and the fire burning, and London and Paris and Portland outdone, and no Milton and no Dante on earth to put the words together!'

"A group of men on the fourth story of this office all write at once on the spectacle and hand sheet after sheet of copy to their faithful compositors, who have not forsaken their posts.

"The first form was locked and the forms went to press. By this time human courage gave way. The first pages were worked off, the outside last pages put on the press. Steam was up and there the work ended.

"The fire cut a new swath across the city at Taylor Street and swept like a prairie flame up State Street. The stately Palmer House came down like a castle of cards. McVickers put on its last spectacular effect, and, attacked in the rear, by the treachery of a rear wall, THE TRIBUNE succumbed."

In another special edition, that of February 1, 1891, the recollections of various members of the staff were gathered and a picture given of the building at 15 Canal Street. The inside pages of the edition of October 9, 1871, had been printed, and the story of the fire had been written and set up when the workers were forced to drop everything and flee. Elias Colbert grabbed up a copy of the half-issue as he passed the press room and this was the only copy saved. It was reprinted in this 1891 memorial edition under the caption "While the Fire Raged."

Joseph Medill, who was then living at Morgan and Washington Streets, was awakened by his family on the night of

October 9 and told that a great fire was raging. He made his way downtown and stood on the Randolph Street bridge and saw the Court House catch fire. He became alarmed for the *Tribune* building and arrived there a little after midnight. Printers were at work setting up the story of the fire. By 3 or 4 o'clock in the morning the fire had swept Clark Street as far south as Monroe. The roof of the *Tribune* building was constantly catching fire from flying brands and Medill went up there and worked for hours with Colbert, Conrad Kahler of the press room and others, stamping out the sparks. At 7 a.m. it was found that the rollers on the presses had melted and the great story would never be printed. Medill ordered everyone out and told them to save the files prior to 1860, as he had the files after that date in his home. But the books had to be dropped on the sidewalk as the men fled, because the fire was too close. Medill went east on Madison Street with his brother, Samuel, and they got home at about 9 o'clock in the morning. After two hours sleep they were out again and at work.

It was the duty of G. P. English, night police reporter, to cover all important fires, and he tried to do his duty on that night. He went out to the place where the fire started and stood in the alley where the O'Leary barn had been and talked with people around there. The story of the cow and the lantern had already been sent out by the correspondent of the *New York Herald*. English did not believe it then and never did. He went back to the office.

"Where is the fire?" asked City Editor Samuel Medill.

"Everywhere."

"Write it up."

He wrote until he was ordered to the roof to help save the building. When the work was over he wandered out and borrowed $10 from a desk sergeant and went home.

Elias Colbert was on the roof dictating notes on the progress of the fire when Medill ordered them all out. He saved the little telescope he had set up on the roof to study sun spots, also his scientific note book, and got home safely.

Critic George P. Upton had great faith in the security of the building. All he did was to lock the door on his valuable collection of manuscripts and notes. He saw the men in the press room working by candle light at 3:30 a.m. City Editor Medill was asleep on the couch in his office. The work on the fire edition was over and he thought it would soon be on the presses. "It would have been a wonderful paper," said Upton, who returned to what was left of his office a few days later and found only a pair of scissors.

Joseph Medill set to work the next morning. He heard of an old job printing office on Canal Street and leased it. He heard of a press in the neighborhood, hunted up the owner and bought it just ahead of the agent of another newspaper. He sent out word to his staff to come to Canal Street and they began to get out a paper, working for a few days in partnership with the *Journal*. For a few weeks they had to cart the forms several blocks to the press. Medill heard of a four-cylinder press in Baltimore and bought it by telegraph and in a few hours it was on its way by express to Chicago. Murat Halstead sent on a font of old type from Cincinnati. And so the rebuilding of the *Tribune* began.

In an article on "Brethren of the Press" on October 12, the *Tribune* said:

"No time will be lost in getting to work again at Madison and Dearborn. The Cincinnati Commercial sent us a complete font of type, distributed in cases. The St. Louis Democrat sent us 65 bundles of paper. The Cincinnati Gazette and Enquirer offered us anything we need. The Aurora Beacon offered to print our paper. Among our brethren of the press a spirit of liberality is equalled only by the magnificent charity which has flowed in to the suffering people of Chicago from all quarters of this blessed land. God be praised for such loving hearts."

The advertisments of the October 12 edition were chiefly cards of new addresses of burned out firms. In this issue Joseph Medill's famous editorial, "Rebuild the City," was printed, as follows:

"All is not lost. Though four hundred million dollars worth of property has been destroyed, Chicago still exists. She was not a mere collection of stone, and bricks and lumber.

"These are but the evidence of the power that produced those things; they were but the external proof of the high courage, unconquerable energy, strong faith and restless perseverance which have built up here a commercial metropolis.

"The great natural resources are all in existence; the lake, with its navies, the spacious harbor, the vast empire of production, extending westward to the Pacific; the great outlet from the lakes to the ocean, the thirty-six lines of railway connecting the city with every part of the continent — these, the great arteries of trade and commerce, all remain unimpaired, undiminished and all ready for immediate resumption.

"What, therefore, has been lost? We have lost the accumulated profits of twenty years of prosperous growth. We have lost the stock of trade we had on hand the night of the fire. We have lost money — but we have saved life, health, vigor and industry. We have a dozen grain elevators yet remaining. We have the materials on hand with which to replace those we have lost. We have, within 36 hours' time, the whole country to draw upon for supplies of every description of goods.

"In two weeks from the date of the fire our merchants can fill almost any order for merchandise that may be sent them. The credit of Chicago is saved. When the whole country has faith, and hope and confidence in us, there will be no depression in Chicago itself. The wholesale trade of the city can be resumed at once. Temporary warehouses are being erected and business resumed.

"Let no trouble be borrowed from the past. All the losses of the fire will in time be passed into the great clearing house, and the payment of balances will be made easy for everybody. Rich men have become poor; the accumulations of years have been destroyed; but no one will sit down and waste time crying for spilled milk. Labor will be resumed, production will be restored, and the general trade and commerce of the city will at once be resumed.

"Let us avail ourselves of the liberal spirit which the country has shown in our calamity. There are no relentless creditors pressing us for payment, or demanding the full measure of their bonds. On the contrary, the world is asking us to take money — unlimited credit, and go ahead, leaving the past to be taken care of in the future, when Chicago shall have resumed her power and glory. Let the watchword henceforth be — Chicago Shall Rise Again."

The *Tribune* continued to get out a four-page paper at five cents a copy. Lists of casualties were published, some financial and insurance news, but the paper consisted chiefly of small advertisments, and there was not room enough for all of these that were offered.

The *Tribune* suggested on October 13 that Congress appropriate five millions for new public buildings here. It was announced on October 14 that the Sherman House and the Palmer House were to rise again. Rain fell on the ashes and the work of the soldiers and the relief society began to bring some order out of the chaos. The banks resolved to resume payments. The old fire engines were dug up, with cylinders unharmed and preparations began to combat the next fire. The courts went into high school buildings.

The *Tribune* apologized to its country customers on October 19, saying that the postoffice was disorganized and they were sending out all they could by train boys. Examination of the *Tribune* building showed that $50,000 would repair the damages and it was announced that rebuilding would begin soon. Thirty-five thousand people were being helped each day by the relief society.

On October 20, 1871, it was estimated that 13,500 buildings, out of 60,000, had been destroyed, 92,000 people driven from their homes. But the west division was almost intact, while a great mass of dwellings and factories remained in the south division. Subscribers were served by mail beginning October 23. The *Tribune* on October 27 said it expected to move into the old building about January 1. Editorials appeared on page one again and politics began to take attention.

The *Tribune* printed six pages on November 1. Fire sales had begun and there was a deluge of advertising. John V. Farwell led with sales offers. Field, Leiter & Company had taken a street-car barn at State and 20th Streets and were transacting business there.

The "Union-Fireproof" ticket was advocated by the *Tribune* as better for the credit of the city. Politics was "out" as in war, it was argued. N. B. Judd and Carter H. Harrison were on the executive committee of the Union organization. This ticket, it was announced on November 2, was headed by Joseph Medill for mayor. The *Tribune* announced increased printing facilities and restored rates on display advertising, which meant a three- or four-inch card. The courts and theatres were open. By November 4 the paper was almost back to normal in appearance.

There was no special personal campaign begun for the election of Medill. The opposition, however, was attacked as "the bummer ticket" and the election of the "Union-Fireproof" group was made one with good credit and rebuilding of the city.

Medill's majority over "the bummers" was 10,000, it was announced on November 8. General Beveridge was elected Congressman-at-large. Fourteen "fireproof" aldermen were elected.

"Chicago has indeed risen from her ashes," said the

Tribune, "and today she stands the object of admiration and approval of the world, as a magnificent illustration of determination and ability of her citizens to help themselves, and, by an example of political magnanimity and unselfishness almost without parallel, to begin at the very foundation and restore their beloved city to more than her former greatness."

Mayor-elect Medill said, when the returns came in at Union headquarters: "I have been called to the head of the city government by the almost unanimous expression of the entire community. I accepted the nomination diffidently, but hopefully. I shall not deny that I felt flattered in the confidence expressed in my fitness.

"I shall enter on the discharge of my duties under the most trying and difficult circumstances. All records, reports, proceedings, books, vouchers, almost the entire municipal history, have been destroyed, blotted out. The various offices are scattered all over the city. The office at present is stripped of many of its powers and is almost an ornamental appendage. It requires power necessary to enable it to discharge powers effectively. If the people desire to hold me responsible we must ask the legislature to have these powers restored. We now have independent departments spending the largest possible amounts. Economy and retrenchment are imperative. The mayor should be clothed with power to make reforms. The only pledge I make is that I will be governed in all official actions by an eye to the public good. I have given no promises or pledges to any person or corporation. The affairs of this city must hereafter be conducted as a prudent and wise man manages his own affairs."

Four weeks after the fire, the *Tribune* said, "Chicago no longer needs the forbearance of her commercial rivals. We are once more on our feet with a full stomach and we welcome them to a friendly contest for commercial supremacy." This was addressed particularly to St. Louis and Cincinnati. "We have money to rebuild and faith in God."

Medill's majority over C. P. Holden, his rival, was 11,337, it was announced on November 9. At least 17 out of the 20 aldermen were deemed "trustworthy" by the *Tribune*. New York went Republican that year as a protest against the Tweed exposures and Republican victories were general. The *Tribune* said the party was stronger than ever.

"No more wooden buildings — let us now commence to built a first class city," cried the *Tribune* on November 11. The loss of 20 years of criminal records of the Pinkerton agency was learned, also 20 years of Chicago newspaper files had been burned. One hundred and twenty-two miles of pine sidewalks were gone.

Chicago's reform bill was introduced in the legislature November 18. "We should confer enough power on the mayor to make him a mayor instead of a mere stick," said the *Tribune*. This bill gave the mayor power to name the members of municipal boards.

The prospectus for 1872, printed on November 20, told of the news features of the *Tribune* and promised a weekly report of the rebuilding of Chicago.

"This is a presidential year and the campaign will in all probability be as exciting as any since the outbreak of the late war. THE CHICAGO TRIBUNE will uphold and defend the principles of the Republican party with its accustomed earnestness. Our platform: Equal and exact justice at the ballot box for all men, without distinction of race or color. Amnesty for political offenses connected with the rebellion. Tariff for revenue only. Preservation of public lands for actual settlers. Opposition to monopolies of every description and corruption in every form."

Arrangements had been made, it was stated, for machinery which would give the *Tribune* the same facilities as before the fire. On the occupation of the new building and the installation of the machinery, the *Tribune* said it would issue an eight-page newspaper.

An investigation of the great fire was reported on November 25. Mrs. O'Leary had been examined. She and her husband and five children were in bed on that Sunday night. A neighbor, Sullivan, awoke them and told them their barn was on fire. A neighboring family named McLaughlin had been having a special oyster supper that evening and she had been told that one of the party went into the barn to milk the cow. She saw nothing until the fire engines came.

The subject of the fire was taken off the first page December 1. The town was getting back to normal interests. Dancing academies were open. The Sir Roger Tichborne case in London claimed attention. The question of a free public library was taken up again. A new poem by Longfellow, *The Divine Tragedy*, was published.

English friends had sent a contribution of books to Chicago. The Grace Methodist congregation, La Salle Street and Chicago Avenue, was again at worship in a temporary building.

Medill's inaugural address was printed on December 5, 1871. He was for brick instead of pine structures. The fire limits must be co-extensive with the limits of the city. There must be a better water supply. "Happily there is left that which the fire cannot consume," said the mayor. "Habits of industry and self reliance, personal integrity, business aptitude, mechanical skill, and unconquerable will. These created what the flames devoured and these can speedily recreate more than was swept away."

The legislature was urged, in an editorial of December 9, to pass the legislation giving more power to the mayor. The *Tribune* on December 11 thanked the railroads for bringing in their new Hoe press from New York.

In connection with a *New York Times* article on Grant's nepotism and gift taking, the *Tribune* on December 12 printed the evidence, the list of appointees, and said: "We are constrained to say that acceptance of presents and the appointment of certain of the donors to office, and the appointment of relatives and family connections to office, are breaches of public decorum and constitute a pernicious example to the President's subordinate officers in all branches of the public service."

The board of police and fire commissioners on December 12 found that the fire originated in a barn in the rear of 137 DeKoven Street, on the premises of Patrick O'Leary. It crossed the river between Van Buren and Adams Streets by flying brands. The loss was about 200 millions, and 2,150 acres had been burned over. The fire department did all it could, it was reported, but the wind and the wooden buildings, too few engines, and the burning of the pumping works did the work of destruction.

Eighty-three cases of smallpox were reported in the city on December 13. The *Tribune* said the city council was controlled by corruptionists and the selling of offices had begun. An investigation of city hall corruption was demanded and got under way in a week. A special grand jury was appointed for this job on December 20. Smallpox was becoming epidemic.

A report of the Relief and Aid Society, of which George M. Pullman was treasurer, was made on December 21. Eighteen thousand families had been succored since the fire. Gifts from the United States totaled $1,875,062. Foreign gifts were $610,821, more than half of this from England.

Mayor Medill closed up all unlicensed saloons on December 24. There was a big snow storm and no paper the day after Christmas. Holiday gifts to the fire sufferers came from all over the world, including $10,000 from Lima and Callao, Peru.

Four aldermen and an ex-alderman of the City Hall "ring" were indicted on December 30, 1871. The Grand Duke Alexis of Russia was in Chicago and was received by the Mayor.

Chapter Ten

THE TRIBUNE SEEKS TO SAVE THE SOUTH

WHILE Mayor Medill was occupied with the problems of relief and the rebuilding of Chicago, the *Tribune* in 1872 entered a unique political campaign, taking the side of "the people" and the white South against the candidacy of President Grant for re-election. Under Editor White's guidance the paper attacked the "Old Guard" of the administration as imperialists, and pictured the President as a one-man power, bent on destroying the South through military support of carpet-bag rule.

The *Tribune* was led by this view of the national situation into a somewhat belated and hesitant support of Horace Greeley as an independent Republican candidate for the presidency. Once committed to him, however, the paper gave him its usual vigorous campaign aid. It was 1860 and the liberal Lincoln period all over again, according to the *Tribune* editorial view.

In its issue of January 1, 1872, the *Tribune* said: "THE TRIBUNE will henceforth as always, labor for the best interests of the new city; will still continue to be the people's TRIBUNE, advocating the Right without regard to men; and, in the administration of city, state and national affairs, demand only the Truth, Justice and Right, for these are higher than Party, Creed or Sect.

"To be opposed to the nomination of Grant is now something akin to disloyalty or Ku Kluxury. A man must be in

141

favor of putting the south under martial law and suspending the writ of habeas corpus in times of peace. A senator must get his ideas from a secret caucus and must not seek to investigate frauds in opposition to the wishes of the caucus. He must be obedient to the administration. Pretty soon we shall have a house of lords without any commons."

The first big news sensation of the year was the killing of Jim Fisk by Edward Stokes in the lobby of the Grand Central Hotel in New York. This was given on page 1 on January 7. "Nemesis has come at last and claimed her own," said the *Tribune.* "Fisk's career of open, unblushing debauchery and corruption is fitly closed by death at the hands of a rival profligate and on account of a worse than worthless woman."

The subject of new buildings in Chicago received attention. The *Tribune* said that the new ones being rushed were firetraps, that the city council was in a condition of paralysis on the question and a meeting of citizens was suggested.

The January 8 issue contained a long account of the death and career of Fisk.

Senator Carl Schurz of Wisconsin was defended by the *Tribune* on January 11 against attacks by the *New York Times.* The *Tribune* agreed with the *Springfield Republican* that it might be well to nominate someone other than Grant. "Nothing could be worse for the party than to nominate a man forced on the party by the agency of office holders."

The Republican national convention was called to meet in Philadelphia on June 5. The Washington correspondent was sent to New York to cover the Fisk story. "The history of an unholy love," that of Josie Mansfield and Fisk, was printed on January 15, documented by letters.

Opponents of the new fire prevention ordinance created a "temporary reign of terror" in the city hall, according to the January 16 issue. They raided the hall and threw brickbats at the council members, who fled. No such mob intimidations should be allowed, the *Tribune* said, adding that "even the

Chicago, Oct 5, 1872

My Dear Mr. Vice President:

It is only within a few days that I began to think the charge was any doubt about the passage of the Cheap whiskey that bill. It did not seem probable that Congress would deny this important measure I and to our trust our people. We especially seems to me the very animal and heartless thing a man when he is here is not even indeed a slave or commend action men whereby if he is a great and neighbor. A great city lies fallen by the agency of some devil, and is struggling to "rise and the Cheer—So-vit fellow" are tracking and pulling it. What a spectacle for gods and men!

This is the only letter I have written to any one in or out of Congress on this subject. Indeed I have no time to write except that I took from the news that I should be invited to believe. But that that I must act so I am how can people feel about this master. What I have said is a feeble and imperfect way of proving it. But we shall have that, and surrow on calamity and not again even with the heavy additional load laid on us by the government under the Michigan influence of the prohibitionists. But make it predestined; we shall live to get even with them, our fund turn devenus on other. We expect to arm but it is simply the beginning of the end.

Very truly, yours,
J. Medill.

A characteristically hard-hitting letter written by Joseph Medill to Schuyler Colfax, Vice-President of the United States. Medill wrote in his capacity of Mayor of Chicago.

Decalogue could not be passed under such conditions." The news story on the riot was headed "Communism."

Trial of aldermen indicted for bribery began before Judge Lambert Tree. It was announced on January 17 that Mayor Medill would take the rioting case to the grand jury. It was referred to as the "fire bugs riot," and compared with the "lager beer war" of 1855. Armed police were on hand at the next council meeting. The legislature was asked to increase the power of Chicago's mayor. Alderman Herman O. Glade of the eleventh ward was found guilty of bribery. The row over fire limits continued in the council.

Advance sheets of *The Poet at the Breakfast Table* by Oliver Wendell Holmes were printed on January 21. Relief work was reviewed on January 24. Seventy thousand had been fed, clothed and sheltered. New hotels and theatres were under way. Another alderman was found guilty on January 31.

The mayor's bill was passed in the House, it was reported on February 1. Alderman Gustave A. Busse was convicted of bribery in connection with school lots. The Union Republican party called for a convention. Horace Greeley opposed the nomination of Grant.

The fourth aldermanic conviction was reported on February 2. The testimony indicated that nineteen aldermen had received a hundred dollars each for their influence and votes. The *Tribune* printed six columns on this and said that this marked a new epoch in the government of cities. One hundred dollars fine and six months in jail were meted out to the guilty four. Three were sent to the county jail, where "they began to realize that something had happened," according to the *Tribune*.

A bill to remit duties on imported building material was introduced in Congress as a Chicago relief bill. "The so-called protective tariff," said the *Tribune* on February 14 in connection with an editorial on this bill, "is the foul fiend of

American politics today, as much so as slavery was ten years ago." It told of 20,000 families trying to build new dwellings and how the tariff raised their prices.

A mass meeting was held at the Tremont House on February 17 to urge Congress to pass the relief bill. The Ku Klux Klan investigating committee of Congress reported on February 19.

"Letters from the People," became a feature of the *Tribune*, also a new column headed "Apiary."

Opposition from certain manufacturers in Chicago to the relief bill was commented on in the February 20 issue. This was based on the argument that the manufacturers could not be destroyed and the city remain prosperous. This would be worse than the fire.

The *Tribune* begged its advertisers to condense their copy for the Sunday issue. The Sunday paper of February 8 consisted of eight pages.

The first signed article on sporting news appeared on February 26. This was an article on a rowing contest by Robert B. Johnson. The dramatic column was unsigned.

The Japanese embassy visited Chicago on February 27, and was received by Mayor Medill. It was announced next day it had given $5,000 to the fire sufferers. Retrenchment was ordered in relief and the able bodied were to be taken from the rolls by March 10.

Chicago merchants presented attractive stocks for the spring trade in the March issues. The paper of March 3 carried a page and a half of want ads.

The *Tribune* objected on March 4 to stories about Chicago which had been sent to the *New York Times* by its correspondent here, quoting from the *Times* article: "We [Chicago] are showing our gratitude to a liberal world by supporting 2,000 saloons, five theatres and still further to exhibit our poverty and need of assistance, plans are being drawn for a $400,000 opera house. So you see we intend to keep up with the civilization of the age, notwithstanding the great destruction which came upon us last October." The *Tribune* told of efforts to get a new temperance act and considered the criticism unjustified.

The Japanese visitors purchased a quarter of a million dollars' worth of livestock and farm implements to be shipped from Chicago.

The mayor's bill was passed in the Illinois House. Trumbull was mentioned as a presidential candidate.

Mayor Medill on March 10 wrote a letter to the *New York Tribune* telling of the government of Chicago. This was in answer to a series of questions. Ten new hotels and a west side theatre were being built.

President Grant on March 17 was reported as in favor of the Chicago relief bill, but it was said he thought the passage of the bill was endangered by allusions to its tariff features in the *Chicago Tribune*. The *Tribune* said it had no apologies.

Greeley came out against Grant for re-election and the *Tribune* said that if Greeley were nominated he would get a good many votes in the back country that nobody else could get.

The mayor's bill was passed and signed. On March 20 the *Tribune* said: "The Mayor of Chicago is to be the Mayor in fact as well as in name."

In an editorial on Liberal Republicans on March 29 the *Tribune* said: "We, THE CHICAGO TRIBUNE, are now exactly where we were in the second year of Andrew Johnson's efforts to re-elect himself, when we were rebuked and read out of the party by scores of Crossroads Gazettes and Bungtown Chronicles. . . . The majority of Republicans favor the one term principle and the reform of existing abuses."

The call for a convention of Liberal Republicans at Cincinnati came from the best men, the *Tribune* said on April 1. "The Liberal Republicans today are in the same situation the Republicans were in 1860."

The Chicago relief bill was passed in Congress, but lumber was excepted from its benefits. The *Tribune* quarreled with a Detroit paper over this and with the *Albany Evening Journal*, which, in commenting on the *Tribune's* present position toward Grant asked what the *Tribune* did about Lincoln.

"What THE CHICAGO TRIBUNE did relative to Lincoln was this": said the *Tribune* of April 13. "It was the first to nominate him, the most ardent to elect him, the freest and most independent to advise and criticize him, and the one which he most uniformly read and respected. As to Johnson we were the first daily in the country to oppose his reconstruction policy, the most persistent and effective in working for his overthrow."

This writer was a bit over-enthusiastic in his statement that the *Tribune* was the first to nominate Lincoln, as this history shows. (Vol. I, Chapters 18 and 19.)

The old business district was rapidly assuming the appearance of a city, it was reported in the weekly review of building. The *Tribune* sought to get the city to clean its streets. "French flats may come to Chicago," it was predicted. "These are combined stores and upper dwelling rooms, for several families." Real estate business was bigger than ever and Chicago, it was stated, would soon become larger and more prosperous than ever.

The *Tribune* editors observed closely the growing impact of scientific discoveries and theories upon philosophical and religious thought. They found at this time that there was no conflict between Darwinism and Christianity. "There is no science of the soul, any more than there is a prayer in mathematics."

Forty columns of advertisments were published on April 8 and it was necessary to exclude one page more of advertising. The *Tribune* said this was sufficient answer to the "small-pox circulars" sent out from St. Louis. The ancient rivalry between the two cities, which had died down during the fire relief period, had now blazed up again.

In an editorial on Grant's mistakes, on April 12, the *Tribune* listed his appointments, his neglect of the wise leaders of his party, his "kitchen cabinet" and attempts to control state politics. The reform tide was rising, it was stated, like that of 1860 in Chicago. "All we ask is for people to think for themselves, as in 1860, instead of office holders telling them what to think."

Organization of the Chicago Baseball Association, with Samuel J. Medill as president, was noted on April 14, 1872. They were selling stock and looking for grounds near State and 23rd Streets.

Senator Trumbull, who had made a speech in New York, was hailed as the liberal leader of 1872. The *Tribune* called for organization to back up the Cincinnati convention. Carl Schurz was for it. A campaign against Grant was opened in Chicago among the Germans. The "Old Guard" Republicans were to meet in Philadelphia.

Five columns were printed on April 18 on the Illinois Republican call for the Cincinnati convention, signed by 300. Among the signers of the call were Horace White and William Bross, and such old Lincoln men as Jesse W. Fell, Leonard Swett, O. M. Hatch, Gustav Koerner and William H. Herndon.

Wendell Phillips in Boston delivered an address on the labor question, reported on April 20. He predicted the downfall of Republicanism, and lauded the efforts of workingmen to organize, promising them if they stood by each other faithfully they could elect their President in 1876. He wanted to see the financial system of the country so reconstructed that money could be had at three per cent, instead of ten, and gardens and books and beautiful things given to the working classes, who, in his opinion, ought never to work more than eight hours a day.

The opposition to the Liberal Republican movement, the Tribune said at this time, is "the imperialists who believe in one-man power."

The *Tribune* came to the defense of the white South against carpetbaggers. It would stop swindling and revive industry there.

Henry Ward Beecher, leader of liberal church thought, came out in favor of Sunday reading and against a personal devil. The *Tribune* commended this attitude.

A movement was noted for the nomination of Charles Francis Adams as liberal standard bearer at Cincinnati. Governor Palmer came out for "Cincinnati," declining to let the regulars name him as a delegate to Philadelphia.

The Washington correspondent, on the Cincinnati scene, wrote on April 27 that "the gathering disgusts of three years are about to drive from office an administration elected with unanimity, tried patiently and found incurably vicious."

Horace Greeley's stock appeared to be rising at Cincinnati according to the May 2 report. Carl Schurz was presiding and there was much talk. Nine columns on this appeared in the *Tribune* on May 3. On May 4 it was reported that Greeley had won the presidential nomination on the 6th ballot. B. Gratz Brown of Missouri was the nominee for Vice-President.

Editor White wrote a letter from Cincinnati on this development. It was printed on page one in leaded type and stated that nobody had thought this would happen, that the convention was stunned. The politicians were not for Greeley, White said, but he had convention strength and "the opinion of the best judges this evening is that he will be a popular candidate and the ticket will sweep the country."

The editorial writer at home, calling attention to the White letter, said that Greeley had entered the field as the foe of politicians, that his selection "means a new era in politics. . . . To his support will rally all who really want reform. He is an advocate of amnesty and impartial suffrage. It was a declaration by Republicans that the war has closed."

On May 5 the *Tribune* printed countrywide comment on the nomination. The nomination was at first thought fatal, it was stated, "but now grows in favor and will continue to do so. Greeley will be elected without doubt."

New attacks on Grant began on May 6. "Cincinnati is the true conservation of Republican principles," said the *Tribune.* "We insist that this government can only be rescued from the perils by which it is surrounded, by a complete change of the men who have abused their trusts, been false to the party, have used the machinery of government for their personal ends, and who have done all they can to substitute arbitrary power for the popular will. The Republican party cannot sustain such an administration. . . . The job at Philadelphia is merely to defend the administration. . . . Horace Greeley is the people's candidate and it is useless to oppose him."

Mayor Medill vetoed a fire limits ordinance which had been passed over his objections. Chicago's reconstruction brought attendant labor troubles. Various strikes were in prospect, carpenters, for instance, asking $3.50 a day. A description of Potter Palmer's new $3,000,000 hotel was printed on May 12, 1872.

South Carolina finances were reviewed on May 13, and the *Tribune* said the Liberal Republicans were in favor of rescuing the South from carpetbag rule before it was completely ruined.

On May 14 the death of Alexander Robinson, Pottawatamie chief, at his homestead on the Des Plaines River, was recorded, with a sketch of his history.

The *New York Times*, a Grant organ, accused the *Tribune* of "cheap, coarse, political practices" in pressing the Greeley candidacy. The *Tribune* asked the *Times* to be specific.

A countrywide unrest in labor was noted at this time. A

demonstration was held in Chicago for the eight-hour day. The employers were determined not to yield. Strikes were spreading. The *Tribune* pointed out that the strikers were losing $678,000 a week and said this was not a time to strike as the employers needed full-time work.

A lake shore drive north to Evanston was promoted by citizens, with the support of the *Tribune*, which had always advocated more parks and drives.

It was announced on May 15 that the *Tribune* campaign weekly would be issued until November 15 at a cost of 50 cents a copy.

A Sons of Labor procession was held in Chicago. The *Tribune* said this was a failure as a demonstration, that only 3,154 men were in line. Mayor Medill addressed the marchers. He advocated unions but said they could not compel other men to work at the wages they set. He said it was unwise to strike at this time. He suggested arbitration and co-operation and added:

"I have nothing better to offer than the course I pursued myself; to work steadily at the best wages offered, to practice economy in personal expenditure, drink water instead of whisky, keep out of debt, put your surplus earnings at interest until you have enough make a payment on a lot, build a cottage on it the earliest day possible, go with your wife to church on Sunday and send your children to school. If you have no wife court some worthy girl and marry her; push forward, hopefully and perseveringly, and there is no fear that you can better your condition and become independent men long before old age overtakes you."

The Mayor said he would keep order in Chicago whatever happened. The *Tribune* at this time was in accord with Cyrus H. McCormick, who supported Greeley and asked for an end of sectional strife.

A biography of Dwight L. Moody was printed in the "church intelligence" column of May 19. He had long been known in connection with YMCA work. The Rev. Robert W. Patterson was quoted on the subject of science and religion. He took the attitude which the *Tribune* consistently followed, that religion must keep abreast of science and commend itself to intelligence.

The state Republican convention on May 23 nominated Richard J. Oglesby for Governor and endorsed Grant. The Liberals were to meet at Springfield on June 26. The *Tribune* said the Republican state central committee was largely made up of those who fed from the public service.

A "grand uprising" for Greeley and Brown was hailed in the campaign notes of May 24. The state Republican platform was said to be a "cowardly evasion of the issues."

A two-column review of Longfellow's new book, *Tales of a Wayside Inn*, was printed on May 26. John M. Palmer was given a page on May 27 on the opening of the campaign in the state. The new grounds of the Chicago Baseball Association near 23rd and State Streets were opened on May 29. Two thousand attended the game between Baltimore and Cleveland.

A speech by Senator Charles Sumner, arraigning the Grant administration and giving a history of the Republican party, was given most of the first page on June 1. The *Tribune* saw the end of the reign of national conventions and hoped to see "both parties rent like the Veil of the Temple from top to bottom, so that all members will feel free to follow personal convictions untrammeled by party lash or convention."

A special dispatch from Philadelphia on the eve of the convention, June 2, predicted the renomination of Grant and Colfax.

In the June 4 report Colfax stock was said to be lower. The convention was called "the brother-in-law convention."

A life of Lincoln edited by Ward H. Lamon was criticized as a book for gossips, in bad taste.

Most of the news space for June 5 and 6 was given to the Philadelphia convention. The *Tribune* declared that Greeley represented intelligence, progress, and morality, while Grant represented brute force, disregard of law, fraud and corruption.

The nomination of Grant, with Henry Wilson of Massachusetts for Vice-President, was reported on June 7, 1872. Wilson was referred to as the head of the Know Nothings in Massachusetts.

A Liberal Republican central committee was organized in Chicago to support the Greeley movement. West side labor was said to be for Greeley, with the "Grant tide ebbing."

Gustave H. Koerner was nominated for Governor by Liberal Republicans and Democrats at Springfield. Outside of politics, the *Tribune* featured the opening of the Edward Stokes trial in New York, while "Peregrine Pickle" covered the world's "peace jubilee," a great music festival in Boston. "Aaron About," travelling correspondent in the West, wrote about Brigham Young's wives, listing twenty-five by name, describing each one.

Mayor Medill on July 2 resigned as presiding officer of the council because of defective hearing.

New York was held up as a strike-ridden city, while Chicago was pictured as free from strikes. The threats had not materialized. The workers apparently had taken the Mayor's advice and put their money in the banks.

Mayor Medill's proclamation against fireworks on July 4 put something of a damper on that celebration in the opinion of small boys, but the list of accidents on July 5 was much smaller than usual.

The Democratic national convention at Baltimore was now the center of interest. The question was whether it would endorse the Cincinnati ticket and platform. The Cincinnati program was to be adopted, the *Tribune* reported on July 9, declaring "the battle already won — the only business of the convention is to ratify the people's candidate, Honest Horace Greeley."

This prediction, so far as nominations was concerned, was verified on July 11 by formal action of the convention. From Greeley headquarters at Long Branch, the *Tribune* pictured "consternation among Southern office holders and carpetbaggers."

Reports of the Stokes trial were carried daily. Liberal meetings were played up, Grant meetings regarded as inspired by postmasters. "Pete Green, the postmaster at Skunk Hollow, is a dreadful enthusiast for President Grant," is a sample of campaign humor in the news.

The opening of the campaign in Chicago was reported on July 20. The next day the *Tribune* said that the most important thing to do was to effect a complete reconciliation between the North and South, adding: "THE CHICAGO TRIBUNE proposes to act in the living present and leave the Dead Past to bury its dead. It claims for its course the merit of honesty and independence. It has no affiliations with any class of office holders or office seekers. Its relations are with the people only. It seeks to elevate the standard of political intelligence and morality and to encourage independence of thought among its readers. In this endeavor it has been amply sustained. From this course it will not be swerved."

"Grant a Swindler" was the heading over a New York story of the President's financial dealings. Senator Lyman Trumbull and Gustave Koerner, candidate for governor, were the chief speakers at a big mass meeting on Market Street on July 29, 1872. The Koerner speech was referred to in the *Tribune* as an "inaugural address." The meeting was pictured as "ablaze with patriotism," while a "few Grant tugs in the river kept up an unearthly whistling."

Straw votes showed Greeley in the lead, the *Tribune* announced on August 1. An election in North Carolina indi-

cated to the editors "the end of the Personal [Grant] Party."
Reformers in Chicago were called upon to organize in every
ward. Joy over the North Carolina election was abated with
later returns, which put the result in doubt and by August
16 it was found that the Grant forces had won after all.
Fraud was charged.

The *Tribune* territory was carefully canvassed for signs
of the Liberal uprising. "We will never help build up a
theory which makes us a Personal government, controlled by
Federal patronage and a subsidized press, tempered by quad-
rennial elections," said the *Tribune* on August 8.

Ten thousand Germans turned out to hear Carl Schurz
speak for Greeley. Reopening of McVickers theatre on
August 16 was an event.

The new city directory gave the population as over
400,000. A police commissioner showed up intoxicated at a
board meeting. The mayor said he had not made up his mind
what to do about it.

The death of Samuel Van Rensselaer Hickcox was
reported on August 18. He was 59 years old and had been
for 15 years on the *Tribune* editorial staff. He had been
Chicago agent of the Associated Press and his last duty was
to send east the news of the great fire.

A wheat-corner scandal occupied attention on August 21.
The *Tribune* advised the Chicago Board of Trade, which
was to open a new building on October 9, to dedicate it to
the suppression of gambling.

News of the death of Rev. Henry Fowler, at one time
editor and part owner of the *Tribune*, was published on
August 22. He had left the *Tribune* to take a pastorate in
Auburn, New York.

The first Japanese vessel ever to come to this country arrived in San Francisco on August 23 with a cargo
of tea.

The *Tribune* quoted Henry Wilson, Grant's campaign

partner, as saying that Grant drank too much, and ought to sign the pledge.

A Greeley and Brown headquarters was opened at Canal and Washington Streets with F. H. Winston as president. The Liberal ticket was printed at the *Tribune* masthead. William Bross was candidate for elector-at-large. The *Tribune* published the speeches of Sumner, Schurz and Trumbull as campaign documents. Wilson was attacked on his Know Nothing record. Andrew Johnson was campaigning in Tennessee for Congressman-at-large. General John A. Logan was for Greeley. Greeley speeches were printed every day, even in the "dog days" of August. A reporter was sent to cover the elections in Maine.

In an editorial on constitutional limitations of power on September 2, the *Tribune* said: "We have reached a point where we shall soon have to decide whether this is a government of law or one of absolute power; whether we are to be protected and governed by a written constitution or by excessive proclamations; whether we are to continue a Republic, such as our fathers established, or fall into the chaos and anarchy of Mexico and the South American republics."

The Washington correspondent was sent to the regular Democratic convention at Louisville, which on September 5 nominated Charles O'Conor of New York for President and John Quincy Adams for Vice-President. They declined to run. The Maine election, although a Grant victory, was taken as ground for Liberal hope. On September 13, 1872, the Tribune announced:

"On or about the 9th of October next, THE TRIBUNE will be issued from its new building, on the corner of Madison and Dearborn Streets, the location which it occupied before the fire. It will be printed on a quarto sheet of the size and shape of the New York Times and will be the largest and handsomest newspaper west of New York City.

"No pains or expense will be spared in making it equal to

the first journals of the world in every department of literary, political and commercial excellence, while, as a newspaper, it will continue in the foremost rank. In announcing this new start after the conflagration which so disastrously affected ourselves, in common with our contemporaries and business men of Chicago generally, we deem it a fitting occasion to repeat that we intend, while helping forward with all our energies the public measures and policies which we deem right, and sustaining the men who fitly represented them, to be independent of party domination, and free from control or influence of caucuses, cliques or conventions, local or national."

Chapter Eleven

THE ATOM OF COURAGE AT WORK

CHICAGO took stock of itself in the latter part of 1872, particularly on the anniversary of the great fire, and found that it was indeed fulfilling the prophecy of Joseph Medill that it would rise from its ashes in greater glory. The "indestructible atom of courage" was at work. There were more houses in Chicago than on the day before the fire. The work of reconstruction was in full blast but it would be a year more, it was predicted, before all the waste places were covered.

On the anniversary of the fire the *Tribune* began moving into its new home at Madison and Dearborn Streets, and published a 16-page edition which attracted wide attention. The formal opening of the new Chamber of Commerce was also held, and the stores were packed with holiday goods and spending crowds.

The Greeley campaign was carried on to its bitter end, which was the defeat of the principles upheld by the *Tribune*. The *Tribune* said it would go ahead on the same lines and that the future lay in the hands of the liberals. The campaign was complicated in Chicago by the Sunday saloon closing question, which had come to plague Mayor Medill as long as he remained at the head of government.

The mayor was forced by circumstances, against his better judgment, into issuing an order for the enforcement of the Sunday ordinance, and thus began a war with the Germans and so-called "bummer" elements which lasted not only through his administration but extended into future campaigns, when he again was at the helm of the *Tribune*. On this issue the *Tribune* was between two fires—its inevitable support of "law and order" and its belief that prohibition by force would not work.

A series of murders in Chicago led to the appointment of a citizens' committee to consider crime and its causes. They came to the conclusion on September 27 that whisky was the chief cause of crime and that Sunday liquor law enforcement was one way to lessen its use. The committee, dominated by clergymen, interviewed the mayor on this question, and they were soon at odds with him. There were 2,300 saloons in Chicago at this time. The mayor told the committee that the citizens had done nothing toward enforcing the Sunday law, that two-thirds of the men of Chicago were of European birth, and regarded it as no more immoral to drink liquor on Sundays than on weekdays.

Chicago saloons, Medill said to the committee, had never ceased to furnish liquor to their customers on any Sunday since the city was incorporated. While deploring intemperance he did not believe the use of an inadequate police force was a practicable way to bring about temperance. Efforts had been made by some of his predecessors to enforce this law, he said, but the most that had been accomplished was the closing of the front doors, and the serving of liquor at the back doors. "I am willing to issue an order to the police to close the saloons on Sunday," he said, "but I can give you no assurance nor hold out any hope that drinking in them can be prevented."

In the meantime the Greeley campaign was carried on in the columns of the *Tribune*. A reporter was sent to Pennsylvania on October 1, 1872, to report on the operations of the political ring there. He attacked Senator Cameron, presidential pardons and the practice of "convict canvassers."

The Credit Mobilier scandal, in which various members of Congress were accused of taking bribes to aid Union Pacific legislation, received much news attention at this time. Greeley campaign items were printed under the head "Our Next President." The Republican regulars and liberals nominated separate county tickets. The regulars were referred to in the *Tribune* as "bummers and professional political barnacles."

Asa Mahan, former president of Oberlin College, wrote a letter on the moral and religious aspects of the campaign, marveling that "any well-informed Christian man can advocate a vote for Grant."

Georgia was captured by the Liberals, it was reported on October 4, and the state was "secure for Greeley." The *Tribune* saw a tidal wave for the New York editor moving in the South. The Washington correspondent went south to report the wavelets.

The musical season interrupted by the fire was to be reopened with Theodore Thomas' orchestra, it was announced on October 6.

On October 8 the *Tribune* issued only four pages on account of the difficulties in moving the editorial, composing and press rooms to the new building. A 16-page anniversary

One year to the day after the destruction of its home in the Chicago fire, the Tribune moved into the building pictured above. It was built on the same site as its predecessor, and was one story higher.

issue was printed on October 9 containing the history of Chicago up to the time of the fire. The *Tribune* said:

"One year ago this morning the newspaper press of Chicago was literally wiped out of existence by a calamity as sudden as it was terrible. On that morning THE TRIBUNE found itself with nothing but its name, its subscribers and a rather picturesque heap of stone, brick and iron in ruins. It was without presses, without engines, without type, files, without furniture, without a home or an abiding place. . . . In less than 48 hours from the destruction of its office THE TRIBUNE was issued again. The fire had destroyed everything but the indestructible atom of courage. From that morning until this it has labored against many obstacles, the chief of which was the want of machinery and room to accommodate its constantly increasing business.

"Time works wonders. . . . The same press in the same room which issued THE TRIBUNE of October 8, 1871, and would have printed the issue of the 9th had the gas burned a few minutes longer, has issued THE CHICAGO TRIBUNE of October 9, 1872. Editors, reporters, printers and pressmen are in their old places and where they stopped work a year ago now resume under better auspices and with stronger resources than ever before. THE TRIBUNE of this morning is an earnest of what it will be hereafter."

This issue was commented on by other papers as the finest newspaper ever published in the United States.

The regular Republican tickets were elected in Pennsylvania, Ohio and Nebraska, with Indiana doubtful. The *Tribune* talked of frauds, and said that "the administration party had all the money, office holders, election machinery and large corporations back of it."

"To Liberals we say — Go on bravely in the path you have entered. Your cause is just. It is still possible to elect your ticket in Illinois."

The history of Chicago contained in this issue filled eight

pages. There were three illustrations of *Tribune* buildings. The latest building was one story higher than the first one on this site and had cost, it was stated, about $165,000 above what could be salvaged out of the old one, which was estimated at $100,000.

The regular edition now became eight pages, with many advertisments still on the first page and editorials taking most of page four. A new printing of the special edition was demanded, as there were orders for 36,000 copies.

Mayor Medill, in speaking at the formal opening of the new Chamber of Commerce building on October 9 said that the time of the fire now seemed like a hideous dream.

"The day after the conflagration," he said, "I made my way with difficulty up the bent, twisted, melted iron stairway of THE TRIBUNE building to the upper story, from the front corner of which I obtained a view of more wide-spread, soul-sickening desolation than mortal eye ever beheld since the destruction of Jerusalem. The proud and stately city of yesterday for miles around had sunk into the cellars and basements. What had hours before been the mart of commerce was now an indescribable chaos of broken columns, fallen walls, streets covered with debris, melted metal, charred and blackened trees standing up like spectres. Thousands of columns of smoke and enveloping tongues of flame still rose out of the tumbling ruins that crashed to earth, throwing up clouds of dust. Great elevators had disappeared. The tall spires of the churches, the court house dome, the stately blocks that were the pride of the city and the admiration of visitors, the noted land marks, your own broad chamber — everything had disappeared."

He estimated a loss of $190,000,000 as the result of this day's work of the fire fiend. He told of the rebuilding that had been accomplished and predicted that in another year Chicago would be ready to receive its friends again, all its wounds healed. He suggested a "house warming" on the second anniversary, a great musical festival and an industrial fair. Under the old fire laws and conditions, he said, the old city was sure to burn up.

"Our sin was in the disuse of the brains given us by the Creator to observe the natural laws that govern our relations to matter. It was a fearful punishment but, in time, will prove a public good. The city will grow faster in population and commerce and become more safe, solid and beautiful than ever was imagined before that event."

Mayor Medill, in an interview with a *Tribune* reporter on October 11, explained that he relied on moral and spiritual agencies rather than physical force to deal with the temperance question. The interview was in response to public criticism of him by the citizens' committee. The committee had visited Superintendent of Police Washburne and the commissioners and had been told that the police would have no trouble in enforcing the order if the Mayor issued it. On that same day, therefore, Mayor Medill issued the formal order to close the saloons on Sunday.

Sales of the special October 9 edition went to 60,000. It had attracted worldwide interest with the story of Chicago's rebuilding.

Hooley's Opera House at Clark and Randolph Streets was completed. Weather reports from Washington became almost a daily feature.

Balzac's *Eugenie Grandet*, translated from the French for the *Tribune*, was published beginning in the October 14 issue.

Beer selling continued as usual in the north division of the city on Sunday, it was reported. The police had not received any new orders on the subject. The October 20 issue contained a review of political parties and presidential votes from 1787 to 1869. Two pages of want ads were printed. This Sunday was a dry day, with the liquor law generally observed.

On October 23 Mayor Medill found himself in trouble

with the Germans, which he had anticipated. A mass meeting of 8,000 was held in Market Street Square to protest the action. They called on the Council to pass a resolution not to enforce the law. The mayor stood firm, telling the Germans on October 27 that the best way to repeal an obnoxious law was to enforce it. Many violations were reported and the police courts were kept busy. The *Tribune* questioned whether any good could come from prohibition. The Personal Liberty League was organized late in the month to combat the efforts of the Temperance Committee.

A mysterious "horse disease," a sort of flu, was first noted on November 1 when one thousand or more horses in the city were said to be stricken. "We will perhaps hear of veloci-pedes and ox carts again," said the Tribune, exhorting the people to bear it cheerfully.

Sunday closing became an issue in the Greeley campaign in the city. The temperance forces put a ticket in the field for legislature and council. As election day approached busi-ness was brought almost to a standstill by the horse epidemic. Horse-drawn buses and streetcars were withdrawn from service.

Election results, announced November 6, gave Grant's majority in Chicago at more than 6,000, with Republican majorities in 18 states out of the 26 returned. "The election is over," said the *Tribune*. "A long tedious and latterly driz-zling campaign has come to a close. General Grant is re-elected. THE TRIBUNE still holds to its principles and the Cincin-nati platform."

The administration majority grew with later reports and Greeley went back as editor of the *New York Tribune*. The Liberals were defeated everywhere. Grant's majority in Illinois was 55,000, with Oglesby elected Governor.

A great fire in Boston absorbed much of the November 11 issue of the *Tribune*, and a relief fund was at once started in Chicago. This grew to $150,000.

"The New Deal" was the heading on a political story of November 14 on the Illinois Senatorship.

The *Tribune* saw no danger from a revived Democratic party. A new water pumping engine, "the largest in the world," was ready for work on November 15.

The *Tribune* completed its removal from 15 Canal Street by November 18. "Having all its forces under one roof again," it stated, "THE TRIBUNE proposes to stay and will be at home to all comers as usual. Housed once more in its own building, comfortably situated in all respects, having a clear conscience, and being under no obligations of any sort, except to furnish its readers with a first class newspaper, tied down to no man or set of men, and independent of all politicians, it sets all sails to the favorable breezes of the coming years."

Horace Greeley's fatal illness was reported on November 29 and his death the next day. "It is done," were his last words. The campaign, it was said, had killed him. The *Tribune* carried two and a half columns of editorial eulogy.

Returning to New York, Henry M. Stanley was the hero of the hour because of his exploit in discovering David Livingstone in Africa. Weekly weather reports from the War Department were printed.

The new city council met and heard Mayor Medill's second annual message. After reviewing the financial condition of the city and suggesting certain improvements, the mayor said: "All that I predicted in my inaugural message, concerning the rapidity of the recovery of this city from the fearful losses of the fire of October, 1871, has more than come to pass. We can look around on a city almost restored in the brief period of a year; with taxable property equal to that before the fire; with a trade and commerce largely increased; with tens of thousands of newcomers added to our population; with general good health; with hopes and prospects of continued growth and a progressive future as in the past; and, is it too much to add, with a zealous and prudent municipal administration to protect and promote the rights and interests of the people?"

President Grant's message to Congress was printed. The tone of it was superior to previous communications, the *Tribune* said, but they did not agree with him on subsidies and the postal telegraph service.

The first train on the Milwaukee and St. Paul railroad arrived in Chicago and the Lake Superior iron regions were open to rail.

Many opinions were printed at this time on the character of the late Horace Greeley. Henry Watterson, Louisville editor, was quoted for two columns. His opinion was that Greeley could not have been elected, that he did not really represent the new movement in American politics. If elected, however, Greeley would have grown into a good President, he declared.

Political turmoil was reported in Louisiana on December 7, with United States soldiers in possession of the state house. The President was determined to sustain the courts there.

A picture of Chicago restored, with banks, insurance, groceries, iron and drygoods men at home in the old stands, was printed on December 8, 1872.

The temperance societies attacked beer as intoxicating and appealed to the Germans to stand by the law. The council tabled a midnight saloon closing ordinance.

A report on the state prison on December 19 showed a population of 1,239 males, 13 females, with a surplus of $36,000 of earnings over expenses. Prison labor was let out by contract at 65 cents a day.

"The present winter," said the *Tribune* on December 22, "finds the theatres rebuilt, with a larger capacity and greater comfort, and more elegance than ever; and the run of amusements includes all the resources that the country affords. Society has opened its doors once more. The retail stores reflect en grosse the revival of social taste. Never before in any western city was there so much capital invested in stocks of jewelry, toys and fancy goods. The very advertisements that are to be found from day to day in THE TRIBUNE will suffice to indicate a degree of social progress that is without parallel in the history of old Chicago."

The first full-page advertisment of modern form to appear in the *Tribune* (see Vol. I, page 336, for an account of an earlier full-page advertisment) was printed on December 23, that of Stanton & Company, family grocers.

Among the Christmas items to be thankful for, the *Tribune* noted "necktie sociables, fluting irons, hay in the horse cars, no-beer Sundays and Theodore Thomas."

Whitelaw Reid took control of the *New York Tribune* and it was reported on December 25 that the sum of $550,000 had been paid for 51 shares of stock in that paper. This would make the value of the entire property $1,100,000, and it was said to be the highest price ever paid for a newspaper on this continent. The *Chicago Tribune* pointed out that this was not exactly correct, that shares in this paper were sold before the fire on the basis of $1,000,000 for the whole and after the fire, when $300,000 of tangible property had been destroyed, without insurance, sales were made on the basis of a valuation of $900,000.

"Gath" was ordered to New Orleans on December 27, 1872. The *New Orleans Times* had been suppressed by Judge Durell in the struggle for political control of the state. The *Tribune* called for impeachment of the judge but the trouble was settled in a few days and the paper resumed publication.

As the year closed, Susan B. Anthony was arrested for illegal voting. The reported death of the King of the Sandwich Isles (now the Hawaiian Islands) brought a story of revolution and annexation. The *Tribune* discouraged the taking of these islands as United States territory.

Chapter Twelve

THE TRIBUNE FALLS FROM REPUBLICAN HEAVEN

LIFE proceeded at an accelerated pace in the Chicago of 1873. It was a year of enormous physical achievement, the opening of great business blocks and palatial hotels, and it was accomplished in the midst of a financial panic which swept over the country following spectacular Wall Street failures. The eight-hour day movement raised its head timidly but was slapped down.

The rebuilding of the city was celebrated in June with the opening of a great exposition on the lake front. There were 60,000 in attendance on the anniversary of the fire.

The Tribune accepted the Grant victory philosophically but snapped at any suggestion of a third term. It called the President the "chief grabber" of the now useless Republican party. A third party was in the making with the backing of the farmers, who were up in arms against the railroad and other monopolies. The *Tribune* gave enthusiastic support to this movement.

Locally the political situation centered around the saloon question. Mayor Medill came out firmly for law and order and had to quell a police revolt as well as deal with the opposition of the saloon keepers and German leaders, represented by the *Illinois Staats-Zeitung*. The *Tribune* supported the law and order group, called the Committee of Seventy, but regretted that it had to alienate so many good people. It had

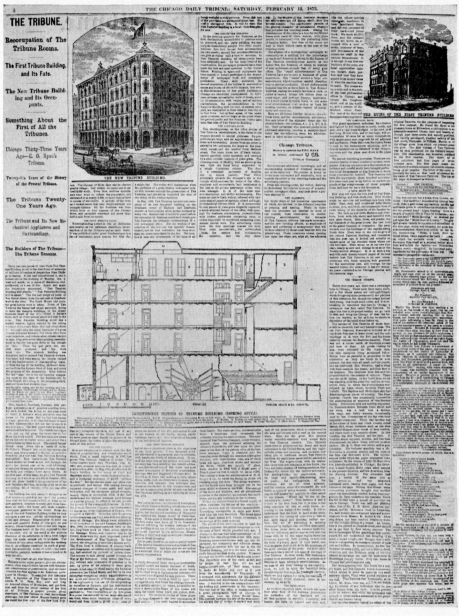

THE TRIBUNE.

Reoccupation of The Tribune Rooms.

The First Tribune Building, and Its Fate.

The New Tribune Building and Its Occupants.

Something About the First of All the Tribunes.

Chicago Thirty-Three Years Ago—E. S. Ryan's Tribune.

Twenty-Six Years of the History of the Present Tribune.

The Tribune Twenty-One Years Ago.

The Tribune and Its New Mechanical Appliances and Surroundings.

The Builders of The Tribune—The Tribune Tenants.

THE NEW TRIBUNE BUILDING.

LONGITUDINAL SECTION OF TRIBUNE BUILDING (LOOKING SOUTH).

THE RUINS OF THE FIRST TRIBUNE BUILDING.

The first of two pages of the issue of February 15, 1873, which were devoted to a concise account of the Tribune's new building, previous homes, and a sketch of its history from June 10, 1847.

little heart in the campaign between the law and order candidate and the so-called "bummer" candidate, and was not surprised when the latter ticket won and this effort at enforced temperance failed.

The year 1873 began with a financial stringency more severe than any since 1857, the *Tribune* said. "The financial situation is bad," it was stated in the January 1 issue, "and it is difficult to see how liabilities are to be met." Chicago was said to be in better shape than other parts of the country. For the New Year, the *Tribune* made a general commendation of "honesty, probity, humanity to man and love to God. We have but one resolution to make and that is to continue issuing the best paper in Chicago or anywhere else," said the paper.

Mayor Medill vetoed the Sunday liquor ordinance of the Personal Liberty League.

Chicago's free library was opened on January 2 with 30,000 books. "Biblomania, Chicago has gone crazy on the subject of books," was the heading on the account of this event. "She proposes to pile up the largest library in America. And she will do it too, or the Hon. Joseph Medill and Hon. Thomas Hoyne are no prophets." Hoyne was president of the library board, on which Medill had labored. Mayor Medill in his address on this occasion pictured this as the start of a great central library, with branches in various parts of the city. He also advocated free lecture courses. All this was for the purpose of leading youth to a wider life.

"There are growing up in this city," he said, "thousands of neglected young men of immature and inchoate mind. They are looked after by the caterers of licentiousness and dissipation, and are rapidly graduating into roughs and rowdies, and grog shop habitues. I have strong hopes that our public library, when well established and its books well circulated, will be the means of rescuing many young men from the downward road they are now traveling, and preventing thousands of others from entering upon paths of vice and dissipation."

A twelve-page Sunday paper was issued on January 12. An account of old Chicago, "the lost city," was printed with this comment: "The long, low red block best known as the quarters for so many years of THE CHICAGO TRIBUNE and the postoffice. The old figures — we see again the slender, active form of Thomas A. Stewart — John L. Scripps, dark-eyed, with silver hair and beard and silver-headed cane, and the full and vigorous figure of Dr. Charles Ray, earnest with a power of expression with tongue and pen that never missed the mark, kindly when kindliness was most beautiful, resistless when worthy occasion was offered and wrath was righteous."

The *Tribune* found a hopeful sign for the punishment of murder in the conviction of Edward Stokes in New York. "Boss" Tweed was to go on trial on criminal charges of fraud.

Grant's popular majority was found to be 759,137. In 1868 it had been 369,588.

New Orleans suspended business. Two legislatures were in session. It was a war of races, with troops held in readiness.

Governor Richard J. Oglesby was named United States Senator by the Republican caucus at Springfield and was elected. The *Tribune* said that the country had been robbed of $30,000,000 in the Union Pacific bond scandal — Credit Mobilier — which was still upsetting Washington.

The so-called "perfumery war," growing out of stockyard stenches, began between Hyde Park citizens and the packers. Railroads were denounced by the farmers' meeting at Bloomington. The First Congregational Church at Ann and Washington Streets was destroyed by fire.

Vice-President Colfax became tangled in the Credit Mobilier scandal. The *Tribune* called for a clean job of investigation. It expressed sorrow over Colfax, but said his acts had not been explained and a smooth career had been broken. The police board was in a row with Superintendent Elmer Washburne, and the mayor suggested that the board be abolished.

On February 1, Mayor Medill stepped out for the law. The police commissioners who would not support Washburne in his efforts to enforce the Sunday law were fired and the police captains who would not support the law and order element were demoted. "The police revolt" was big news. It was announced that the mayor had the support of the Governor and that soldiers would take over if necessary. Merchants came to the support of the mayor. The gamblers tried to bribe Washburne. The mayor's action was referred to in the *Staats-Zeitung* as a "coup d'etat" and he was called "Joseph I, Dictator." The German element was incited against him.

Attention was called in the religious news to a scandal in connection with Henry Ward Beecher, then considered the greatest living preacher. The *Tribune* said this should be investigated. Blackmailers were after him, it was suggested in the New York column. Beecher was making $50,000 a year.

The mayor named two new police commissioners. A law and order mass meeting in support of the mayor was held on February 5. J. V. Farwell and John Wentworth were among the speakers.

Commenting on Credit Mobilier on February 7, the *Tribune* said: "The only public safety is found in the broad principle that government must abandon all business of private nature. For the future let us have no more subsidies, loans, land grants, government aids or protection over industrial enterprise of any sort. People are never so well protected as when they protect themselves."

A full page recounting the history of the *Tribune* was printed on February 13. It told of the first *Chicago Tribune*, established April 4, 1840, by E. C. Ryan, and discontinued August 21, 1841, and of the beginning of the present *Tribune* in 1847.

An impeachment resolution was introduced against Vice-President Colfax on February 21. The *Tribune* said that "even the administration organs could not stand for him longer." The House Judiciary Committee said there was no authority to impeach. Congressmen Oakes Ames and James Brooks, the central figures in Credit Mobilier, were censured but not expelled.

A story that Harvard had abolished morning prayers was printed on February 22. A two-column report on a lecture by Henry Ward Beecher at Union Park Congregational Church was carried on March 1. He talked on "Manhood and Money." The fight against the mayor extended to Springfield in efforts to repeal the law giving him appointment power over boards.

Citizens began to discuss a grand fair, a $300,000 "crystal palace" at Dexter Park.

President Grant was inaugurated for his second term. Colfax returned to his home at South Bend, saying he was guiltless. He was given a grand reception and received a letter from Grant a few days later in which the President expressed his sympathy with and confidence in him. The *Tribune* said of the Colfax demonstration: "The South Benders or those who participated in the ovation have advertised themselves either as ignorant persons, unable to judge of the value of testimony, or those possessing no valuable standard of moral measurement."

Oscar C. Pratt, a former Chicago reporter, killed himself in Omaha. "It is not to be presumed," said the Tribune obituary, "that the grass will refuse to grow over his grave because he was not absolutely faultless, and failed in the solution of life's problems, which perplexes all."

"It Is Done," was the heading on a nine-column descriptive story of the execution of two men for murder on March 15. The Interstate Industrial Exposition planned for the fall got under way.

The *Tribune* printed an exposé on March 18, 1873, of how the country had been swindled in bail bonds without any property back of them. The states attorney moved to correct the law.

James R. Casey, brother-in-law of the President, was renominated for collector of customs at New Orleans. This was a disgrace to civil service, the *Tribune* said, and hoped the Senate would refuse confirmation.

A $500,000 libel suit started by Joel H. Wicker against J. Y. Scammon, publisher of the *Inter-Ocean*, with whom the *Tribune* kept up an intermittent warfare on various grounds, was published on March 23. The *Inter-Ocean* had been started the year before.

Mayor Medill and the new police commission recommended the closing of saloons at 11 p.m.

Three hundred anti-monopoly clubs were organized among the farmers of the state. Revealing articles were printed on the practices of justices and constables in Chicago. Medill resigned as a member of the United States Civil Service Commission. A war with the Modoc Indians began in California. The 11 o'clock closing ordinance was passed. In Washington Speaker James G. Blaine was discussed as a presidential candidate and Congress was busy explaining its "salary grab" action.

Superintendent Washburne issued orders for the closing of saloons on Sundays. Merchants on Clark Street paved the street in front of their own houses of business at $5 a running foot instead of the $7 authorized by city ordinance. The *Tribune* economists figured a 35 to 50 per cent tax on all those who spent $1 a year for suspenders, for protecting labor. The death of Chief Justice Chase was recorded and his career called a shining record.

The Tribune on May 12 demanded a congressional investigation into the blackmailing of Phelps, Dodge & Co., New York importers, by a customs house ring. A story on the murders of the Bender gang in Kansas appeared on May 13. Preparations were made for Jubilee week, to celebrate the great rebuilding, the first week in June. This was to be a countrywide attraction.

The Germans fired the first gun in the saloon war by announcing that they would change the city government for one more to their liking in the fall campaign. The 11 o'clock ordinance went into effect. Chapin and Gore, saloonkeepers, made a test of the law by keeping one of their places open.

A two-column description of the new Grand Pacific Hotel, which was about ready to open, was printed on May 16. A $250,000 "crystal palace" was to be built by September for the exposition. The fashion writer told the women what kind of dresses they might wear at the Jubilee ball.

The German political group attacked the anti-saloon group behind Medill as the "so-called Puritan element in the Republican party," and went out after it. The "Puritans" were denounced in mass meetings and in the German language newspapers, particularly the *Staats-Zeitung*, whose publisher, A. C. Hesing, was the leader of the new political movement.

The Rev. Robert Collyer, discoursing on May 26, on what is a good newspaper, found that the *Tribune* filled the bill. Such newspapers, he said, were the true leaders of the people, and journalism was a sacred calling.

The Committee of Seventy reported on the saloon situation for the law and order forces and told the people they must choose that way or the liberal way, which led to crime.

The *Tribune* on May 27 condemned the G.A.R. for refusing to decorate the graves of the Confederate dead at Arlington on Decoration Day. "The Union and the Confederate soldiers sleep side by side in that dark and silent rest where all men are brothers and the same flowers blossom over them. . . . The G.A.R. is a secret political, not a military organization. Its purpose is to get offices for some members of the Republican party and withhold them from others."

The deadhead system of giving free travel passes to editors and others was condemned by the *Tribune*. "Where is the railroad that will refuse to give passes to anybody? That is the one to be puffed."

On June 1 the mayor revoked the licenses of ten German saloons which had refused to close on Sundays. The revolt grew during Jubilee week, when the city was filled with visitors.

The New York correspondent on June 6 called attention to the eight or nine months old Beecher-Tilton scandal, which he said must be threshed out in the light. Nobody knew what the scandal was, but the "greatest living preacher" had been made the subject of it in connection with the family of Theodore Tilton, editor of the *Independent* and a member of Beecher's Plymouth Church.

Business was dull and real estate moved slowly that summer. The farmers adopted a "Declaration of Independence" of all monopolists. The *Tribune* warned the saloonkeepers they could not control the city and make its laws.

A series of articles on the city's health was printed during June, and the danger of sewage and dirty streets emphasized. The mayor asked for an appropriation of $700,000 for new sewers.

Susan B. Anthony was found guilty of illegal voting in the East and fined $100. The *Tribune* said this should teach the advocates of women's rights a useful lesson — "the folly of attempting to carry out their notions by breaking the law."

Weather began to be a first-page feature, the government reports telling of winds and temperatures appearing frequently. The *Tribune* quoted Henry Ward Beecher on the virtues of journalism as a profession, opposed to servile and party journalism. Beecher made blanket denial of the widespread charges against him.

A duel between R. B. Rhett, Jr., editor of the *New Orleans Picayune* and former Judge William H. Cooley, in which

Cooley was killed, was reported on July 2. The *Tribune* thought that duelling should be outlawed and Rhett should be treated as any other murderer.

Mayor Medill issued a warning against violations of the anti-fireworks and firearms ordinance on July 4, 1873.

On the movement of the farmers away from the Republican party, the *Tribune* said on July 4: "The Republican party was organized by men for a specific purpose. That purpose having been accomplished it has not had, since then, any function but to hold offices, and divide among its managers the plunder resulting from reckless and corrupt administration of government."

Iowa papers, among others, wanted to know why the *Tribune* was trying to hurt the Republican party. "Of what use the cry of reform when fraud and corruption go on as usual?" the *Tribune* asked on July 7. "The time has gone by when the people of America believe that whatever one party proposes must necessarily be right."

A third-term movement for Grant was reported. It was said he had been promised three terms when he left the army. "Grant is the biggest grabber of all and a fitting nomination," said the *Tribune*. The President denied that he had any third-term ambitions.

A 6-cent damage verdict was returned in a libel suit brought by Linda Gilbert against the *Chicago Post*. Mayor Medill announced on July 16 that he was not a candidate for re-election, and would not accept the office if elected.

A staff correspondent was sent to a boat regatta in the East. The *Tribune* on July 17 described an evening on South Park Boulevard, "where the fashionables take the air, beautiful women, gallant men and handsome equipages."

In connection with an editorial on city politics the *Tribune* said that the *Staats-Zeitung* seemed to be impressed that Mayor Medill had either written or inspired the article. This impression was called "an entire mistake."

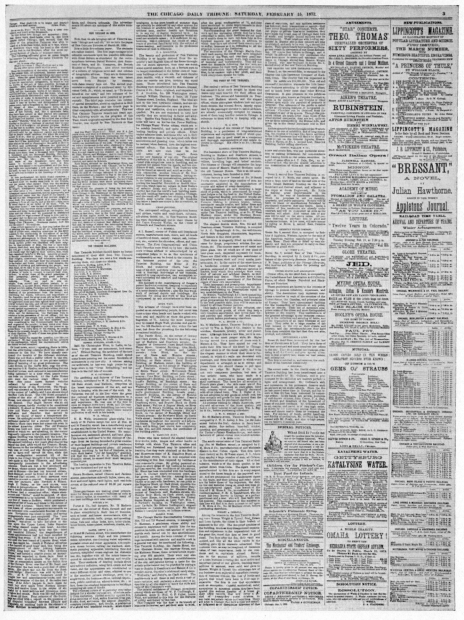

The second of the two pages which in the issue of February 15, 1873, told about
the new Tribune building. It also carried reviews of the various tenants of the building and the construction companies which built it.

"Protected classes" in the United States were listed in the Tribune of July 17 at 782,421, the non-protected at 11,723,-502. Plans were completed for a new City Hall. The temperance committee began to take interest in the campaign. There was another police board row in the mayor's office. The growth of the city toward Humboldt Park was noted. On the subject of why the races at Dexter Park did not pay, the Tribune said on July 20: "It is understood by the public that the gentlemen who have control of the track are not proper persons to cater to their tastes, and THE TRIBUNE, which is read by every person of social standing in the city, puts its foot down on practices indulged in by these gentlemen at a recent meeting."

The Tribune and the Nation were in long-distance controversy over what the Tribune had called watered stocks in railroad financing.

The third-term movement was reported making headway in July. Chicago was suggested as a summer residence for the President. The city council laid on the table a resolution for eight hours of labor daily.

Reporters were sent on August 1 to farmers' meetings at Fort Dodge and Des Moines and all anti-monopoly and liberal meetings in the central west were given attention and space in the Tribune. The reporter who went to Des Moines was accused there of unduly magnifying the anti-monopoly situation. The Tribune editorially backed up its reporter.

A third-party convention in Cincinnati adopted a platform condemning both Republican and Democratic parties for having outlived their usefulness, condemned the congressional salary grab, corruptions in railroads and banks, demanded that the government attend to its own business and leave the people to theirs, declared for duties for revenue only and for the repeal of laws that favor capital to the prejudice of labor.

The superintendent of schools reported that disuse of corporal punishment, which had been tried for a year, had been successful. A sort of reform school for incorrigibles was suggested.

The city population was estimated at 465,170.

Interesting experiments with a young Iowan in mind reading were carried on, in which the young man found hidden articles. This was a forerunner of modern telepathic experiments. "Such a mysterious force exists," the *Tribune* said.

It was madness, the *Tribune* said on August 14, for any party to violate the third-term tradition. On the subject of a national university, which President Eliot of Harvard had reported against, the *Tribune* said:

"A paternal government means a dependent people—that accursed inheritance from the days of the divine right of kings. The greatest and most insidious danger to our institutions and our liberties is the system of subsidies. A paternal government destroys individual enterprise, paralyzes personal industry and creates a nation of dependents and mendicants."

A notice on the editorial page stated that Mayor Medill had asked and obtained leave of absence for the remainder of his term, which expired the first Monday in December. His plan was to visit Europe with his family. One exigency, it was stated, that might cause an early return would be the election of an unfit person for acting-mayor. The mayor would be responsible for the rest of his term to the extent of not permitting the powers of acting-mayor to pass into dangerous hands.

Alderman L. L. Bond, who was acceptable to Medill, was chosen acting-mayor on August 18. "This selection is such," said the *Tribune*, "as to render it unlikely that the mayor will find it necessary to return during the remainder of his term in office. He will sail from New York on the 27th to be gone a year or more, with his family."

A special article, carrying affidavits, was printed on the life and career of Mike McDonald, Chicago's boss gambler. It was said that "probably no man in the city has been responsible for so much misery."

The *Minneapolis Tribune* said that the *Chicago Tribune*, "like Lucifer has fallen head foremost out of heaven." It referred to the Republican heaven.

How each of Brigham Young's 25 wives lived was described in an article by "Aaron About," the *Tribune's* roving Western correspondent.

Double tracks, better watches, better telegraphic service, were discussed as a result of an Alton train wreck at Lemont, Illinois.

Plans were adopted for a new court house and city hall. A staff correspondent was sent to the American Association of Science meeting at Portland, Oregon, and wired detailed reports.

The mayoralty campaign got under way in September. The local Germans were on the war path. The meeting of the Committee of Seventy, the law and order group, was given much space on September 6. A two-column history of the University of Chicago (not today's institution of similar name) was printed the next day. It was announced in the musical news that Theodore Thomas was to go from building an orchestra into the work of building a great chorus for the projected new opera house.

An excursion over the Northwestern to the new Dakota Territory was reported on September 16. Congressman-elect Joseph G. Cannon of Illinois was scolded for his attitude on the salary grab bill. The *Tribune* intimated that he would lose his seat as a result of his attitude.

A so-called grand rally of the Chicago Republicans netted, according to the *Tribune* "7 whites, 3 colored men and a *Times* reporter."

The general business of the city in 1872 had been greater than that of any other year, it was reported. A fire in which ten acres of shanties were burned was reported on September

17. The failure of Jay Cooke & Company, reported on September 19, caused intense excitement. The *Tribune* thought it nothing to make a general panic, and gave much attention to a convention of spiritualists.

President Grant rushed back to Washington to halt the threatened panic. Banks toppled in the East and 19 failures were reported on "Black Friday" in New York. The *Tribune* said that appeals to the Treasury should be met with prompt refusal, that the government should not meddle in business. There was no unusual run on the Chicago banks.

The *Sunday Tribune* of September 21, which had printed several articles by Professor Agassiz, who had not accepted Darwinism, now printed a defense of the evolutionary theory by John Fiske. The *Tribune* kept well abreast of scientific and philosophical thought, as well as printing many orthodox sermons each week.

The presence of President Grant in New York, to deal with the panic, was the big news of September 22, 1873. He ordered the Treasury to buy bonds in any amount and nine millions' worth were purchased on September 24. The panic, however, continued. The *Tribune* advised the people to keep cool and said Chicago was in better shape than any other large city.

The opening of the Interstate Exposition was heralded with a big story, illustrated by a picture of the industrial palace, with flags flying. This was held on the lake front near Michigan and Adams Streets. Governor Beveridge, Senators Logan and Oglesby, and other notables went to the opening, which was attended by 15,000.

On September 26 the *Tribune* wrote scornfully of a sensational story in the *Times* on the closing of banks here. "Chicago yesterday received the Judas kiss and the traitor in her household that betrayed her interests, her business and reputation into the hands of the Philistines is that newspaper sheet which is nothing if not sensational, and insipid when not weak."

Chicago became the center of bank excitement the next day. Five banks suspended temporarily. Loan certificates and checks became currency.

The situation looked brighter the next day. The *Tribune* printed two pages of financial news and advised the people to read "The Holy Book, Plato or Marcus Aurelius." Four million dollars were shipped in here and the President ordered the prepayment of November interest and promised greenbacks if necessary. The situation improved daily and the Exposition continued to draw good attendance.

On October 1, the thirteenth day of the panic, the *Tribune* interviewed business leaders such as Leiter, Farwell, and Mac-Veagh, who presented an optimistic view of the situation. The closing of the Union National Bank had a depressing effect but a hopeful view was taken of business in the West. Public confidence was said to be coming back.

The financial "patient" recovered early in October and life went back to normal. Evanston citizens protested the lighting of Davis Street with gas instead of kerosene on account of the increase in taxes. Racing was featured on the first page. The People's Party met and adopted a platform read by J. K. C. Forrest (one of the original founders of the *Tribune* in 1847), with A. C. Hesing of the *Staats-Zeitung* in the leader's chair. The *Tribune* thought it would be well for them to disband and take places on the broad basis of American citizenship rather than on the narrow issue of Sunday closing. The Committee of Seventy adopted a platform calling for enforcement of the closing laws.

A detailed description of the new Chicago, featuring Palmer's new hotel and the new store of Field, Leiter & Company was published on October 9. In a letter to his friend, A. H. Burley, city controller, Medill in Edinburgh wrote: "There will be a stringent money market for some time to come and Chicago must feel the effects as severely as any other city, in consequence of the sudden rebuilding. Collecting taxes will be as hard as pulling teeth. There is only one course to pursue — shorten up expenditures for the present. Shut off every expense that can be retrenched. Economy and retrenchment are the sheet anchors during this fiscal storm. Postpone public works for the present."

In studying the political situation the *Tribune* saw danger in the extreme platform of the Committee of Seventy. Many good people would refuse to go with them in this and they did not see the necessity of this raid upon the lager-beer people.

A Citizens Independent Movement was started on October 10. The secretary of the organization was Victor F. Lawson, who, three years later was among the founders of the *Chicago Daily News*. The anniversary of the fire, it was reported, had been celebrated at the Exposition by an attendance of 60,000. A charity night was held there for the victims of yellow fever in Memphis. There was a new stock panic in New York. Goldsmith Maid trotted a mile in 2.18 at Dexter Park. Iowa elected an anti-monopoly legislature. California and Ohio also repudiated the Republican party.

Medill in London wrote to a friend in the Chicago Public Library on a day at the British Museum, where there were over a million volumes. "Our poor little nest egg of a library in Chicago shrank into insignificance," he wrote. "I would not think of going abroad if I were at home now but it is not advisable to return home in a panic. When I heard of the collapse of Jay Cooke I took in the situation at a glance. I have seen and known, for a year or more, that things were rotten financially, as well as politically and morally, in America; and that we were approaching a repetition of the experience of 1857, and would soon 'shoot Niagara,' as Carlyle would call it. But the hurricane came a year or two sooner than I had anticipated. It will do good, and is needed to purify

the moral atmosphere. Bankruptcy and hard times will promote piety and honesty."

Opponents of the saloon keepers and their friends nominated Acting-Mayor Bond for mayor. The *Tribune* said on
October 20 that the only thing to do was to unite on the
Bond ticket, which represented good citizenship as against
lawlessness and disorder.

The convention of the People's party was referred to in the
Tribune as "the sample room convention," and the par-
ticipants were called "bummers." "Bummer" H. C. Colvin
was nominated for mayor.

Medill in London wrote on his general impressions of Great
Britain on October 24. It was not a free country, he said, as
only 50,000 persons were interested in ownership of the soil,
and 31 millions were practically hewers of wood and drawers
of water for the aristocrats, who drew 730 millions annually
in ground rents from them. Titles had been founded solely on
robbery.

Medill wrote on the wealth of British capitalists on October
27. They were creditors of eight billions throughout the
world, and the value of their property was estimated at fifty
billions. By way of contrast, there were a million paupers
in the country. Everybody was educated to useful employment except the hereditary aristocrats. "The British are a
peculiar people and have made a mighty impression on the
human race," wrote Medill. "Their power and influence is
not yet exhausted."

The *Tribune* said on October 29 that Acting-Mayor Bond
had succeeded in carrying out the Medill policies, had
enforced the law and had given the city harmonious government.

On November 1, 1873, the *Tribune* began talking about
naturalization frauds in connection with the election. The
naturalization office, it was stated, was a mill that turned
out 500 voters a day. The German leaders called on the

people to unite to defeat the " Puritans." The *Tribune* warned the Citizens Committee that they had a formidable enemy, headed by 2,500 saloon keepers.

Another letter from Medill in London on November 2 told of a conspiracy to keep up the price of coal in England and of the English agricultural serfs. " The people have not yet learned to walk alone or think for themselves."

The *Tribune* asked the people on the eve of election: " Do you want your city converted into a German principality? We believe the great mass of citizens are opposed to the German conquest, but will they go to the polls to prevent it? " A raid on the city treasury was planned, the *Tribune* warned, by an organized " German-Know-Nothing movement."

Theodore Tilton was dropped from membership in Plymouth Church and the Beecher scandal again made the headlines, still without any specification.

On November 5 it was announced that the Hesing ticket had carried the election by a majority of 12,000. Colvin was the new mayor and Daniel O'Hara the city treasurer.

The "Bummers" held a ratification meeting at Kingsbury Hall. Mayor-elect Colvin, the *Tribune* reporter said, was sober, and announced that he would show himself a merciful victor. Hesing announced that he had sent a telegram to Medill in Paris stating that Medill's policy had been defeated by 10,000 majority.

Chapter Thirteen

THE HENRY WARD BEECHER SCANDAL

GREAT and perhaps insoluble problems arose in the social matrix of 1873 and 1874. These were reflected clearly in the rapid industrial growth of Chicago, and in the culture which rested on this base.

In foreign affairs, trouble with Spain over Cuba came to a crisis, foreshadowing the Spanish-American War. In national affairs the question of inflation had to be met, although prosperity was in sight again. In social fields a crusade against the demon rum led by praying women took news precedence. Relief for the poor and unemployed became a big problem in Chicago and in connection with the eight-hour movement led to what the *Tribune* called the "danger of Communism."

The cities must be prepared to meet the ideas of Karl Marx, expressed in the International labor organization, the *Tribune* warned again and again. At the same time it proposed practical measures for relieving the condition of the poor in order to cut the ground from under these dangerous doctrines.

In the religious world the country was shaken by the Henry Ward Beecher scandal, which simmered for months, finally breaking into a trial. The *Tribune*, sympathetic with Beecher, insisted that he meet the situation clearly and unevasively. In Chicago the heresy trial of Professor David Swing occupied the stage for weeks. Letters from Joseph Medill in Europe appeared regularly in the *Tribune*, but his political enemies

183

were in control of the city. As to the aftermath of the November election, the *Tribune* said:

"The election proves that the ignorant and vicious classes, added to the entire German vote, are a majority of the entire population and they have the power to govern and will exercise it whenever any influence is brought to bear that will coalesce them. The election of H. C. Colvin as mayor at any time could only be regarded as a huge practical joke. The Sunday ordinance will go overboard and the police will fall into the hands of a bad and dangerous set of men. The new council, we judge, will be worse than the average."

The political reporter said that the candidates who were defeated would never again rely on good weather. "Weather is very good in its own way," he wrote, "but when it is opposed by a powerful combination it cannot win on its own hook. It wasn't backed up by law and order votes. The Committee of Seventy relied solely upon Providence, forgetting, as Napoleon remarked, that Providence was on the side of the heaviest artillery and helps those who help themselves."

Hesing's victory was proclaimed, it was reported, by the flying of the Prussian flag from the *Staats-Zeitung* building, with an American flag in the background. "Mr. Hesing was elected King and why should he not flaunt his bunting?"

The *Staats-Zeitung* had much to say, such as this: "Seven dailies, the weeklies, all the pastors, were against the People's Party. Such lies and vilification! It was an honest election and means an improvement in city government.

"It most decidedly signifies that Chicago is not a wretched Yankee village, but a cosmopolitan world city; that the citizens of the United States not born in Chicago who helped to make Chicago that which it is, have the majority of power here, and they are not willing to allow themselves to be bound by the special isms and outrageous demands which their fellow citizens, born in the New England states, think decency demands."

The *Freie-Presse* said: "The voters decided by an overwhelming majority that the narrow minded and ignorant Puritans should be stripped of their power and that the government of the city and county is to be conducted on liberal minded principles."

The *Tribune* explained that it did not support the views of the Committee of Seventy and was not intolerant. "Forcible Sabbatarianism and coercive temperance are against TRIBUNE principles too. But this became the issue. THE TRIBUNE was conscious of this before the election and endeavored to modify the issue in accord with commonsense, scientific demonstration and the experience of other communities. Its judgment did not prevail and it was constrained to support the ticket which in its judgment best represented the taxpayers. The result will not have been without avail if it shall teach certain extremists and the impracticable never again to force these issues upon the people."

A history of the Committee of Seventy was published on November 9. Mayor Medill had told the committee on October 2, it was related: "I am endeavoring to do what is practicable to punish drunkenness, preserve order and suppress crime with the small police force at command. But we have to deal with opposing forces, — appetite and cupidity — which are as persistent and unblushing as depravity, and, if your meeting suppose that drinking may be freely indulged in six days of the week, and can be suppressed on the recurring seventh, they have studied human nature to little purpose, and have yet their first lesson to learn."

The charity organizations of the city came together in a co-operative relief effort, the forerunner of United Charities.

Medill wrote three columns from Ireland on November 9. These were a poor and discontented people, he said, ruled by the bayonet, living under a system of land monopoly and absentee landlords. The purpose of the Home Rulers was independence from Great Britain.

185

Anti-monopoly victories in Illinois counties were reported on November 10. As the Exposition closed business was poor and the financial outlook still gloomy. Spanish "butchers" were at work in Cuba. Americans were shot there and feeling in Chicago ran high.

The *Tribune* called attention to the fact that the powers under the mayor's bill expired on March 9 and suggested that these be made permanent.

In reply to complaints from subscribers that the paper had been delivered late for the last six months, the *Tribune* said on November 15, 1873:

"About a year ago THE TRIBUNE invested nearly $300,-000 in building and machinery to take the place of that destroyed by the fire. We left space for more machines but did not anticipate the demand so soon. For the first six months our printing machinery has been wholly inadequate to meet the demands of increasing business. We determined on the addition of three new presses. We have already placed one of the latest improved Bullock printing machines with double delivery and other improvements, a capacity of 15,000 impressions an hour. A single issue of THE TRIBUNE with supplementary sheet requires 140,000 impressions."

The *Philadelphia Press* was quoted on the question as to whether the *Tribune* or the *New York Herald* was entitled to precedence in journalism in this country. The New York paper had printed a 20-page paper containing 120 columns and claimed this the greatest feat in American journalism. The *Chicago Tribune*, the Philadelphia paper said, on the same day had printed 16 pages of 112 columns and had said nothing about it. "The Tribune of the day mentioned [the fire anniversary issue] in all features, news, editorial, literary and local, was probably the best paper ever issued in America," added the *Press*. The *Tribune* said its net receipts probably equaled those of all the other daily papers in Chicago, English and German.

In commenting on the Cuban situation, the *Tribune* said the United States had 26 wooden steamers carrying 530 guns for effective use in foreign war, and that "we may have to create a navy to defend our rights in Cuba."

There was a scramble for offices in the city administration, with a rift developing in the People's party. The *Tribune* said that Mayor Colvin had so far shown a purpose to make the public interest paramount.

The American vessel *Virginius* was captured in Cuban waters and its crew shot or imprisoned. The Church of the Messiah at 23rd Street and Michigan Avenue was dedicated. Medill wrote a letter on the wonders of London. The *Tribune* scolded the *Chicago Times* for indecent and smutty stories. There were war preparations in the navy yards and Governor Beveridge offered artillery, infantry and cavalry for war with Spain. Navy recruiting offices were opened. On November 18, 1873, the *Tribune* printed eight columns of news and comment on this crisis with a four-column map of Cuba.

Elias Colbert had a three-column story on the conjunction of Mars and Saturn, whether the planets were inhabited and how the universe was formed and governed, something of a large subject.

The *Tribune* was against annexation of Cuba and said it must be shown that our rights had been invaded and that Spain refused reparation before war was declared. A correspondent "Walda" was heard from in Peru. Boss Tweed in New York was sentenced to 12 years in prison.

"Let us have peace," was the note of the November 24 issue. President Grant was said to have the war fever. "A war," said the *Tribune*, "would serve as a cover for fraud and corruption, direct thoughts from hard times, etc."

Grant gave an ultimatum to Spain on November 27. "If Grant listens to the evil promptings of men who favor war with Spain as a means of salvation of the Republican party, he will make the most serious mistake of his life," said the

Tribune. On November 30 "Peace" was the news head. Spain had acceded to the demands.

A page on Chicago's transportation system was printed on December 1, with maps of where the cars ran. The Spanish crisis was over. The *Tribune* said it was high time the Beecher scandal was settled. Henry C. Bowen, trustee of the Congregational Union, had fanned the flames of this scandal by questioning the action of Plymouth Church in the Tilton dismissal.

The 42nd Congress came to life and Blaine was re-elected Speaker. Mayor Colvin's inaugural was held in Chicago. He called for economy, a reduction of the tax levy to 15 mills, repeal or modification of the Sunday closing ordinance. He wanted the city gas contract set aside and building of the new court house postponed.

A creditable and satisfactory document, said the *Tribune*, "but his good promises are not borne out by committee appointments." Two indicted aldermen had been named to head the finance and public building committees. The President's message was given a page. The chief trouble, according to the *Tribune*, was that it was too long.

A speech by Medill at a banquet in Paris was reported on December 7. "I came abroad," he said, "to study the institutions, methods and customs of the old world. I expect to return home much changed and modified in previous estimates of men and things, methods and manners. Not a little conceit has already evaporated. It has not modified, however, my love for America, the freest, happiest and most glorious country on earth." In the same issue a letter he had written from Paris was printed, showing how paper money could be made equal to gold.

A lecture by William H. Herndon in Springfield was printed on December 14 on Lincoln as a religious man. Professor William Matthews of the University of Chicago became a regular Sunday contributor on literary subjects.

City Treasurer David A. Gage, it was reported on December 15, was short about $300,000 in his accounts. His books had been examined just before the election on demand of the People's party. This was a painful disclosure to the law and order ticket backers. The *Tribune* acknowledged that the People's party had been right in insisting that the money be counted, an item which had been overlooked. The deficit reached $350,000 in succeeding days and the mayor was ready to enforce the law. He exonerated former Mayor Medill from any knowledge of the Gage transactions. Gage turned over all his property to the city and the question of criminal prosecution was discussed. His case went to the grand jury on December 18. The *Tribune* and the *Staats-Zeitung* engaged in heated controversy. The *Tribune* said that Gage was not a dishonest man but his fault had been in allowing others to cheat him. The German paper wrote of the "whited sepulchres" who had supported Gage.

Illinois farmers at Decatur organized a campaign against monopolies. "It is a movement," said the *Tribune* on December 20, "of the people to overthrow the despotism of the politicians who use the party machinery for the spoliation of the country and their own aggrandizement."

Trade revived as Christmas approached and it was said the corner of the depression had been turned.

On December 22, from 5,000 to 7,000 workingmen gathered at Vorwaerts Turner Hall demanding work. A party was to be organized and the speakers told of "bloated aristocrats and capitalists rolling in wealth" while they were starving. The distribution of surplus wealth was demanded. On this and succeeding days the *Tribune* gave first-page attention to this demonstration. Interviews with leaders of the movement were printed.

The meeting sounded "Communistic," the *Tribune* said, "but probably does not represent the opinions of a large number. Denunciations of the rich and the middle class are absurd. We have no privileged class in this country. Ninety-nine per cent of the rich began life in poverty. The remedy for labor's wrongs is at the ballot box."

The question of relief was taken up at the city council and finally given to the Relief and Aid Society which took care of all real cases of need. There was hope for the early opening of many closed plants. On December 25 the *Tribune* printed a historical sketch of the Communist movement here and in Europe, a four-column page-one story. Karl Marx was the founder, it was stated. "The principles and demands of these men are wild and subversive to society," said the *Tribune*. "Land will save us for a time but the cities must prepare to meet the dangers of Internationalism."

The annual review of business was printed. Wholesale trade had been 530 millions for the year. The growth of the packing industry was given special attention.

The *Tribune* was in controversy at this time with Chief Justice Melville W. Fuller of the Illinois Supreme Court over the action of the court in granting a *supersedeas* in the murder case of Christopher Rafferty, who had shot and killed a police officer serving a warrant. The *Tribune* called the writ an outrage. Justice Fuller said that "we cannot hope to offset Communism if we take away respect for the courts." The *Tribune* said no court was above criticism.

The unemployed did not like the relief set-up and denounced the press and the aristocrats. The city council passed an ordinance permitting the selling of liquor on Sunday behind closed doors.

The year 1874 opened with the unemployed, led by Communists, considering a political program in Chicago, with Communists being guillotined in Paris, and the Beecher case occupying the center of attention at home. All branches of business were prospering in Chicago, the *Tribune* review said. Collections were good and a large spring trade was expected. Pressure for relief continued. The opening of the Fourth

SAMUEL MEDILL

*Youngest brother of Joseph Medill, he was a member of the Tribune staff
for fifteen years. He was managing editor for nine years until his death
in 1883 at the age of 42.*

Presbyterian Church was noted on January 3. The Rev. J. C. Burroughs resigned as president of the University of Chicago and the Gage case was at last presented to the grand jury.

"It is time," said the *Tribune* on January 5, "that every state in the Union should go earnestly to work to prepare for the onset of the followers of Karl Marx, for they mean business, not in Paris and Berlin merely, but in New York and Chicago."

The former city treasurer was indicted for perjury and embezzlement on January 8. The railroads made an offer of $800,000 for the lake front. The mayor and council were said to be in favor of accepting.

Medill in London wrote on labor in England on January 11. He found a lesson for Americans in the co-operatives of England. "Emptiness of stomach — emptiness of mind — these are the workingman's woes," he wrote. "Co-operation will give him physical and mental food. Will he take what it offers and learn to help himself?"

The *Tribune* noted the growth of instalment buying and pointed out its dangers.

A history of Chicago's clubs was published on January 12. Rev. Robert W. Patterson, noted Chicago Presbyterian minister, preached a farewell sermon. Medill, now in Paris, wrote a letter of comment on Mayor Colvin's inaugural address. There was no need, he said, for Colvin to take such a gloomy view of city affairs. He told of how much better off Colvin was than he was when he became mayor and recited the financial achievements of the last two years.

Had he (Medill) found the city in the condition that Colvin found it, he wrote, he would have "felt like writing a message of congratulation at the happy improvement in municipal affairs and thanking those officials who had faced the music in the days that tried men's souls and brought order out of chaos, credit out of bankruptcy, and furnished protection, aid and encouragement to the citizens in the great work of converting a city of debris into a city of palaces in the brief season of two years."

Congress voted to repeal the salary grab bill, which the *Tribune* had persistently fought. The *Tribune* advertised its annual review as a business guide and reference book. It was edited by Elias Colbert.

Medill on January 16 wrote on the characteristics of the French people. A novel method of travel devised by a Chicago inventor — an elevated railroad — was described on January 21. A stock company was formed to promote it.

The *Tribune* said that the lake front ought not to be sold or exposed to sale and opposed a bill to this end presented at Springfield. Medill wrote on the people's banks of Germany on January 25. This was a safe and simple system, he said, under which American workingmen could find escape from the tyranny of capital.

A *Tribune* reporter interviewed Wilbur F. Storey, publisher of the *Chicago Times*, on the subject of spiritualism, to which that editor had become a convert.

There was a controversy over the management and future of the University of Chicago. The *Tribune* said the trouble with it was that it was a sectarian institution; that it might become a success if secularized from head to foot.

On January 26, former Mayor R. B. Mason had a two-column letter in the *Tribune* in reply to Medill's recent letter on conditions in the city. Medill was at fault in several items, he said, on conditions that existed when he took over the city. The *Tribune* waged a war on several fronts with J. Y. Scammon, publisher of the *Inter-Ocean*, who had said 18 months before that the *Tribune* was fast hurrying to bankruptcy.

The Illinois Supreme Court finally decided that the murderer Rafferty might be hanged. The *Tribune* on February 1 said this decision would have a more wholesome effect on the criminal element than a thousand new police.

Crime and vice were on the increase in Chicago, the

Tribune found in a series of articles. They related how a lead-ing gambler had once tried to get Medill as mayor to ease up on gambling raids, with some of the arguments used. "What the police pretend not to know, THE TRIBUNE has now pointed out to them," it was stated. There were four col-umns on faro as it was then played.

A story on the old and new Tremont House was printed on February 2. The Illinois Supreme Court upheld Medill's position on revoking licenses for violations of the Sunday ordinance.

The system of assessing personal property and other tax questions was discussed in an eight-column story on February 9, with radical changes proposed.

The Gage indictment was upheld and a council commit-tee reported against selling the lake front. The new First Con-gregational Church was dedicated. Much space was given to discussions of evolution and theology, which were subjects then engaging many minds. A new county jail and court-house were approaching completion on the city's north side.

The *New York Herald* boasted that its current Sunday issue carried 54 columns of advertising. The *Tribune* on the same date carried advertisments equal to 48 columns of *Herald* space, in a territory one-fourth as populous.

A description of a night of horror in the Cook County poorhouse where 400 were lodged in one "vermin-infested room," was printed on February 21, 1874.

An anti-rum crusade was sweeping the East at this time, particularly in Ohio and the *Tribune* gave it first-page atten-tion almost daily. Attempts to organize along this line in Chicago were feeble, it was reported. Chicago saloonkeepers were on a strike against $12 a barrel beer.

Religious journals, particularly the *Interior*, attacked the *Tribune* for some of its want ads. One was pointed out which was called an assignation date. The *Tribune* said it handled 2,000 advertisments a day and might have made a mistake, but in turn it attacked these weeklies for the kind of advertising they permitted. The *Interior* was controlled financially by Cyrus H. McCormick, whom the *Tribune* had fought for Congress.

It was reported on February 26 that a women's movement was to start in Chicago against saloons. In the East bands of praying women were visiting saloons, in an effort to arouse a temperance sentiment.

On March 1 the *Tribune* said that this was an advertising dodge, the Chicago saloonkeepers had engaged women to come to their places and pray in order to attract trade. The church leaders were divided as to whether to aid the sincere women of the city in such a crusade.

George Alfred Townsend ("Gath") the *Tribune's* Washington correspondent, was reported on March 4 in a scuffle with W. S. Walker, *Chicago Times* correspondent. Walker had attacked Townsend as being in the pay of "the ring" in Washington and as living in a house bought by them. The *Tribune* said this was a lie. The fight was with umbrellas and fists and did no damage.

The workings of the policy system in Chicago were described on March 9. The death of Charles Sumner was reported on March 12. An ordinance repealing Sunday closing of saloons was introduced in the city council. Temperance leagues were organized in Chicago and meetings were held in protest against the Sunday action. The temperance women marched on the council on March 17, but the Sunday opening ordinance was passed. Arthur Dixon, a "law and order man" was chosen presiding officer of the council. The ladies moved in force on the mayor, but he said he was pledged to the open Sunday saloons.

"Mayor Colvin's heart is as hardened as those of the members of the Council," said the *Tribune*, while declaring the women's movement impracticable. A mass meeting of temperance advocates was held in the Methodist Church block and while the women prayed the mayor signed the ordinance. A reporter was sent to Ohio and Indiana to review the temperance crusades there.

The Beecher case came before the Congregational Council in New York. Beecher was blamed for not denying the charges against him (still unspecified) and the church was blamed for dropping a member without trial. "While our sympathies have been with Mr. Beecher right along," said the *Tribune* on March 27, "they have been so on the presumption that an investigation would do him no harm. That is our present belief, but we do say that to longer resist an investigation will bring a reproach upon the Congregational Church in the person of its most distinguished representative."

A Chicago Sunday Afternoon Lecture Association was started on March 29. There were to be education and music for all on a basis of four cents a membership ticket.

The Congregational Council, it was reported, was to force Plymouth Church to investigate its year-old scandal. Withdrawal of fellowship from the church was justified if the scandal was not investigated.

A mass meeting was held in the First Methodist Church on March 31, with Frances Willard of Northwestern University among the temperance speakers. She said it was her first temperance speech and advocated the pledge method of reform, the use of loving persuasion.

Popular demonstration and crusades should be discouraged, the *Tribune* said on April 5, lest they become as dangerous as the Commune. Medical opinions on the use of alcohol were printed, indicating that it was not a poison except when a certain "safety line" was passed, varying with each patient.

The *Tribune* fought "inflation" legislation in Congress, but Congress on April 7 passed a new bill fixing the legal tender limit at 44 millions. It was the Southern Republicans, the ones from the "Africanized states" that had turned the vote for inflation, the *Tribune* said in its analysis.

The Republican party showed losses in the April elections. "It has grown so rotten that the people for the moment will turn to anything to escape from it," said the *Tribune*.

A story on the terrorism of the Molly Maguires in the Pennsylvania coal fields was published on April 11.

The controversy between Professor David Swing and the Rev. Francis L. Patton, Presbyterian leader and editor of the *Interior*, occupied much space during April and later. Professor Swing, Chicago's most popular preacher, was to be tried by the Chicago Presbytery for heresy. Swing said he was first a Christian and then a Presbyterian, one of the "new school." Dr. Patton had been brought to Chicago at the instance of Cyrus H. McCormick, owner of the *Interior*, the *Tribune* stated.

President Grant's veto of the currency bill brought him high commendation from the *Tribune*. It was like a "thunder clap" to the inflationists.

The Swing trial opened May 5. It brought one of the most thorough discussions of religious issues ever heard in this country. The *Tribune* devoted pages to it daily and was evidently in sympathy with Professor Swing.

On May 7, the Tribune printed results of its circularization of the newspapers of nine western states on the inflation issue. Grant's veto was sustained by 504 and opposed by 408, with 11 on the fence.

A page-story on the beauties and advantages of Chicago, the "Garden City," was printed on May 9 in answer to critics, chiefly in St. Louis, who had pictured Chicago as ruined, with miles of empty stores and heavily mortgaged property.

As the Swing trial neared its close various side discussions arose. Swing had eulogized the late John Stuart Mill and this was taken as heretical and unfaithful, as the opposition said that Mill was an atheist. The *Tribune*, which had greatly admired Mill, disputed this, showing that Mill had declared the origins of life unknowable, which was not atheism.

At the Chicago Academy of Sciences, city editor Elias Colbert read a paper on the velocity of light and William Bross discussed the Mississippi floods.

Closing arguments in the Swing case took pages of *Tribune* space. "He is so much of a Christian," said the *Tribune* of Swing on May 16, "so little of a pettifogger, so abounding in his love of the good and beautiful in every creature, so little skilled in the trickeries of theological finesse, that, if he be not a good Presbyterian, the misfortune is not his but that of the Presbyterian Church."

The trial opened the question of the revision of the Westminster creed. Professor Swing won the case in this court by a vote of 48 to 15.

Henry Watterson said that Grant was a candidate for a third term, and the *Tribune* commented on May 22:

"Although there is an obvious tendency toward centralization and personal government, — a tendency which is fraught with the gravest dangers toward civil liberties, — it is not likely to crystalize during the short time that remains to General Grant's term. Such revolutions are of slow growth. The sapping and mining process which made Caesarism possible in Rome, was more than 80 years in accomplishing its baleful end. The same elements are at work among us — enormous wealth, corruption in office, repeated violations of the Constitution, Communism, cynicism and a 'debtor class.'"

Professor Swing after his vindication withdrew from the Fourth Presbyterian Church, although he was asked to remain. He eventually became an independent minister. The opposition to him won the case in the Illinois Synod.

Moody and Sankey were at that time touring Scotland in a great series of revivals and the question arose as to whether "Brother Moody was a heretic too?"

The breakdown of the old creeds was forecast in the *Tribune*, which was considered good in many ways, yet the shallow cynicism which was taking the place of these creeds was called a dangerous thing. The Swing case as reported in the *Tribune* might be called an index of the religious future of the country. Communistic thought was growing. The *Tribune* said on May 24: "Our tendency toward Communism must be checked by giving the workingman comfort, mental and physical. Secure him a larger share in the products of labor, build school houses and make education compulsory, put sewers in the streets, ventilate his houses, etc."

James W. Sheahan, chief editorial writer, addressed the Illinois Press Association on May 27 on how the press had been emancipated from political slavery.

The *Tribune* opposed the admission of New Mexico as a state on the ground that it was merely an aid to the Republicans in Congress. On June 6 the Washington correspondent said that Grant did not want to be the next President and could not be elected if he did. The Republicans were pictured as in mourning over the currency bill veto. The Republican state convention was referred to as the "Office Holders' convention."

Theodore Tilton's charges against Beecher were made public on June 26. He said that his wife had confessed to him her improper relations with her pastor. An excerpt from a letter written by Beecher on January 1, 1871, was given, in which Beecher humbled himself and asked Tilton's forgiveness, adding: "I can ask nothing except that he can remember all the other breasts that would ache. I cannot plead for myself. I even wish that I were dead."

Beecher and his church were silent. The *Tribune* said the matter could not rest there. "While if guilty he can never be the same Henry Ward Beecher to the public that he was before, still friends will gather about him, not to condone a fault which morality must condemn, but to encourage him to a life more befitting his great endowments and his high calling; and among these THE CHICAGO TRIBUNE will be found, if his course shall be frank, manly and honorable.

A quibbling and evasive policy will now complete his ruin."

In discussing Blaine's chances for the presidency the *Tribune* questioned whether the Republican party would not fall into a minority in the whole Union before it got a chance to vote for him.

Dr. Lemuel Moss of Crozier Theological Seminary was made president of the University of Chicago on July 3.

Chicago was becoming a "Stygian pit," the *Tribune* said in an attack on the smoke nuisance. Special dispatches were printed on July 9 on the drought in seven western states.

A secret trial, it developed on July 10, was under way in Beecher's church, with Beecher naming his own jurors.

The *Tribune* began investigations into the adulteration of food and drugs in July, printing much evidence along this line. A report on Elisha Gray's electrical inventions was published on July 12. He was able to telegraph music from Paris to Chicago, it was stated. Special reports on Indian battles in the Wind River country of Wyoming were carried on July 14.

On July 15, another big Chicago fire was reported. Sixty acres were burned with a loss of $5,000,000. "The sad lesson of 1871 has been in vain," said the *Tribune*. "In wooden buildings there is no safety for us." The fire originated in a rag shop on Taylor Street. The Continental, Woods and St. James' Hotels were gone. The list of small business houses destroyed made three columns. "We hope that henceforth no man will justify or tolerate erection of frame buildings for any purpose within the limits of Chicago."

Chapter Fourteen

MEDILL RETURNS TO THE TRIBUNE HELM

ON NOVEMBER 9, 1874, control of the *Tribune* and its policies was taken by Joseph Medill through the purchase of a majority stock interest. Horace White retired from the Chicago field of journalism and the *Tribune* from that time to the present day became an independent Republican journal, always free to criticize individuals or programs but supporting the principles of the party. Its criticism of men was not lessened, but it never again strayed into opposition to the party in national election times. This was probably the most important change in the paper since Medill had first assumed its leadership in 1855. His personality as one of the great journalists of the age was stamped on the paper from that time until his death and lived on in his successors.

The latter part of 1874 saw other important developments in the history of the *Tribune*. Medill began a long and determined war against municipal corruption in Chicago. This purpose was probably one of the chief motives that led him to return from Europe and to find the money to buy control of the paper. In time he drove out "the bummers," those who had boasted of defeating his policies. Aldermanic and county graft rings were the objectives of many *Tribune* campaigns in the interest of the taxpayers.

Sharp criticism of President Grant was changed during this period into a sustained support of administrative policies, even the strong hand again in the South. The drift toward the

Democratic party was blocked so far as the *Tribune* was able to influence the voters of the Middle West. At the same time there was a call for reform and purification of the Republican party. Medill would not stand for corruption there any more than among the Democrats. He supported Republican principles but not always Republican office holders, and never the crooked ones.

An explosion occurred in the Beecher case during this period and the *Tribune's* Washington correspondent, "Gath," scooped the New York and all other papers with five pages of love letters of the Tiltons. Susan B. Anthony got new and less dignified fame by being accused of once having sat in Tilton's lap.

A question of immediate interest in Chicago was that of fire protection and new building ordinances and fire zones. Medill had contributed to this debate from Berlin and now entered the fight in Chicago.

The *Tribune* saw Chicago reduced to a second- or third-rate city unless first-rate fire protection was adopted at once. Floating steam fire engines on the river were called for. A map was printed comparing the limits of recent fires with the great fire, showing much of the same territory burned.

A *Tribune* reporter was sent to New York to interview the Tiltons who had separated. The investigation had gone beyond Beecher's control, it was stated. Tilton promised a sworn statement soon.

A mass meeting was called in Chicago on July 18 to consider the threats of the board of fire underwriters to leave the city unless the fire department was reorganized and the fire limits extended. It was resolved to extend the limits, and pull down illegally erected wooden buildings.

With the burning of hundreds of shanties, the *Tribune* saw State Street emerging purified from the fire and entering its destiny as the great retail business street of the city.

Five columns were printed on July 18 on the new order in

Japan and that country's emergence from feudalism. Medill wrote of the population and resources of Bavaria. The abduction of a boy named Charley Ross in Philadelphia was reported. He had been missing 18 days and stern measures against kidnaping were called for. The city council made the fire limits coextensive with the city limits.

Six columns on "the Beecher Explosion" were printed on July 22. Tilton formally charged the pastor with criminal intercourse with his wife, Elizabeth R. Tilton, and that she had confessed. She had been under Beecher's sway, it was charged, and did not think she was doing wrong. Letters were included in the statement of Tilton. "It bears the impress of truth," said the *Tribune*, "and, fortified by a chain of circumstances, will carry dismay into religious and family circles everywhere. But don't be taken off your feet about religion. The same divine laws exist now as they did before, even as the sun gilds the heavens."

Both Beecher and Mrs. Tilton entered denials. "If the documents are not forgeries," said the *Tribune* on July 23, "there is scarcely a doubt as to Beecher's guilt. There is no defense except that Tilton is a forger and a perjurer. It is sad to think that this great preacher, almost adored by the American people, has been so long a whited sepulchre, fair to the eye but within full of dead men's bones." A libel action was started against Tilton.

Organization of the Citizens' Association was announced on August 1. This was to be a permanent organization to help with municipal problems as they arose. Thomas Hoyne and E. A. Storrs were the leaders. Franklin MacVeagh was made the first president.

A new feature column, "Sparks of Science," was published weekly. August 7 was referred to as "judgment day for the Republican party," when the Democrats were reported as taking a North Carolina election.

George Alfred Townsend ("Gath"), Washington correspondent who had been summering at Saratoga, was ordered to New York to investigate the Beecher scandal. He spent a night at the Tilton home, came to the conclusion that Tilton was a bigger man morally than Beecher and got an armful of letters which had passed between Tilton and his wife for a term of years. Five pages of these letters were published in the *Tribune* of August 13. They covered the life of the couple until within three months of the alleged confession. There was great excitement in New York over these letters. The *Tribune* said they were among the celebrated love letters of the world, that the case had been taken away from the church committee and turned over to the people by the *Tribune* exposure. Orders for the Beecher extra edition poured into the office. The *New York Tribune* took three columns of the letters by telegraph. The *New York Sun* asked that a special messenger be placed on a train with a copy of the *Tribune*.

An interview with Tilton in his home was published on August 15 as to how the "confession" of Mrs. Tilton was made. The *Tribune* said that Beecher's defense was defective and incomplete.

A page was printed on August 16 on the decision in the case of Rev. Charles Edward Cheney, Episcopal rector who was put out of his church by the presbytery and put back by the civil court.

Regular Sunday articles were contributed on "the woman question."

A column of countrywide comment was printed on August 17, on the *Tribune's* Beecher scoop. An interview with Frank Moulton, close friend of Tilton, which "Gath" had also obtained, was denied by New York and other newspapers. Townsend, who had returned to Saratoga, was interviewed by the *Brooklyn Argus*.

"What do you think of the newspapers pitching into you so hard?" he was asked. "O, that is a mere pout. The metropolitan papers got beaten. The fact is all this shallow talk about THE CHICAGO TRIBUNE as a western paper is a mere fanfaronade. THE CHICAGO TRIBUNE is worth $1,200,000, pays the best dividends in America, pays me $6,000 a year, and I consider that when Mr. Tilton gave those letters to that paper he showed more good judgment than generosity."

A second interview with Moulton was obtained by "Gath," in which it was stated that Beecher's relations with Mrs. Tilton had been a subject of conversation between Beecher and Moulton for years. Beecher was pictured as one of the most licentious men in the country, with many amours.

It was admitted by Townsend that in his first interview with Moulton he had used expressions which possibly might not have been meant for publication at that time and that the statements of others had entered into the general picture. A statement by Moulton made to the church committee followed and Moulton made a third statement to Townsend for exclusive use in the West. The *Tribune* said that it was not likely that Townsend's interview would again be questioned.

In the testimony before the church committee it was stated that Susan B. Anthony, a friend of Mrs. Tilton, had once sat on Tilton's lap. It was the statement of a serving girl. Miss Anthony said the girl was a halfwit and the story was ridiculous.

The Plymouth Church committee found Beecher innocent on August 24. The *Tribune* said that Beecher was unfit for further pastoral work and should step out. The pastor went to Twin Mountains House, New Hampshire, for the summer and preached occasionally.

Discovery of gold in the Black Hills was reported on September 1.

Medill in a letter to W. F. Coolbaugh in Chicago, written from Germany, suggested how Chicago might be made fireproof. He looked on the recent fire as a blessing in disguise, but said it had given a shock to outside confidence in the safety of business in the "Queen City of the West. The time has come to look this great question in the face," he wrote. "All the precautions proposed recently are not enough while the business center remains encircled by pine structures miles deep and ready to go off."

He suggested that the insurance companies withdraw protection until pine roofs were covered with cement or tiles and the wooden cottages lined outside with brick. "I am acquainted with one man," he added, "who will lend enough money to put a hundred poor men's cottages in a condition of safety and there are plenty of others who will do the same." The "one man" was probably himself.

The *Tribune* questioned where to get the right kind of cement for all this labor and pointed out the difficulties of flat roofs for slate or tile. The Citizens Association began to look into the question. The *Tribune* said this organization had its hearty support.

Medill from Berlin wrote on September 5 of how the people there enjoyed a feeling of security against fire "which would be a perfect luxury in Chicago."

On September 8 three pages were devoted to description of the Second Annual Industrial Exposition. Medill described the military system of Germany and said that country was not a military despotism but a constitutional monarchy and that the people were contented. New Orleans rose against carpetbag government, and there was war on Canal Street.

Tilton on September 19 made a second statement, including parts of Mrs. Tilton's diary. The *Tribune* described this as a fearful indictment of Beecher, and printed three pages of the statement. Beecher appeared in his church again on October 3 after his summer rest, and great crowds attended his first sermon.

Medill in Switzerland wrote of the beauties of that country. The board of fire insurance underwriters voted to leave Chicago because of non-compliance with its wishes in fire protection. Many companies, however, decided to remain. The *Tribune* on October 3 gave 6,000 words to the opening meeting of the Philosophical Society. The women suffrage movement was advised on October 8 to rid itself of "free lovers and fools" and get a little more commonsense.

The fall campaign was under way and the parties were jockeying for position in the legislative and congressional races. The *Tribune* printed the news and the debates but said that the Democrats probably would win in an apathetic election.

A column was printed on October 11 about Miss Midy Morgan, livestock reporter for the *New York Times*.

Susan B. Anthony, who had come to Chicago for a woman's congress, was interviewed on whether she had sat in Tilton's lap. "Why should I not sit on Mr. Tilton's knee?" she asked. "All the men had said that Susan was so sour she couldn't get a husband and I thought I would show them I could sit on a young man's knee just like any foolish girl."

The apparent drift toward the Democratic party brought this comment from the *Tribune* on October 15: "This does not mean that the country is warming toward the Democratic party per se, but rather that the sins of the present administration are too grievous to be borne, and unless there is speedy and radical reformation from that quarter, the people will even vote for an old line Democrat for President in order to have a change."

Police and gamblers were in league to govern the city, the *Tribune* charged.

The Lincoln monument was dedicated at Springfield on October 16, 1874. Two pages were given to a description of this event. The *Tribune* said that the best monument to Lincoln would be to conform government to his principles.

In considering the future the *Tribune* said that all power was in the masses and that these must be raised, physically and mentally.

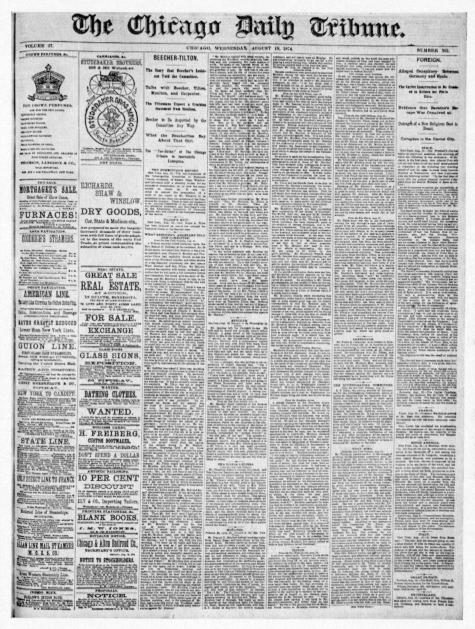

Chicago took a special interest in the Beecher-Tilton scandal because of the publication by the Tribune of letters obtained in what the newspaper described as a "ten-strike in journalistic enterprise."

Chicago's most fashionable wedding was reported in great detail on October 21 when Lieutenant Colonel Fred Grant married the daughter of H. H. Honore.

On the eve of election, November 2, the *Tribune* advised voters: "We think the Republican party is the safer of the two, but we also think it needs thorough investigation and overhauling, and if it gets such surgery in the next Congress it will meet in national convention and enter the presidential race in a much healthier condition than it now is."

Great Democratic gains were reported on November 4. The lower House was to be Democratic by thirty and they had gained six United States Senators. A tidal wave against Republicanism was reported on November 5. Where woman suffrage and prohibition were issues they had been lost in the ruins. The independents held the balance of power in the Illinois Legislature. It was at this critical time, politically, that Joseph Medill re-entered the active field of Chicago journalism.

An announcement to readers of the *Tribune* appeared on the editorial page of November 9, signed by Medill. It follows:

"With this issue of THE TRIBUNE I resume its editorial control. Having within the past fortnight purchased enough shares, added to what I previously owned, to control the majority of the stock, the responsibility of the future management of THE TRIBUNE will necessarily devolve on me. With what degree of ability and success I shall discharge the new obligations, time alone can make known, for—'Let him not boast who putteth on his armor but rather him that taketh it off.'

"A few words of explanation may not be inappropriate in this connection. Shortly after the close of the Great Rebellion I was obliged by ill-health, caused by overwork, to resign the managing editorship of THE TRIBUNE, first to the late Dr. C. H. Ray, and, after he vacated his post, to Mr. Horace White, who has since then had chief control of the paper.

After a brief rest I took an editorial chair and wrote for its columns for several years.

"At first, the political course of THE TRIBUNE, under the new management received my approval in the main, but questions began to arise about which we sharply differed. Both being men tenacious of their opinions, it was difficult to harmonize our conflicting views, and agree as to the course THE TRIBUNE should pursue. These disagreements became more irreconcilable as the paper drifted away from the Republican party and approached the position of an Opposition journal. Finding myself circumscribed with a gradually narrowing circle of topics in which we were in accord, I retired altogether from the editorial columns of THE TRIBUNE. Our differences, however, were always political and not personal.

"My predecessor has pursued the course which he believed to be the path of duty with a courage which challenged the respect of those who condemned it, and supported his views with an ability which extorted their admiration; and he leaves his editorial chair after having achieved a national reputation.

"The readers of THE TRIBUNE will naturally desire to be informed, at the outset, of the probable line of conduct of THE TRIBUNE under the change of management. A full explanation cannot be given on the instant. Men's opinions and actions are more or less influenced and controlled by the circumstances which surround them, and always by unforeseen causes. But this much may now be safely promised: THE TRIBUNE will hereafter be, as it formerly was, when under my direction, an independent Republican journal. It will be the organ of no man, however high; no clique or ring, however influential; or faction, however fanatical or demonstrative.

"While giving to the Republican party and its principles a hearty and generous support, it will criticize the actions and records of Republican leaders as freely and fearlessly as in

208

days of yore. But it has seemed to me unwise for a great representative journal, for the purpose of correcting some alleged abuses of administration, to desert its party organization and turn its guns on its old friends, or help into power and places the leaders of the organization whose political records and whose official conduct show that they are insincere in their professions of desire for administrative purification.

"As a general rule a man can exercise more influence among his friends by remaining en rapport with them than by assailing and traducing them. The same rule holds true in regard to newspapers.

"The Government of the nation must be conducted through the instrumentality of parties. I know of no other agency which has succeeded in free countries. The party in the majority must assume the responsibility of governing. A party is simply a voluntary organization of citizens united to carry into effect certain principles and purposes. It must employ and intrust individuals to collect and disburse taxes, to perform executive and police duties for the protection and security of person and property; men must be engaged to construct public works, carry the mails, administer justice, and make and execute laws and do a thousand other things which the public well-being requires; and these individuals will often prove careless, inefficient and corrupt.

"But a party whose aims and purposes are good and patriotic, and whose record is grand and glorious, should not be condemned and thrown out of power on account of the defective work or misconduct of a few of its employes, in order to make place for an antagonistic organization whose record cannot be defended, but is regarded with sorrow and shame by its best members, and whose conduct when in power never fails to show that its reformatory professions when out of power are a delusion and a snare.

"Such being the case in regard to the necessity and machinery of parties in free countries, the Press, to be useful, cannot avoid being partisan in greater or less degree. If an editor undertakes the role of supporting both sides, his position is equivalent to a double affirmative, which amounts to a negative. If he habitually censures and condemns both, he is soon regarded as a common scold and nuisance. To be entirely unpartisan leaves him in the condition of a cipher; and when a newspaper undertakes to be wholly 'independent' of its party and yet discusses politics, it is on the high road to the camp of its political opponents, whether its conductor so intended at the outset or not, — unless, indeed, he takes refuge in the coward's harbor of neutrality and abdicates his duties altogether, which is a most contemptible and despicable position.

"But it is not essential to the prosperity and influence of a party that it should wilfully misrepresent its opponents, and behold nothing but evil and depravity in all their actions, or discover only treasonable designs in all they propose to do. Candor and frankness in the treatment of political opponents will detract nothing from the influence of a paper, nor will it injure the prospects of its own party.

"Such, in brief, are the views I have long entertained of parties, and the relation which the Press should bear toward them. A political newspaper, to be of service to the public, must give one party or the other the preference. And, while the Democratic party embraces many excellent and worthy members, who would be an honor to any organization, yet I sincerely believe the Republican party comprises a much larger proportion of the intelligent and educated classes, of moral worth and business enterprise, as well as of the patriotic elements, of the nation; and therefore the Government of the country and the civic rights of the poor and weak can be more safely and prudently committed to its keeping than to that of its antagonist, whose past history and antecedents furnish so much cause for misgivings and dread of its future behavior.

"Looking, then, at the individual composition of the two great parties, — all other parties being mere fragments, ephemeral in duration and narrow in object, — and at their respective records and underlying principles, I cannot hesitate to give the preference to the Republican party. Hence, THE TRIBUNE will be conducted as a Republican journal.

"Having said this much in a general way, it only remains to be added, that no labor or expense will be spared to keep THE TRIBUNE in the very front ranks of journalism as a newspaper in all departments of intelligence and activity. The high position it has attained as an advocate of the material, moral and intellectual progress of the people, will be maintained and advanced as far as possible. It will be my constant aim and endeavor to make THE TRIBUNE not only a welcome but useful visitor to the fireside, as well as the counting room, shop and office.

"For the cordial greetings with which the brethren of the Press have welcomed me back to the editorial arena, I tender them my most heartfelt acknowledgment, and for the hundreds of congratulatory telegrams and letters received from old friends, they have my sincere thanks for their kind expressions and good wishes."

In an adjoining column in this issue an item from the *Interior* was printed which stated in part: "Now that Mr. Medill has assumed control of THE CHICAGO TRIBUNE, would it be too much to ask, very respectfully, that wholesale and retail slander of the ministry in the columns of that able paper be stopped?" The editor denied the premises and asked for specifications.

An editorial on prohibition appeared in the same issue. It was called a ruinous policy. "To persist in bolstering up this mischievous and insane movement any longer is simply suicidal. If it is made a law it cannot be enforced."

A ten-page paper was published on November 10, with the general make-up as usual. The news space on page one was

given to a lecture by Professor Bonomy Price, political economist of Oxford University, at Standard Hall. In an editorial
on the political outlook the attitude was taken that the recent
election was a blessing in disguise, like the fire. It was like a
thunderstorm clearing the air, preparing the way for the
1876 struggle.

"Nothing in the facts," it was stated, "is indicative of the
disruption or disbandment of the Republican party or that
that party is any less strong in the affections of the people
than it was in previous years. Principles are unchanged."

The hard times and a few corruptionists were given as
causes of the Democratic victory, which was not underrated.

There were no advertisements on the first page of the
November 11 issue, which was given to details of the election
returns. On the question of the tariff, it was stated editorially,
the *Tribune* would take the Republican state platform of 1870
as its platform. This stated that the best system of protection
to industry "is that which imposes the lightest burdens and
the fewest restrictions on the property and business of the
people."

On the currency question, the *Tribune* accepted the Demo-
cratic-Liberal platform of 1874 in Springfield. "The restoration of gold and silver as the basis of the currency, the
resumption of specie payments as soon as possible without
disaster to the business of the country, by steadily opposing
inflation, and by the payment of the national indebtedness in
the money of the civilized world."

A firm and optimistic Republican tone characterized the
paper. "The Republican party will elect the next President;
that much is as certain as any future event can be," it was
stated on November 12, 1874.

In a survey of the relief needs for the winter the *Tribune*
said there was an effort to compel the community to carry
through the winter those who had saved nothing during the
summer. "Loafers, vagabonds, Communists, which have taken

deep root here since the fire, and street beggars should be discountenanced by the relief and aid society during the winter."

An analysis of the growth of municipal expenditures, published November 13, showed that this "exceeded in all proportion the increase in actual service performed."

Medill was elected a vice-president of the Industrial Exposition, which reported a balance on hand of $585.

The city authorities were advised on November 14, that if the police did not protect the people from a steady increase in burglaries and other crimes that the people would protect themselves in the manner of the San Francisco vigilantes. The police toleration of gamblers, it was charged, was a disgrace to the city.

The trial of the defaulting city treasurer, Gage, opened at Waukegan. Crime in the city was laid at the feet of the People's party policies, and a story was printed relating in much glee that "Long John" Wentworth, and A. C. Hesing, two party leaders, had recently been robbed. A visit to Mike McDonald's gambling den was described on November 20. On November 22 a list of gambling houses, with names of owners, was printed "for the information of the police."

Testimony in the Gage trial, which began December 1, was printed in full for several days, two pages being given to the case on December 2. Gage was acquitted on December 5. The *Tribune* said: "When the taking of $600,000 of public money ceases to be a crime, then it is time that there should be some law enacted directly applicable to such cases and to protect the city against loss pecuniarily. Here is work for the Citizens' committee."

The Washington correspondent, "Gath," who had not written anything but a few columns of gossip since the change in the *Tribune's* political policy, had a story on December 5 reviewing the Grant administration.

"His administration stands out intelligibly and conspicuously amongst the best reigns of contemporary rulers, and comparable with Lincoln's work. . . . Strange as it is, to speak well of the President is startling. Decency has got to be sensational. Abuse is a poor old drab, cursed out with inherent malignity. Take this sensation then, thou drab, and curse at me." Many of "Gath's" old friends took this occasion to curse him and he was given space in the paper to answer them.

The *Tribune* was in daily controversy with prohibitionists and also found itself in a quarrel with the *Western Catholic* over its attitude on church and state relationship. It was stated on December 8: "THE TRIBUNE opposes any church, Catholic or Protestant, Jewish or Mohammedan, or any religious organization of any kind, which encroaches upon, meddles with or interferes in secular affairs. It has no war to make against dogma or religious belief."

A correspondent in Omaha wrote on December 18: "Much interest has been manifested here in the recent change in the management of THE TRIBUNE and there is a disposition here to give it a warm welcome by the Republicans, as the steady champion of their pure principles. Though our people felt sore at its course in support of 'Liberalism' and its attitude toward us in matters of deep local interest, yet some think now that the great journal which did so much for the cause of humanity in the dark days of national history will yet give this thrifty young city the right hand of fellowship, and treat her with the justice she deserves."

At a lecture at the Sunday Afternoon Association, Colonel Edmund Juessen, who spoke against Sunday laws as a growth of Puritan intolerance, was introduced to the audience by A. B. Mason of the *Tribune* staff.

Washington letters began to be signed by "Ouisel." The *Tribune* was in editorial controversy with "Bourbon" newspapers over the question of states rights, which had been resurrected in politics by the situation in Louisiana and the strong line of action which Grant took there. The *Tribune's* stand that the United States was a "nation" was taken as an argument in favor of centralized power.

"There is no danger," said the *Tribune* on December, 23, 1874, "that we will ever have such a centralized government as that of the Grand Roi who claimed that he was the state. Such a government is simply impossible in this country and ever will be impossible. But if we are a people, if, as we claim, we constitute a nation, we need a government strong enough and centralized enough to make its will obeyed."

Chapter Fifteen

BUILDING A SOLID NORTH

THE *Tribune* entered upon the year 1875 with a new political orientation provided by Joseph Medill. Its business supremacy increased month by month and under Samuel Medill as managing editor the paper provided many new features for its readers and a keen news coverage.

The political position taken by Medill was that the Republican party must not only be supported but purified. This was the year of growing whisky and Indian ring scandals that had been years in forming, and public trials which seemed to put the Grant administration in a bad light. The position of the *Tribune* was that this proved the Republicans were honest as a whole. At the same time the third term talk was discouraged. The *Tribune* wanted no taint of monarchy or Caesarism in America.

In Chicago Medill entered upon one of the most spirited

battles of his career, against the Colvin machine that had defeated his candidate and his policies while mayor of Chicago. He went after the "bummers" and the "devil-fish crew" with persistency and courage, seeking to bring the Germans back into the Republican party and apparently succeeding. The *Tribune* led the fight for a clean ballot in Chicago and went into the courts against the Colvin machine in a charter election contest.

The *Tribune* continued its fight against monopolies. Medill came out for a government-owned telegraph system against the Western Union monopoly. At the same time he was against paternalism in government. His position was that of "fraternalism" instead of paternalism, that individual enterprise was to be encouraged wherever possible.

The 1875 prospectus of the *Tribune* took on a new significance with the advent of Medill as controlling editor. Its principles and the application of them to current problems were stated firmly, as follows:

"THE CHICAGO TRIBUNE, under the guidance of its former editor, has resumed its old position at the head of Republican journals, and will do battle in the future for the true principles of free government, and for a purified and honest administration of national, state and municipal affairs.

"While giving to the Republican party a cordial and earnest support in all wise measures and to all fit candidates, THE TRIBUNE will never be the organ of any individual, faction or ism, nor will it cease to combat oppressive monopolies or fail to expose and denounce all corrupt schemes for plundering the treasury or the people. It will wage perpetual war on lobby rings who prowl around the halls of legislation in quest of spoil.

"The recent elections, while inflicting a temporary defeat on the Republican party, have done a great good in sweeping away fanatical and side issues which embarrassed its freedom of action, and in crushing out those baleful and corrupting

influences known as 'Butlerisms' which poisoned the channels of national life. Purified, as by fire, of the evil things
which had infested its garments, the Republican party will
enter upon the tremendous struggle of 1876 with renewed
vigor for the possession of the government and the shaping
of the policy of the nation when it enters the second century
of its existence.

"The Democratic leaders, misinterpreting the real cause
of their triumph, are proclaiming the result a 'reaction' of
the popular mind against the principles of the Republican
party and an endorsement of the fundamental doctrines of
the Democratic party, which means 'state sovereignty' and
all that expression includes.

"When that party obtains possession of the government,
under the assumed leadership of the Southern right wing,
steps will be taken in Congress to refund the cotton war tax
from the federal treasury, principal and interest amounting
to $100,000,000 or more. A bill will be passed to compensate
the Democratic rebels for losses and damages sustained by
them while resisting the Union armies and upholding the sov-
ereign state right of secession. And lastly will come a demand
for the value of the emancipated slaves, who, under the doctrine of state sovereignty, are alleged to have been unconsti-
tutionally liberated. These claims will more than double the
national debt. In the meantime what will become of the
rights and freedom of the colored race thus placed under
absolute control of their old masters? Against these perils to
the future peace and welfare of the country all true Republicans must present a solid front."

For a specific "platform" the *Tribune* stated:

"As agriculture is the basis of national wealth, whatever
policy benefits that great interest promotes the prosperity
of the whole country.

"THE TRIBUNE will advocate adoption of such measures as will cheapen transportation and reduce the taxes on

goods. The lightest tariff which will provide the government with the necessary funds to carry it on and maintain its credit should only be imposed on imports, and the national highways should be improved to create a stronger competition with the railroad monopolies, which will compel them to lower their tariff charges.

"The utmost reduction of all direct taxes must be insisted upon by the people, and retrenchment in county, township and municipal taxation.

"Plenty of currency for all the legitimate wants of the country with elasticity as to quantity and stability as to value by convertibility into coin.

"THE TRIBUNE will sternly combat repudiation of public obligations in the form of watering and debasing the currency or any other guise it may assume.

"Subsidies and bounties of public lands, money or credit to enrich rings, run steamship companies or furnish capital to other corporations, are flagrant abuses of the powers of government and tend to promote corruption, extravagance and speculation."

The annual review of trade and commerce, which had grown in importance with the years, was printed on January 1 in a four-page supplement. The business situation was found satisfactory despite the panic of 1873. The total business of Chicago in produce and manufactures was 639 millions as against 596 millions for the previous year. This extra edition was soon sold out and new copies had to be printed.

The writer "Reno" was sent to Louisiana, then in a miserable period of reconstruction. The *Tribune* said on January 4 that it was not satisfied with the Associated Press reports from the South, that "the truth about the southern Republicans is bad enough but that about the Democrats is probably worse and suppressed."

Locally the *Tribune* sought to keep the Germans, after the fall of the People's party, out of the Democratic ranks.

A strong Republican stand was taken in state affairs. A *Tribune* "commissioner" was sent out to investigate the stench nuisance in the stockyards district.

The big news of the month was the opening of the Beecher-Tilton trial in Brooklyn. This became what the *Tribune* called a "menagerie." Admission at first was for ticketholders only. The *Tribune* criticized Beecher's attitude at this time as "a curious way to establish innocence." The preacher's table was loaded with flowers each day. The report of the trial was signed by "Dr. Syntax" and was ably written, with much fine description and character reading. As the trial developed this writer saw Dr. Beecher in a poorer light each day. The testimony of Beecher's accuser was given from three to six columns a day during late January and early in February. On February 20, 1875, it was reported that Beecher had confessed and had threatened suicide.

On the enactment of a new "Force bill," designed to give teeth to the Fifteenth Amendment, the *Tribune* said on February 27 that this would be a gigantic political blunder. "This bill is demanded by carpetbaggers and other adventurers who have used the Republican party for their own selfish and corrupt ends. It gives the President authority to move in on any state on his own notion of rebellion." It was suggested that this bill be talked to death in the Senate and when this particular bill was defeated early in March the *Tribune* said: "THE TRIBUNE is a safe prophet and its views have been in the main in accordance with the acts of Congress."

Nearly three pages were devoted on March 6 to the 400th anniversary of Michelangelo and a sketch of his life by Frances H. Bruck. A page in the Sunday paper was given to news from neighboring cities, such as Milwaukee, Waukegan and Evanston.

"Social honors to Chicago's favorite colored citizen, John Jones of the county board," was a report of March 11. This was described as a "brilliant, fashionable and enjoyable occasion." The prison at Joliet was described as a self-sustaining convict system. A reporter for the *Tribune* spent four days in the county poor house and wrote a description of the inmates and the management giving many instances of abuse and neglect.

"Scandal" was the standing head on the Beecher trial reports. It was a continued exhibition of a puny and irrelevant defense, according to the report of March 17.

Republicans were not in favor of "third term nonsense," the *Tribune* said on March 18: "As well attempt to repel an accusation of a purpose to establish a monarchy, as to deny the shadowy imputation of favoring the third term."

J. K. Magie of Springfield sent a letter to Medill with a photograph of Lincoln taken at Macomb, Illinois, on August 27, 1858. This was for Medill's album and the editor replied in a letter, one column long, which was printed on March 18. Medill recalled the occasion of the picture-taking and then recalled other Lincoln incidents in which he played an intimate part. He told of the argument with Lincoln over putting a certain question to Senator Douglas in the Freeport debate. Lincoln ignored the advice of Medill and other Republicans in this matter and the issue was made.

"When I returned to the hotel that day," Medill wrote, "Lincoln said to me, 'Well, Medill, how do you like the way I hoed the row with Douglas today?' 'Mr. Lincoln,' I replied, 'before you spoke you had three chances out of four for the Senate. Now I think Douglas has three chances out of four. I am going back to Chicago in the morning and will make the best fight I can for you in THE TRIBUNE, but I fear you have let Douglas steal your chances of winning.' The reply Lincoln made to me I shall never forget, as he looked at me with a singular expression of countenance.

" 'If my question about excluding slavery from a territory has beaten me for Senator, as you seem to think it has, his answer to it has beaten him for President, and that is really the stake he is playing for.'

"The result turned out exactly as each predicted it would."

All talk about a new party at this time was shallow nonsense, the *Tribune* said on March 25. "The rotten wood will be thrown away in the Republican party and it will be as near perfect as anything in this imperfect world."

The *Sunday Tribune* of March 28 had nearly 50 columns of advertising matter, in 2,150 separate announcements. This, it was stated, went to 150,000 readers, counting four readers to each copy sold. The 16-page paper might have to be enlarged, it was announced, and the whole was taken as a business barometer of Chicago.

Editor Storey of the *Times* got ten days in jail for contempt. In connection with this the *Tribune* said editorially on March 30:

"The freedom of the press is more than anything else dependent on the independence and fearlessness of the courts. Without the protection of a fearless and upright judiciary the rights of the press and of all citizens would be frail indeed. The liberty of the press does not consist of the mere privilege of the editor, it is a liberty pertaining to the general public."

Dr. Beecher was on the witness stand in his own defense during the first two weeks in April. The reports of the examination were given in great detail, taking some days two or three pages of *Tribune* space. Beecher made an absolute and unqualified denial of the charges of adultery brought by Tilton, whom he called a monstrous liar. The *Tribune* said the denials would make a difference of opinion for all time. "Mr. Beecher's testimony stands alone. If the case ended today a great majority of the people would have the comforting assurance in their own minds that Beecher was an innocent man. But the case may not end here and his testimony may not stand."

Beecher closed his direct testimony with another solemn denial. His attitude on cross examination was not so smooth and easy, it was reported, but it revealed him as an intellectual giant. The lights and shadows of this melodrama were presented with full effects in the *Tribune* accounts.

In a city charter election on April 23 the advice of the *Tribune* to vote against the charter of 1872 was not followed and the charter carried by a majority of 600. Fraud was at once charged and the counting of votes was stopped by an injunction. A mass protest meeting was held but the council counted the vote despite the injunction. The *Tribune* said the contest would be continued.

Whisky ring frauds came to the surface and the *Tribune* printed an exclusive story on this on March 12. This exposé was regarded as a victory for Grant and the Republican party, a house cleaning which showed no intention of third-term politics.

The *Tribune* investigated, through a special commissioner, the stone used in the construction of the Custom House and came to the conclusion that a big price had been paid for poor stone. This was more Republican housecleaning.

On May 30, 1875 Grant was reported as saying he did not want a third term and would not accept it. After one hundred days the Beecher trial was still on. Dr. Syntax had grown tired of it and had put his reportorial abilities at work on a big financial scandal, that of B. F. Allen of Iowa and Chicago.

The *Tribune* won its case in the lower court in its effort to punish the aldermen who violated the court injunction in the charter election case. The case was to go to the Illinois Supreme Court.

There was talk of jury bribery in the Beecher case. On July 25 the jury had been out 9 hours and was reported ten to two in favor of Beecher. There were seven days and nights of speculation, with no verdict and on July 2 the jury was reported as disagreed and was discharged. At the last it was

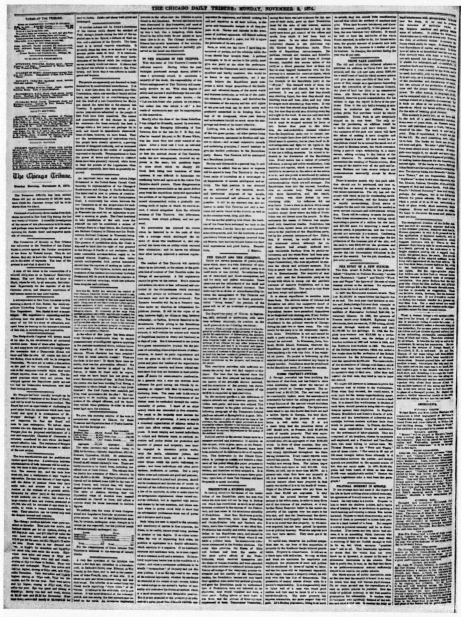

As far as is known, the only signed editorial ever to appear in the Tribune *was on November 9, 1874, in which Joseph Medill announced: "With this issue of the* Tribune, *I resume its editorial control."*

said to be nine to three for Beecher. The *Tribune* said the case was not clear, that it was Beecher's duty to prosecute Tilton for slander and to win his vindication in that way. Plymouth Church reacted to this situation by voting Beecher a salary of $100,000.

The South was advised on July 12 to follow New England ideas, that is, take off their coats and go to work. "They must wake up," said the *Tribune*, "to the realization of the fact that it is no longer the duty of the nigger to support them in ease and luxury."

A tariff for revenue only, even if it furnished incidental protection to a few favored industries, was the stand of the *Tribune* at this time.

P. T. Barnum came to Chicago and his press agent, D. S. Thomas, arranged a balloon ascension to advertise the lake front circus. Professor Washington Donaldson and a companion, Newton S. Grimwold, a reporter for the *Journal*, ascended on July 17 and on the 21st the balloon was still missing.

A United States protectorate was established over the Samoan Islands. Cuban patriots should be recognized, the *Tribune* advised, declaring that the manifest destiny of Cuba was home rule, with an alliance of friendship and commerce with the United States.

The University of Chicago was again hunting for a new president. The *Tribune* told the voters to get ready to drive the "bummers" out of office in the fall, and choose good men for offices.

The death of Andrew Johnson was reported on August 1. The *Tribune* overlooked all it had objected to in his life with this epitaph: "In the day of treason he was an American patriot."

A five-column story of "Bloody Williamson" County in Illinois was published on August 13, containing the full history of the vendetta there.

The problems of young people in marriage and income were discussed in many contributed articles during August. The revivalists Moody and Sankey returned from England and a revival was planned for Chicago. John V. Farwell discussed this at a McCormick Hall meeting. The *Tribune* said on August 31, 1875:

"The moral system of the community has reached a very low ebb. Dishonesty, fraud, theft, gambling, have blunted the moral sense in political and commercial life. A religious revival would prove just the needed tonic. Are Moody and Sankey ready to grapple with the great evil of dishonesty which is sapping the community? Are the churches ready to support them, aid them with practical work?"

"Hands off," the *Tribune* warned Mayor Colvin in an article on the school board on September 1. "Rumors are floating about the city hall that the mayor is disposed to thrust city hall politics into the school board for the first time in the history of the city. The information is too astounding for belief. Does Mayor Colvin seriously propose to inaugurate such an innovation as this, and turn over school board and management of the public school system as mayoral or aldermanic patronage for political bummers?"

On September 2 the *Tribune* issued a warning against the telegraph monopoly of the Western Union and said that the result might be a government telegraph system as in England.

Medill had entered into this controversy in 1873 while mayor of Chicago. In a public letter to William Orton, president of the Western Union, on January 24, 1873, Medill gave his views on this subject in part as follows:

"Let me state, at the outset of this letter, my understanding of the functions and relations of the Government toward the business affairs of the people, which will prevent misunderstanding or perversion in the future.

"I hold that any business or occupation which is or can be conducted by individual enterprise, or by pecuniary corporate efforts, with fair and open competition to regulate prices and prevent extortion, or when the charges can be regulated by law, should be left to the management of such agencies, believing that such course will best promote the public welfare.

"I hold further, that any business essential to the public welfare, and general in its nature and requirements, which cannot be conducted by individual effort and capital, but only by corporate organization, and which is not practicably susceptible of fair and open competition, or whose charges cannot be regulated or limited by law, but which is, or degenerates into, a monopoly, may rightfully be taken control of and managed for the public benefit by one or other of the political corporations best adapted to the performance of the service, whether that be the National, State or Municipal corporation."

Medill said that he was not for a "paternal" government but for a "fraternal" one. He analyzed the telegraph situation in the light of this principle and said that while it was a well-managed corporation under the present management its stock was the football of Wall Street, and it might not continue to be well managed in the interests of the people. "Hence I see no other alternative," he continued, "than that the National corporation must sooner or later take possession of the telegraph, unite it with the postal system, and operate them together for the common good."

Dwight L. Moody began building a church in Chicago at this time and the *Tribune* was in frequent controversy with the *Interior*, a religious weekly, over the distinction between dogma and real religion. Moody was taken as an example of real religion. Bible reading was discontinued in the public schools. A revival was decided upon for Chicago.

The Grand Pacific and the Palmer House each claimed to be the most elegantly furnished hotel in the world. The Grand Pacific had 600 rooms, 200 of them with bath. The

Palmer House advertised room and board at $3 and $4 a day. The *Tribune* on September 18 gave a page to the arrival of the first fast mail from New York.

The *Staats-Zeitung* attempted to revive the Sunday saloon question for political purposes, but the *Tribune*, which had learned this lesson well, said that it would not work, that the People's party was sunk this year. Citizens were rallied to defeat the "bummers," with a warning to taxpayers that unless they did this Chicago would be saddled with graft like New York and an annual expenditure of 44 millions.

A letter from Horace White, describing political conditions in England, was printed on September 25.

A woman reporter was sent out to Field, Leiter & Company and other stores to find out what the best dressed woman should wear. An event of the season was the brilliant opening of Mandel Brothers on October 7.

The charter litigation which had gone to the Supreme Court was decided in favor of the aldermanic group, holding Mayor Colvin in office until April of 1877. "The Supreme Court," said the *Tribune*, "has given the people of Chicago a legacy of fraud from which it will not be easy to escape."

A two-page review of the building progress of the city was printed on October 9, the fourth anniversary of the fire.

"Today," said the *Tribune*, "Chicago is larger, better built, more populous, stronger in all material ways, more beautiful in herself and in the suburbs than ever before. Chicago has risen again and starts on the fifth year of the new birth with the same old Christian faith and western grit."

Republican news was given first-page position each day during October, and Louis Huck was backed for treasurer against "Bummer" A. C. Hesing, the German political overlord. A test could come here if not in a mayoralty campaign. Medill was aching to smite the element which had repudiated his administration. The Hesing group was opposed as tax eaters catering to the criminal classes. "Return the scaly crew to the slums," said the *Tribune*.

A Saturday page of book reviews was inaugurated and a column of gossip for the ladies on Sunday.

Business men were called on by the *Tribune* on October 28 to organize ballot box guards to defeat the tax eaters. The "devil-fish crew" was a new name for the opposition coined in the *Tribune*. Much of the first page was given to the political situation, the call to arms.

"We have no apology for devoting all this space to the election," said the *Tribune*. "The smashing of the ascendancy of the criminal and dishonest classes by the defeat of their ringleader will be accepted by our readers as sufficient excuse." Another page was given to "Hesing's mob" on October 30.

"The only refuge now left to the opposition is fraud," said the *Tribune*, "and [in italics] to attempt that they may just as well understand, now as at any other time, will be worth their lives."

"Long John" Wentworth, who had been in politics for 39 years, lined up on the *Tribune* side in this election. Hesing tried desperately to rally the Germans against the *Tribune*. The governor ordered the First Regiment to be in readiness on election day and demanded an honest ballot. "Kill the devil-fish," was the final word of the *Tribune* on November 2.

A headline of November 3 exulted: "Victory. Huck by 4,000 majority." Medill was revenged for the telegram sent to him in Paris by Hesing after the defeat of Medill's candidate in 1873.

The Republicans had met with a comfortable success throughout the country, it was reported. "Well and nobly have the people of Chicago vindicated the character and credit of their city," said the *Tribune*. "It is a healthful sign of municipal purity and reform."

The *Staats-Zeitung* said the Irish had betrayed the Germans in the election. The *Tribune* said this coalition could never be revived and set out to reform the city council.

Third-term talk for Grant was called a "New York Herald bugaboo." "Take it away. Caesar is dead."

The life of Dwight L. Moody was given a first-page story on November 6 and Professor Swing's sermons were printed in full on Monday mornings. The death of General E. B. Harlan, *Tribune* correspondent at Springfield, was reported on November 8, 1875.

Henry Ward Beecher preached on the heroism of silence and the *Tribune* on November 11 said the history of his case showed him to have a weak nature "and not entitled to that respect and confidence which he had commanded for his supposed strength, boldness and Christian fortitude."

On November 15 six columns were given to a lecture before the Philosophical Society on Voltaire. The cornerstone of the new Rush Medical College was laid and Holy Name Cathedral was dedicated.

"Raconteur" was writing Washington social gossip. The "whisky ring" trials in St. Louis and Milwaukee were followed closely. President Grant in a message advocated free schools without sectarian teaching in all states. A third party was predicted for the 1876 campaign.

The question of the tenure of Mayor H. D. Colvin rose again in December and the Citizens' Association took a hand in the political situation. Carter H. Harrison, just elected to Congress, introduced a bill making ex-presidents senators for life. Harrison was referred to in the *Tribune* as "Our Carter" and was treated jocularly for many years.

At Christmas time the *Tribune* said: "Chicago will have a Merry Christmas notwithstanding unseasonable weather, unpaid bills, unstable finances, unendurable taxes, uncertainty as to paying them, and mingled indignation about them." As to the national situation it said:

"There is no lack of United States customers. New

trade with the South, Mexico and China are coming. If we sell the world will buy, but if we keep out the world by a tariff wall and suffer our business interests to flounder in the quicksands of a shifting currency, we shall effectually prevent our selling and the world's buying."

The *Inter-Ocean* and the *Tribune* were in a row over the whisky ring trials as the year closed. The *Inter-Ocean* was characterized as "The Whisky Thieves' Organ." The *Tribune* opposed sentimental Christmas pardons of Joliet inmates, saying "Sentiment and justice do not mix with the people."

Chapter Sixteen

THE NEW DEAL AND THE "BUMMERS"

VICTORY and defeat came to the *Tribune* banner during 1876, an eventful political year both locally and nationally. Probably the most soul-satisfying event to Editor Medill was the defeat of "The Bummers" in a special mayoralty campaign. It will be recalled that he received a telegram in 1873, in Paris, from "King" A. C. Hesing, leader of the German voters, stating that Medill's policies in Chicago had been defeated by 10,000 votes, and the Prussian flag flew over the American flag at the *Staats-Zeitung* building.

Now the tables were turned. Mayor Colvin, who had been put into office by Hesing, was defeated by the Republicans, and Hesing himself went down in the whisky fraud scandal that featured this part of the Grant administration.

In the national field Medill sought to purify the Republican party and to lead it to victory. He picked out Secretary of

229

the Treasury Benjamin H. Bristow, who had prosecuted the whisky and Indian rings, as the logical leader, the "available man." He turned out a campaign paper that had the flavor of 1860, when Lincoln was picked for the same reason — availability. Bristow was "the man of the hour." But the Republican party thought otherwise and Medill lost this fight. There followed the long struggle between Hayes and Tilden, which led to talk of another civil war, and was reminiscent of the Jefferson-Burr conflict. The *Tribune* fought the growing "Commune" in Chicago, which was their designation of labor strikers, and favored mightily the Dwight L. Moody revival era. While supporting President Grant and declaring him personally honest, the *Tribune* began to discourage any talk of another term for him.

The financial condition of the paper at that time is indicated by a notation of March 13, 1876, when Medill received an 8 per cent dividend on his 1050 shares of stock, in the sum of $8,400. He allowed himself a salary of $100 a week.

The year 1876, the opening of the second century of American national life, was to be characterized, according to the *Tribune*, by two great movements in religion and education. Attention was called to the great revival to be started in Chicago by the evangelists Moody and Sankey and also to President Grant's message on the necessity of free elementary schools and the abolition of sectarian teaching.

"Whisky" was a standing first-page head during January, as the Federal axe had descended on the heads of many prominent Chicagoans in connection with revenue frauds. One of the heads to fall was that of A. C. Hesing, political enemy of the *Tribune*. "The Republican party," said the *Tribune*, "cannot be hurt by exposing and punishing rogues."

The *Tribune's* annual business review showed wholesale business of 639 millions, an increase of 18 millions over the previous year.

A new book by Ralph Waldo Emerson, *Letters and Social Aims*, was given special attention and the *Tribune* said that it was time that America recognized "this man who sits in his house in Concord as poet, philosopher and prophet."

Chicago was hoping to be chosen as the scene of the next Republican national convention. Postmasters and other Republican leaders were forming subscription clubs for the *Weekly Tribune*. Governor Rutherford B. Hayes of Ohio was talked of as a presidential candidate.

The Illinois Supreme Court was unable to decide whether the office of mayor of Chicago was vacant or not, as a result of the charter election, and the *Tribune* sought to get the city council to call an election in April.

The *Journal* printed an item stating that Horace White had received $10,000 from the Cobden Club for his services on free trade as editor of the *Tribune*. The *Tribune* said it was surprised that the *Journal* would ever print such a lie, which was supposed to have come from a former employe of the *Tribune*. "We do not believe that he ever got one cent from any club for his tariff articles," said the *Tribune*. "Certainly the present editor never heard of such a charge." White was not in town for comment.

Henry Ward Beecher was preaching again to a crowded church and defying "man, angels and God himself to speak if they had anything to say against him." The *Tribune* said it was a little strange he did not include women. The *Tribune* ran a weekly column on science and religion and in February started a new department of domestic economy. Its "How to Get Married" articles, it was stated, had attracted so much attention that it was decided to start a department of practical information for the married.

President Grant was warned on February 24 that it would be a fatal error to dismiss Secretary of the Treasury Bristow, who had exposed the whisky ring frauds.

The *Journal* rebuked the *Tribune* for seeking the defeat

of Acting-Governor Beveridge and the *Tribune* said on February 25th:

"THE CHICAGO TRIBUNE has had a life in this city dating back beyond the birth or organization of the Republican party, and during that time has always been in favor of free speech, and of free criticism of all men in office, without reference to what party they may belong, and of all measures and policies, no matter by what party they may be proposed. THE CHICAGO TRIBUNE does not intend to alter its course in this respect. It fearlessly criticizes all public measures, and it defends or opposes them from the standpoint of the public good. It supports Republican policies and Republican candidates because they are preferable to the policies and men proposed by others.

"The fact is that the newspaper which has no opinions, has no concern for the welfare of the party, which dares not warn against error or demand the expurgation of evil, which accepts implicitly what is given it, and is forever pressing the hand that is smiting and crushing the party, is not worthy a name or place in journalism. Its support is that of the bondman and not of the freeman; of the grinning idiot and not of the intellectual mind; and THE CHICAGO TRIBUNE has never been and does not now intend to be a newspaper of that character, and if this is to be considered in opposition to Beveridge, or opposition to any other candidate, we rejoice that we are in opposition."

Secretary of War William Belknap of Iowa was forced to resign on account of his connection with the Indian Agency scandal. "A brilliant career shattered by a woman's extravagance," commented the *Tribune* on March 3. The President, it was stated, knew nothing about the affair until the facts were developed by an investigating committee. Bribes and blackmail, waste and extravagance, were exposed.

"There can be no reformation," said the *Tribune*, "until society shall recognize wealth as disreputable that is not the product of honest toil and skill." The Republican party could not be blamed for this scandal, the *Tribune* held, and pressed for the impeachment of Belknap.

A treaty with the Hawaiian Islands was pending. There was talk of a coaling station and paying sugar planters half a million a year. "Go slow. This is pretty thin," said the *Tribune*. "If this is a question of some time coming into possession of the islands and shouldering the responsibility of fortifying their coasts and defending them in war, then we beg to be excused for the present."

The death of General J. D. Webster, one of the early proprietors of the *Tribune*, was reported on March 12. He was collector of internal revenue in Chicago.

The Republican national convention went to Cincinnati instead of Chicago and early in the spring the *Tribune* began to set the stage for the Republican campaign. The result of all the federal investigations and scandals, it was stated, would be to rid the Republican party of thieves. It showed that the party had the moral strength to purify itself and was at least better than "the reactionary ex-Confederate Democracy."

"Wanted — for President," said the *Tribune* on March 19: "A man of unquestioned honesty, free from all connection with the errors and follies which have exhausted the patience of the people. Is there a statesman in the Republican party with the ability and learning qualifying him for the office, whose nomination will of itself be such a separation from all the past that the country will accept him upon his own character and his own record as the beginning of a new era? Such is the man who should be nominated at Cincinnati."

A Republican city convention was called to nominate a candidate for mayor on April 6. The council did not issue a call for an election. The *Tribune* referred to Colvin as the acting mayor and argued that the election of a new council included a new appointment as mayor. The aldermen had taken the Colvin side of the controversy. Elihu B. Washburne was boosted by the *Tribune* as a candidate for governor. Acting Governor Beveridge had been on the side of Hesing.

The Democrats of Chicago also came out against Colvin in this campaign and recommended Thomas Hoyne for mayor. A meeting of 40,000 citizens was held at the Exposition Building on April 7, expressing the will of citizens in a sort of fusion movement for Hoyne. "Long John" Wentworth, Republican, was in the chair. Colvin was called on to resign. The *Tribune* said the election of Hoyne would be a practical expression of the people's will and called for the hanging of ballot box stuffers. The *Inter-Ocean* was referred to as the "Ballot Box Stuffer and Thieves Organ."

Colvin refused to resign, saying on April 18: "In November, 1873, I was elected by a majority of 10,000 to the office I now hold by the suffrages of the people, irrespective of party, who had become heartily disgusted with the administration of affairs by Mr. Medill."

Hoyne was elected in the special April election and nearly all the Republicans on the local ticket were victorious. Hoyne claimed to be mayor on the theory that the 1875 charter election had repealed the charter under which Colvin had been elected. At the same time it was recognized that there was a legal question involved and the *Tribune* made no attempt to decide it. The matter moved into the courts.

On April 22, 1876, in an editorial on the next governor, the *Tribune* said it had no candidate but favored Washburne, that Beveridge had never been really elected governor and was a machine politician.

"THE TRIBUNE is not committed to any person. THE TRIBUNE is a people's paper, and not a machine paper working in the interest of any particular office holder or office seeker. . . . In a series of murders in southern Illinois it was not until THE TRIBUNE had sent a commissioner to the district, had published the whole history of the crimes [in "Bloody Williamson" county] and had held the governor directly responsible for its continuance, that steps were taken to put a stop to the assassination business. Previously he had gone into conference with the demagogues of the legislature, pleading that he could not maintain order and suppress organized crime because of the want of $12,000 in his contingent fund. THE TRIBUNE taught him his duty differently."

Washburne declined to become a candidate for governor. On May 1, in considering the presidential aspirants, Roscoe Conkling, Levi P. Morton, James G. Blaine and Secretary Bristow, the *Tribune* favored Bristow as "the man of the hour, the candidate of the people, who would smash the political machines." He was commended for the conviction of men of his own party for robbing the Treasury in the whisky frauds. The *Tribune* had general admiration for and confidence in Blaine and would support him if nominated, "notwithstanding some misgivings of the success of the party with him as a candidate."

Two columns were printed on May 1 concerning the relative circulation of the *Tribune* and its rivals. An affidavit by George Clarke Cooper was presented as proof of the number of papers sold during the week ending April 29. This was 219,317, a daily average of 31,331 copies. Cooper had canvassed each district in the city for the *Tribune*, the *Times*, the *Inter Ocean*, and those who took no paper. The *Tribune* said:

"THE TRIBUNE is the business man's newspaper. It is taken and read by all classes of people who have any property or anything to sell, lease or loan, or any money with which to make purchases or investments, or any useful services to hire or engage. Its circulation is not of the back alley sort nor dependent upon occasional sensational or scandalous articles. It is the character of the constituency that determines the quality of circulation and its corresponding value as an advertising medium. . . . Readers in the slums and back alleys who occasionally invest a nickel in a newspaper are not the class whom advertisers desire to reach. Business men, manufacturers, merchants and substantial, respectable citizens who can afford to take their paper regularly, subscribing for it annually, are precisely the people advertisers would reach. Such, precisely, as the figures disclose, are the readers of THE TRIBUNE."

The *Tribune* on May 5 called on the new council to seat Hoyne and let Colvin take the consequences. "Long John" Wentworth lectured on early Chicago at McCormick Hall and was given twelve columns in the *Tribune* of May 8. Henry D. Lloyd was made president of the Sunday Lecture Society. The new council canvassed the vote and declared Hoyne elected. "Now let the people sing a paean of victory," said the *Tribune* of May 9. "The bummers are outwitted."

Colvin decided to stick in the Mayor's chair and department heads were notified by both sides. Colvin blamed the newspapers for his plight, chiefly the *Tribune*.

A strike in the lumber yards was treated in the *Tribune* as the work of "The Commune." A special reporter was sent to Philadelphia to write of the opening of the Centennial Exposition. Whisky fraud trials in Chicago called for pages of testimony. Samuel J. Tilden was looked upon as the Democratic nominee for President and the *Tribune* said on May 18 that New York would be the battlefield, that the Democrats were reasonably certain to carry all the late slave holding states except South Carolina.

Hoyne took his seat as mayor on May 19 as a result of *quo warranto* court proceedings and delivered a message calling for economy and reform. The *Tribune* referred to his prospective changes in the City Hall as "The New Deal." Colvin's attorneys carried his case to the higher court.

In urging the nomination of Bristow the *Tribune* said on May 20: "We submit to thinking and reflecting Republicans that, in rejecting Bristow at Cincinnati, they may throw away the all sufficient and at the same time the only successful answer they can make to the Democratic array of official Republican corruption and extravagance."

Shelby M. Cullom was nominated for governor at the Springfield convention, which chose a delegation favorable to Blaine but uninstructed. Benjamin F. Butler looked like the dark horse of Illinois and the favorite of "rag baby politicians," according to the *Tribune*.

W. F. Storey launched the *Evening Telegraph* on May 31, taking an advertisement in the *Tribune* to announce the fact.

Dwight L. Moody opened his Chicago Avenue Church on June 1. At the organization of a Bristow Club in Chicago, Horace White made a speech and Samuel J. Medill was present.

The circuit court reinstated Colvin as mayor until he should call a special election. He went to court again to get out of calling such an election. Reporter "Harryth" was sent to Cincinnati. There was apprehension over Blaine, who was under fire in the Washington investigation. The *Tribune* said it printed "bad Blaine news" as news, not to hurt him, and in order that the people may understand all. On June 12 the *Tribune* said it would support the Cincinnati nominee, whoever it might be.

"And this not from any slavish submission to the party dictation, but because THE TRIBUNE has an abiding faith in the truth of the doctrines of the Republican party and as deep a conviction that the success of the Democratic party will be perilous to the perpetuity of the freedom of the people and the perpetuity of the Union."

Hayes was growing in favor as a compromise candidate as convention day approached. Medill went to Cincinnati himself and wrote the lead story of June 15, after Hayes and William A. Wheeler of New York had been nominated. The Republican party, he said, had almost miraculously escaped destruction. Don Cameron of Pennsylvania was given the credit for stopping Blaine.

"Let us all rejoice and give thanks," said the *Tribune* of June 17, 1876. "The government is not about to pass into the hands of those who strove to destroy it. The work of official purification will go on, revenue thieves will be hunted down and driven from public life, and honest men will be put in their places. We have no fears for the result of the election of 1876."

A special mayoralty election was ordered on June 22. A ratification meeting was held in Chicago for Hayes and Wheeler. Reporters were sent to St. Louis for the Democratic convention, which the *Tribune* referred to as "the great gathering of the distinguished unwashed," and "Democracy strutting its brief hour."

The *Weekly Campaign Tribune* was announced on June 24, with the formation of clubs. "If the ascendancy of the Republican party is to be maintained," said the *Tribune*, "no agency will be more useful and potential to that end than THE CHICAGO TRIBUNE, which has no superior in power and influence among Republican newspapers. THE TRIBUNE proposes to keep the enemy on the defensive, and to make it a hot campaign for them until a glorious triumph is achieved in November."

Among the results of the Chicago whisky fraud prosecutions was the conviction of A. C. Hesing, who was sentenced to two years' imprisonment and a fine of $5,000.

Monroe Heath and Charles E. Culvert were suggested as mayoralty candidates for the special election which was to take place on July 12.

Samuel J. Tilden of New York was the Democratic nominee for President. The *Tribune* referred to "Sammy's Bar'l" in its headlines and made the dismal prediction that the party never would survive the nomination. "The Republican party now has knowledge of whom they have to deal

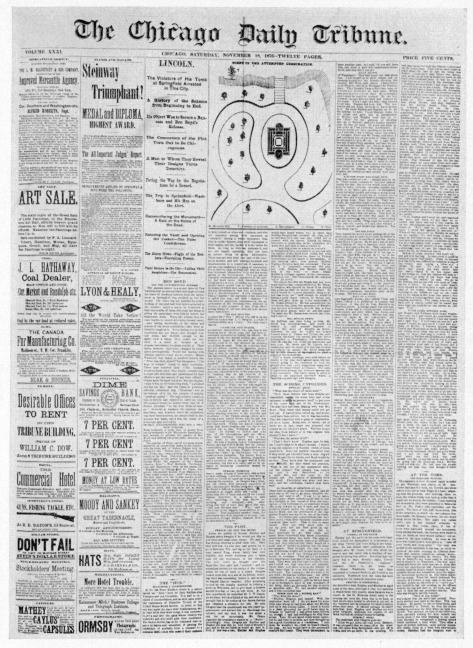

On the front page of the Tribune *of November 18, 1876, began a complete account of one of the most sensational stories in American history, the attempt to steal Lincoln's body from the tomb in Springfield, Illinois.*

with — a desperate, unscrupulous foe, armed with immense wealth, controlling a legion of agents skilled in the machinery of fraud elections, and united to a man for the purpose of defeating the Republican party."

Governor Thomas Hendricks of Indiana was chosen the vice-presidential candidate. "A gathering of roughs, black-guards and incompetents," said the *Tribune* of the St. Louis convention. The *Chicago Times* stories were headed "Honesty's Hosts."

Heath was nominated for mayor by the Republicans on July 2. The *Tribune* advised the acceptance of the Illinois Central offer to buy the lake front property for $800,000. Mark Twain's new book, *Huckleberry Finn*, was given a long review on July 3. On July 5, 1876, the *Tribune* printed a national centennial edition, filled with historical material on the founding of the republic.

A dispatch from Salt Lake City told of the massacre of General Custer and 315 soldiers in Montana. "Too true," said the *Tribune* of this tragedy on July 7, presenting a map of the battlefield and a two-page account.

Mark Kimball was nominated by the Democrats for mayor, with Jim McGrath running as an independent. The only way out was to vote for Heath, the *Tribune* advised the citizens. Hayes in his letter of acceptance printed on July 10, called for an honest currency and for perfect political equality in the South. A letter from a *Tribune* reporter, from a camp in the Big Horn country, told of the Indian war.

"Got 'Em All," was the announcement of election results on July 13. Heath had a small majority. "This is the first gun in the presidential campaign," said the *Tribune*. "Chicago is a Republican city. . . . For the first time since the bummers acquired possession of the city two years ago the city government is in a condition to realize the demands of the people for reform and retrenchment."

Business was poor that summer, with capital seeking investment bargains in vain. The paving of State Street was in prospect. The *Tribune* sent a reporter to St. Louis. He found "To Rent" signs everywhere and wrote that the city's claim to solidity had vanished.

The *Tribune* household department sent a load of jellies to St. Luke's Hospital. Reporter "Harryth" was sent to Columbus to write of Hayes at home. Special dispatches were carried on August 21 on failures and rascality in St. Louis banking and on the story of the Mollie Maguires in Pennsylvania. "Wild Bill" Hickok was given a special story on August 25. A chess department was started in the *Tribune*. A new drive for the German vote began in September, with Carl Schurz taking the headlines.

The *Tribune* printed a four-page supplement on September 1 on Tilden's record, made up of contributions from many other papers, and exposing alleged railroad plunderings, election frauds, "humbug claims to reform, disloyalty to the Union," etc. Hayes' record as a colonel in the Union army was given in contrast. Hendricks' war record was also given and the following excerpt from a letter which he was said to have written on September 14, 1864, stating: "All who favor peace come. All who desire to be free from the death grip of this infamously wicked, imbecile and tyrannical administration [Lincoln's] come and hear the advocate of peace."

It was charged that in 1863 Tilden made a false return on his income tax, putting in $7,118 when he had received a fee of $20,000.

Professor Swing's sermons were presented regularly. "It is only by such harmonizing," said the *Tribune*, "that religion can continue to exercise its beneficent influence over society, and brush away alike the superstitions of the past and the dangers of materialism."

The great issue of the election, as the *Tribune* saw it, was whether the South was to be put in power again and the war lost. Tilden was attacked again on September 16 on his income tax returns for 1862. A special story was carried from Bay-reuth on the triumph of Wagner and a description of the musical festival there.

Lyman Trumbull, who was a Republican leader, spoke at a Farwell Hall Democratic meeting against "Grantism" and said there would be better times under the Democrats and there was no reason to fight the battle of slavery over again. The *Tribune* said it was not worried that he would take many Republicans with him. It took three editorials on September 21 to explain the weakness of the Trumbull arguments and call on the "boys in blue" to rally again. Nine columns were given to a Republican speech by "Long John" Wentworth.

Moody and Sankey started their long awaited revival on October 2 and had 7,000 at the opening meeting. The *Tribune* reported this in four columns. A special correspondent wrote of a trip from Atlanta to the sea, along the line of Sherman's march, and described conditions of the day. Boston capital was reported interested in an elevated railroad to bring Evanston within twenty minutes of downtown Chicago. The new Rush Medical School was opened at Wood and Harrison Streets. Jesse James was being hunted in Missouri.

The October elections showed Ohio Republican by a small majority, with Indiana Democratic. The *Tribune* said this made New York the battlefield.

The revival conducted by Moody and Sankey grew into a great demonstration, with overflow meetings at Farwell Hall and at the First Methodist Church. General Benjamin Harrison and Robert G. Ingersoll came to Chicago, as did several Southern orators. "Let them come," said the *Tribune* on October 20. "Fetch your captains of rifle clubs, your leaders of White Line mobs, your masked Ku Klux."

It was stated on November 2 that there were 62,173 employes in the federal service. A page was given to Tilden's "nefarious career" as a lawyer.

The election, said the *Tribune* on November 7, would decide one of the gravest issues of the age. "The defeat of Tilden today will be a complete overthrow and disruption of the 'Solid South' as a political organization. It will destroy the last hope of the Southern extremists to regain power and undo the results of the war. The election of Hayes will build up a large white Republican party in the South and this party will be composed of native white as well as Negroes."

The *Tribune* guess as to the result was 205 electoral votes for Republicans and 164 for the Democrats.

"Lost" was the first-page heading of November 8, 1876. "The country given over to Democratic greed and plunder. Tilden, Tammany and the Solid South free to rule the nation. New York decides against us." A 4:30 a.m. postscript gave Hayes 181 votes and Tilden 184, with Florida's four votes missing. A gloomy editorial on the probable election of Tilden was printed. "Republican defeat must be only temporary," said the *Tribune*. "Its leading principles are engrafted in the Constitution and are unchangeable."

It was reported the same day that thieves had tried to steal the remains of Abraham Lincoln at Springfield, and that the robbers had been interrupted and had escaped.

Luther Laflin Mills was elected states attorney. There was still hope for the Republicans the next day. "Never give up the ship," said the *Tribune*. "Several doubtful states pan out well. Illinois is Republican by 10,000. Florida is for Hayes."

On November 10 "Victory" was announced, with North Carolina, South Carolina and Florida "knocking the Solid South folly in the head."

The next week was called the most exciting since Grant's campaign in the Wilderness, with the situation changing every day. The uncertainty narrowed to the returns in Louisiana and General Sheridan was sent to New Orleans. Members of the Louisiana returning board were said to have been threatened with death if they did not return for Tilden. The *Tribune* said on November 14 that it looked like Hayes, with the struggle transferred to the electoral college.

The political situation was subordinated on November 18 to the story of the desecration at the Lincoln tomb, and the arrest of the conspirators. It made a six-column thriller.

Hayes was apparently given the South Carolina vote on November 19. An honest count of an honest vote was demanded by the *Tribune*. The next day the result was again in doubt. The scene then shifted to New Orleans, where a reporter was sent to write the stories of election day crimes. "There is no chance of a successful Republican organization in the cotton states," said the *Tribune* of November 27, "while the organization is made up of white carpetbaggers and the mass of black voters. There must be an ultimate division of the white voters on politics."

"Saved," was the *Tribune* headline on December 7, 1876. Hayes now had 185 votes and Tilden 184. The story was decorated with a battle-scarred rooster, feathers torn but triumphantly crowing. Oregon complicated the situation and there was a rumor of bribery there.

All talk of war over the result was bluster, the *Tribune* declared. "The pending question must be decided by law and in a calm, just and upright manner." It was suggested by the *Tribune* that new elections be held in the disputed states.

On President Grant's annual message the *Tribune* commented: "There will be few of his countrymen who will withhold from Grant the tribute of patriotism and honesty of purpose."

Business men were disgusted with the political situation and the financial columns reported hard times as the year closed.

Chapter Seventeen

THE NEW ERA ARRIVES

WHILE 1877 promised to be a most exciting year politically the Hayes-Tilden contest ended peaceably and talk of civil war ceased. This was at the expense, however, of the abandonment of the Radical policy toward the South, and a new era of conciliation was begun, which was supported by the *Tribune*. The South was left largely to its own devices and control of the Negro vote. The *Tribune* fought against disfranchisement of the Negroes but admitted that the states could not be ruled longer by federal bayonets.

Hard times were upon the country. Banks and insurance companies failed in Chicago, but the *Tribune* forged ahead to new records in advertising. The year was made memorable for the paper by the establishment of the first European service, centering in a London bureau. A new appeal to women readers was made in a household department, which proved extremely popular.

Wages were being reduced everywhere and the result was a series of strikes culminating in a great railroad strike in which many lives were lost and millions of dollars' worth of property destroyed. The *Tribune* held that rioting must be severely punished but that the railroads and other employers must pay a living wage. Communism was held responsible for the disorders that followed the effort to get better wages and an eight-hour day. Some method of government guarantee of savings deposits was advocated by the *Tribune*.

The *Tribune* prospectus for 1877 outlined its major policies on the national situation as follows:

"The country has passed through a fierce presidential contest, and the result has been left in a dangerous and unsatisfactory shape, on account of the unprecedented closeness of the election, the angry disputes as to the votes of certain states, and the failure of the Constitution to provide any tribunal to solve doubts or decide contested points.

"From the best light before it THE TRIBUNE believes that Hayes has received 185 electoral votes against 184 for Tilden and is therefore entitled to be inaugurated President on the 4th of March, 1877. The highest good of the South, as well as of the North, would be best promoted by his occupancy of the presidential chair. But there are grave apprehensions that a ruffianly, ravenous crowd of office seekers may resort to lawless and violent means to induct the defeated candidate into the office of Chief Magistrate. All peace loving and law abiding men, irrespective of party, must stand together in this crisis and crush out the incendiary demagogues who are threatening to light the torch of internecine war, which would bring ruin and destruction upon the country.

"The coming year promises to be the most eventful and exciting of any since the war. THE TRIBUNE will do everything in its power to have the new President peacefully and lawfully inaugurated and to restore harmony and confidence in the future. Let us never despair of the Republic.

"While THE CHICAGO TRIBUNE is a Republican newspaper and has contributed as much as any other in the United States to the success of the party, it is always independent and fearless in expression of its views, and aims to be right rather than partisan; and while holding party high it holds the country higher."

The year opened in political confusion but with a tacit recognition of Hayes as the President-elect. The *Tribune* printed a page-history of the electoral college. The question was raised as to whether the House of Representatives had the right to name the President over the electors. The *Tribune* took the position that Congress had no such right and stated: "The great peril to the United States Constitution now and ever has been, the grasping of new and dangerous powers. To assume or admit that either house may by a majority vote reject the vote of a state and defeat the election of a majority candidate, is to assume a power which the Constitution expressly aimed to prohibit."

Democratic conventions throughout the country demanded Tilden's election. A joint committee of Congress was named to count the votes. A new election was still discussed. The commission was composed of eight Republicans and seven Democrats.

In its 6-page annual review the *Tribune* writer noted a great increase in "beef and pork stink factories." There was a 5 per cent gain in manufactures. The total trade was 652 millions. In view of the hard times the editor found the situation satisfactory.

The *Chicago Times* took occasion to criticize the *Tribune's* new household department, which had proved popular and reached 40,000 families every Saturday. "Experience has proved," said the *Tribune*, "that a decent regard for honesty, virtue and home life is not only more creditable, but more popular and more profitable, than pandering to vicious and vulgar tastes."

The Illinois senatorial struggle took shape on January 5. The *Tribune* desired the election of a Republican but had "no candidate." Logan was named by the Republicans and Palmer by the Democrats. In the January 17 voting Logan lacked five votes. The legislature went into a deadlock.

The Moody and Sankey revival ended and the *Tribune* hoped the result would be a revival of plain old-fashioned integrity and uprightness.

The senatorial deadlock continued until January 25. The

Tribune said Logan had become a "Republican Jonah" and a compromise was urged. This resulted in the election of Justice David Davis of the United States Supreme Court by the Democrats and Independents. "Illinois," said the *Tribune*, "should be proud of such a representative." Justice Davis, it will be recalled, was one of the original Lincoln men in Illinois and as such a close collaborator with Medill in 1860.

Special attention was given to a scarlet fever epidemic late in January. The doctors disputed as to how to treat it. "Shame," said the *Tribune*. "Tell us if you have a cure – not that belladonna will cure it and will not cure it. Death is among us."

A baseball league alliance was proposed by A. G. Spaulding. Reporter "Harryth" investigated the Springfield statehouse ring. He wrote of the building lobby, "the bottomless pocket," and how the low-bid law had been evaded. "Monstrous moral obloquy," was disclosed.

Henry Ward Beecher appeared at the new Moody Church on February 12. Crowds sought to get in and five columns were given to his sermons. "He looked old and worn," wrote the *Tribune* reporter. "His hair is long and white and falls on his stooping shoulders. His actions were weary at first and there was an expression in his eyes suggesting that life had become wearisome to him. But as he entered upon his sermon the old look came back to his face and the fire to his eyes." He spoke of the Kingdom of God. In succeeding lectures messenger boys were hired to stand in line to hold places.

Compulsory education was debated at Springfield, with the bill going to a hostile committee.

"Settled," was the *Tribune* page-one "screamer" of February 17. "Rutherford B. Hayes is to be the next President and William A. Wheeler the next Vice-President." The Louisiana vote had settled the matter, with eight members of the congressional committee voting to receive it and seven dissenting.

"The Democrats have decided to act squarely and carry out the law," said the *Tribune*. "The American people have a right to gratitude that a contest of this kind has been settled by lawful and peaceful means."

On February 19 the *Tribune* reported a Southern Hayes movement, and said it looked like a deal to get soldiers out of the South. If this were true it meant the failure of the Radical movement to force equal citizenship rights for colored voters. This was in the law but not in practice.

A leaded editorial was run on February 21 in which the selection of Senator Morton, Radical leader from Indiana, as president of the Senate was urged. The question of the completion of the count by March 3 was raised and the *Tribune* saw "Democratic perfidy" in the offing, a conspiracy to keep Hayes from office. "The government must be prepared for the emergency and the man to act as president for nearly a year, in the emergency, is Oliver P. Morton of Indiana. If a solemn compact is to be broken then there is villainy in the land — villainy that requires a stout heart and a strong hand." It was recalled how Morton had dealt with "fire-in-the-rear Copperheads" during the war.

In answer to criticism of this suggestion the *Tribune* said on February 23: "We are not in favor of keeping a lot of carpetbag, knavish politicians in the South by the power of federal bayonets — no more so now than before — but Morton's methods would be directed against the entire class of perfidious and bulldozing Democrats North and South, who would be responsible for preventing the inauguration of Hayes, maggoty ham and decayed sow-belly office bummers."

A new mayoralty race was coming up with Colvin, a formidable candidate. The *Tribune* urged the organization of the "respectable element" in each ward.

The *Inter-Ocean* on March 1 charged that five acres at 46th Street and Grand Boulevard, adjoining the South Park district, were the property of Alfred Cowles, business manager and one of the proprietors of the *Tribune*. It was also stated that Horace White owned the adjoining eight acres. This was supposed to be a "donation" from the park people.

White came out with a statement that he did not own a foot of this land and had never received a donation from the park promoters. Cowles, then in Europe, said he had not received any donation either, but might have bought the land in the open market.

The electoral count was announced on March 2. All was serene in Washington. Hayes called on Grant. Grant withdrew troops from Louisiana, except enough to keep the peace. As Grant's administration ended, the *Tribune* said he would take his place in American history as "a soldier-president who performed his duties ably, and who, committing mistakes and blunders, had the courage to avow and regret them. Let the new President have a fair trial and opportunity to demonstrate his policy and intentions. Let us all rejoice that the great agony is ended."

A resolution to investigate the South Park district board was passed at Springfield.

The Hayes inaugural address outlined a policy of conciliation to the South. "No abler, more dignified, or so frank and explicit an address was ever made by any President entering office," said the *Tribune*.

What was called "The New Era" was begun, with Hayes announcing that he would not tolerate party dictation. Blaine, with an eye to 1880, declared war on the pacification policy. A commission was to be sent South. "Civil government is to take the place of military rule and honesty and competency take the place of machine dictation in office," said the *Tribune* of March 14.

Frederick Douglass, noted Negro leader, was made marshal of the Washington district. "Our advice to Southern statesmen," said the *Tribune* of March 26, "is that they take active and effectual means to show that while they are unwilling to submit to corrupt and incompetent government under a carpetbag despotism, they mean to concede to the Negro all his legal rights and to encourage his elevation by education and religion."

Mayor Heath was renominated by the Republicans and Perry H. Smith by the Democrats. The *Tribune* said that Smith was one of the manipulators of Tilden's "Bar'l of Money" at St. Louis. Hesing was out of jail and the Germans seemed to be back in the Republican camp. The issue, said the *Tribune*, was an honest and capable government "against a lot of scalawags and bummers."

Tribune correspondents ranged far west in the spring, writing of the agricultural wealth of California and the mines of Nevada and the Black Hills.

Troops were withdrawn from the South Carolina statehouse and the South was left to get state governments that could function. Southern Republicans were in an ugly temper. "We cannot rule by bayonets," said the *Tribune*, "yet the rights of the blacks must be recognized."

"Hallelujah!" was the page-one shout on April 4. "Professional tax eaters take a back seat. Heath and the entire city ticket elected by 12,000 majority."

The *Tribune* found that a majority of the aldermen elected were respectable. They objected to J. H. Hildreth taking a seat in the council, as it was stated he had been convictd of crime as a government whisky gauger. The *Tribune* found only a "few faint vestiges of Democracy" left in Chicago and crowed over "ancient Storey and his defeat."

"Taxation is the political issue of the future," said the *Tribune* of April 9. "Those with property and something to save on one side, the professional office seekers, the ignorant and reckless on the other."

Taxation of capital stock was being debated in Springfield. The *Tribune* was used as an illustration. It was worth a million, it was stated, and yet was only taxed on $240,000 valuation of capital stock. The proponents of the measure wanted to tax it at its real value. The *Tribune* argued that the value of a newspaper depended on the brains of its conductors and that brains should not be taxed.

J. W. Hinton of Milwaukee, lecturing at Waukesha on the press, said the *Chicago Times* left "a great stench" but that the *Tribune* was "solid, sound, strict and respectable." The *Tribune* Sunday edition, it was stated, was not surpassed by any paper in the world. It was selected and arranged by a master hand. "The editor-in-chief," said Hinton, "is a cultivated gentleman, and that sufficiently accounts for the high character of his paper."

The *Tribune* at this time stood against the movement of a reform organization to make Bible reading compulsory in the schools. "The world has moved to a revolution in religion. These men are a generation behind the times."

General Grant was away on a world tour and preparations were made to welcome him in England.

Pointing to its Sunday edition of April 15 the *Tribune* said it was an indication of a steady increase in the volume of business. "The paper becomes the pulse of its constituency, and its columns illustrate with rigid accuracy the extent of the embarrassment or the prosperity which the various lines of industry or mercantile endeavor reach."

There were 63 columns of advertisments in the paper, "an amount of advertising patronage never equaled but by one daily, the New York Herald, and rarely, if at all, surpassed by that paper, considering the greater length of THE TRIBUNE columns."

The *Chicago Daily Courier*, a 2-cent morning newspaper begun in 1873, was laid away in the sepulchre of dead newspapers on April 19. An account of its brief existence was given in the *Tribune*.

The Sunday edition of April 22, twenty pages of 7 columns each, was said to be the largest daily newspaper ever published in this country. There were 70 columns of advertising.

The *Tribune* of the 70's and 80's had a strong literary bent and its columns were open to many struggling young authors. Its editors were easy of approach, and it also had contact with an eastern literary syndicate. Its columns through many years show the names of nearly every writer of note in America, including many whose fame was only in the springtime. Included in this list was a young writer who signed his stories "G. R. G.," and whom later research has shown to be George Gissing, author of *New Grub Street*, and other works of genius. He came to Chicago in the spring of 1877, wandered around the lake front and took rooms in a dingy old boarding house on Wabash Avenue.

Gissing had been expelled from college in England and had only $5 in his pocket when he reached Chicago. He wandered into the *Tribune* office one day and was kindly received. He wrote a story, *Too Dearly Bought*, which was published that April and several others, including *Brownie*, which was published on July 29, 1877. He remained in Chicago for six months, living an existence which was later reflected in one of the characters of his *New Grub Street*. This collection of early stories was published by the Columbia Press in 1931, with an account of how Gissing's early work was discovered in the files of the *Tribune*.

The *Tribune* was in heated argument with several Southern newspapers over its statement that "the curse of the South is sheer, persistent, chronic and hereditary indisposition of the Southern whites to work."

War was declared between Russia and Turkey and the Russian army was on the march. "Happy indeed," said the *Tribune*, "are the United States in their wide geographical and political separation from these disturbed and warlike nations, between whom exist universal jealousy and universal hate."

A storm was caused in Springfield by the *Tribune's* charge of "disgraceful idleness" there and the printing of a list of absentees on roll calls. The legislators retaliated by saying that the correspondent who obtained the list, H. W. Thomson, was a clerk in pay of a committee. The editor of the *Tribune* said he was not aware of this, but the list stood anyway. Thomson said he had done committee clerk work and so had several other newspaper men. There had been no objection until this list was printed. The outraged legislators called the correspondent a thief and the *Tribune* a "dirty, lying sheet."

George Edward Wright of the *Tribune* staff was sent to London to organize a central bureau, with telegraphic lines to the Russo-Turkish war fronts, it was announced on April 28, 1877. "The establishment of a TRIBUNE bureau in London," it was stated, "places this journal on an equal footing with the New York press and beyond its Chicago contemporaries in the freshness and reliability of its news."

A six-column map on the theatre of war was published on May 1 and the paper began to get out frequent extras on war news; one on the first account of the Russian movement of troops, another on the destruction of a Turkish monitor. The *Chicago Times* was accused of stealing these dispatches, "following the ruling passion in the decline of life."

The Southern Pacific railroad was pushing its way to the Colorado River and the *Tribune* said that the road and the people would be better off if it were built as a business enterprise, instead of with a government subsidy.

The death of the old Northern fire-eater, Senator ("Parson") W. G. Brownlow, was reported on May 1. A review of the letters of Elizabeth Barrett Browning made page one on May 5. The Presbyterian General Assembly, meeting in Chicago, selected the *Tribune* as its official organ of the sessions. Nearly two pages were given to this meeting on May 19. The war with the legislature continued. On May 23 it was said that "the misrepresentatives of the people are about to adjourn."

An anti-administration party headed by Blaine was at work in Washington. Grant was the hero of the hour in Europe and daily stories were carried of his travels and receptions.

The first special cables from the *Tribune* London bureau were carried on June 1.

A scandal broke out in the county building. "The outlook for the complete collapse of the ring is good," said the *Tribune* on June 3. "Official crime must be made infamous, legally and socially, or it is futile to attempt to punish the ordinary offender."

Turkey appeared to be collapsing in the war and England moved into Egypt to protect the Suez Canal and the route to India.

St. John, New Brunswick, which had sent Chicago $10,000 in gold after the fire of 1871, was itself destroyed by fire on June 22 and a relief subscription was started here. A page and a half story told of the hanging of six men at Pottsville, Pennsylvania, on June 22, and the end of the reign of terror of the Molly Maguires. Wages were being reduced all over the country.

Charles Landor wrote from London on Wagner and the Bayreuth festival. The *Inter-Ocean* was called a " devil-fish among newspapers" on June 27 and its financial history was given.

Reformers were getting up a petition for the Sunday closing of saloons. "There has never been a time," said the *Tribune* on July 1, "when THE TRIBUNE has refused its sympathy and aid to any movement calculated to promote temperance in the community. . . . The ladies of the WCTU are only repeating the mistake that has been made spasmodically over and over again during the last twenty-five years. It means only political strife and bad feeling."

The *Tribune* sought to have the fireworks ordinance

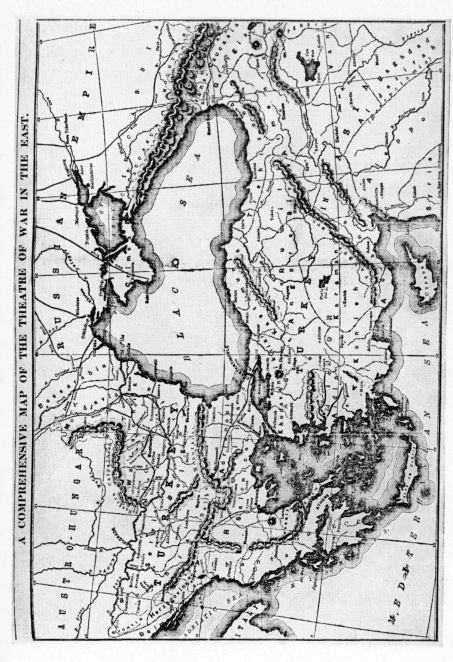

A COMPREHENSIVE MAP OF THE THEATRE OF WAR IN THE EAST.

An early example of Tribune enterprise in providing readers with maps illustrating important news events is this May 1, 1877 map showing the territory involved in the Russo-Turkish War of that year.

enforced on July 4 but did not succeed and there was a long list of accidents.

Progress in lighting by electricity was reported on July 9 and it was prophesied that this would come into domestic use as the light of the future.

The growth of rationalism in Germany was discussed on July 15. There were hundreds of Herbert Spencers and Robert Ingersolls in that country, it was stated. "The church by raising an impenetrable barrier against science continually loses her followers, and the outlook is not an encouraging one."

The fight of the *New York Tribune* with the printers' union was called a complete success on July 15 and the union, it was declared, was doomed.

A railroad strike at Pittsburgh broke into riots on July 22. There was a half column list of dead and wounded. A truce was arranged and in a 6 a.m. extra the *Tribune* proclaimed " Peace — Thank God! " Mob rule must first be stopped, the paper said in discussing the strike. Then the railroad should charge enough to pay their men a living wage.

A nationwide railroad strike was declared on July 24. The *Tribune* carried three pages of news on this. In Chicago the First and Second Regiments of state militia slept under arms and eight companies of United States regulars were reported coming in. "There must be no parley or temporizing with rioters," said the *Tribune*. "Mob rule is a weed to be torn up by the roots." Five million dollars' worth of property had been destroyed in the East. The next day the strike was on in Chicago and traffic was suspended. The *Tribune* said that Communism was at the bottom of the strike and called on the city to organize for the common defense. "Let every man enroll."

Halsted Street was the scene of riots reported on July 26 and the next day there were pitched battles on the southwest side. Eight men were killed and the First Regiment was called out. Seven pages of a 12-page paper were devoted to the strike news.

The *Tribune's* main editorial theme at this time was that the law was supreme. At the same time it distinguished between the railroad workers who were demanding a raise and the "Communistic rabble" that was fomenting riots. Wages which on the Pennsylvania railroad ranged from $41 to $92 a month had been reduced because of hard times. The *Tribune* was commended by the union for demanding decent pay for the men.

All was reported quiet on July 28. The loss in Chicago was seven million dollars. The *Tribune* urged an increase in the national army and said in its lead to a page-one news story:

"THE TRIBUNE is in favor of one more strike, and it ought to be made today, a strike that shall be to the death and to the destruction, bloodshed, gore and all the rest of it. This strike should be against the villainous scoundrels who have incited the mob and who at the same time have been too cowardly to lead or take part in it—men like the one who begged in Market Square like a cringing, dirty, despicable hound, on his knees for his carcass, on the spot where he had been a moment before urging men to take capital by the throat. But very likely he will continue to sponge a living off the workingmen."

There were said to be a million unemployed in the country at this time. The *Tribune* suggested a back to the land movement. "Seek the country, go to work, be sober and industrious and other things will follow as a matter of course." The eight-hour "nostrum," said the *Tribune*, was no cure for hard times.

Reporter "Lynn" visited the Custer battlefield. The Bucharest correspondent cabled of a Russian defeat at Softcha. Julia Ward Howe wrote a letter to the *Tribune* about her visit to the Doré gallery in London. Fiction began to appear in the Saturday supplement.

A history of the Protection Life Insurance Company was published on August 5. The half million dollar failure of this company showed, according to the *Tribune*, that state protection was a delusion and a snare and that it "protects rottenness and mismanagement." Other instances were given in which the *Tribune* had exposed the weakness of insurance companies and forced the state into action.

Blaine's presidential aspirations and his fight on the President and the Southern conciliation policy received criticism on August 11.

Chicago real estate had struck hardpan, it was reported on August 12 and the real estate editor predicted an increase in values. It was suggested that colonies of unemployed city families be organized and helped back to the land. The *Tribune* urged employers to pay a living wage. It continued its denunciation of Communist leadership of the unemployed and the workers. Of a Communist meeting on Market Street the *Tribune* commented on August 22: "A loaf for every loafer. If the chief end of man is to become a lazy lout, a shiftless vagabond, a pestilent putrefaction, a brawling, long-haired idiot, a public nuisance and an enemy of his race, let him turn Communist."

September opened with a bank scandal. The State Savings Bank failed with three million dollars due to 14,000 depositors. There was $600,000 left to divide. The president, D. D. Spencer, fled. There was a run on other banks.

The *Tribune* on September 2 called attention to the insecurity of depositors generally and suggested postoffice banks. The only objection, it was stated, would be a paternal power, the exercise of the authority of government over the business affairs of the people. But this was overcome, it was thought, by the general need and it was the duty of Congress to protect the people's savings.

William Bross read a paper on immortality before the American Association for the Advancement of Science at its Nashville meeting. Two columns of this were published September 8. Bross argued that the thinking principle, the human soul, was permanent in nature. The *Tribune* commenting on the evolution theory said that Christianity was adapting itself to this as it had once done to the Copernican theory. Professor Swing's sermons were a regular feature of the paper, presenting the view of the Divine energy acting on circumstances.

The Republican party in Wisconsin wanted to get the government to settle labor colonies from the cities on government lands. The *Tribune* said this was rank and vicious Communism, that it would cost two billions and it was outside the function of government.

President Hayes was in Kentucky and was given a fine welcome. The Hayes policy, the *Tribune* said, had been a success. This was that the national government was no longer responsible for the acts of state governments and appealed to the magnanimity of the people. Violence had ceased, the Ku Klux disbanded and the Negroes had found protection and employment.

The tariff needed a thorough revision, the *Tribune* said at this time. "It needs to have every tax on every article of foreign product which enters into the use of American manufacture repealed. Remove all laws which limit or restrict or prohibit production."

Editor Medill made a speech before the Ohio Editorial Association at Toledo on September 21, 1877. He gave the history of the press from the earliest days and said that it had obtained its freedom under the wing of political parties. "The press," he said, "owes more to party for its freedom of discussion and exemption from political prosecution than to any other cause. Party is the palladium of their liberty and the shield which saves them from suppression by the potentates in office who always imagine themselves the Lord's anointed, and can brook no criticism or animadversions at the hands of newspapers, but strike them down upon the slightest provocation if not prevented. Talk of the odium theologicum, but it is grace itself compared with the odium politicum of those in power toward the freedom of the press when unrestrained by the strength of the opposing party."

He told how the telegraph and the railroad had extended circulation and said that the task of educating the people had fallen to the press. "The profession that is overshadowing all others in influence and power has no colleges, no professors of journalism — strange is it not? Why not a department of editorship in the colleges. [Medill's grandsons were to help establish years later the Medill School of Journalism at Northwestern University.]

"Effrontery of assertion," Medill continued, "will not hide poverty of information; vituperation will not be accepted as a substitute for argument; defamation of rival editors may gratify vindictive feelings, but the better class of readers are neither edified nor amused thereat. In the survival of the fittest the fish-market style will not secure perpetual existence. Editors who are well stocked with facts and useful information have little need of filling their columns with coarse abuse of their opponents, which when indulged in is a sure sign of feebleness of ideas and paucity of knowledge. With an increase of power there should be an increase of dignity in the conduct of the press.

"The growth of the press in power and influence during the last 25 years in this country has excited the apprehension of some classes, or rather persons of classes. Many politicians, office holders and office seekers declare that it is becoming dictatorial and overbearing, and is wielding a dangerous influence among the people.

"This feeling is inspired by jealousy and resentment. The press interferes with slates and programs and selfish aims and aspirations, and hence these tears and fears. But there is no ground for the belief that the interests of the people will ever be harmed by any influence the press may acquire, for the sufficient reason that the press is never united in behalf of any disputed question. With the press there are always two sides to every proposition, and every cause has its advocates and opponents among the newspapers. Upon all social, political and economical questions they are divided, precisely as the community is divided. In this inevitable and perpetual difference among the newspapers lies the safety of the public from undue or injurious journalistic influence. The press is vastly more in danger of weakening or losing its hold on public confidence by committing excesses and follies and pandering as some of them do to licentious elements than any rights and liberties are in jeopardy from any combination of the newspapers against them. Let it be the ambition of every editor to contribute toward elevating the tone and standard of journalism; to make the profession more honorable as well as useful; to serve the people better; to combat profligacy and corruption more relentlessly and to do their whole duty to society and civilization more fearlessly and effectually. By so doing they will secure the approbation of their own consciences and the gratitude of good men."

Chapter Eighteen

THE SILVER DOLLAR FIGHT

DURING the latter part of 1877 and early in 1878, the *Tribune* was engaged on many fronts by what were considered the forces of evil. At home there was a rising tide of Communism, which was a sort of mixed socialism tinged with the ideology of the Marxian International. Joseph Medill, who had seen these labor forces in action in Paris, following the Commune of 1871, fought this development in the columns of his paper, presenting arguments day after day against this school of thought and seeking to prepare the city and the country for a revolutionary attack. The time would come, the *Tribune* said, when all men must choose for or against Communism.

The county ring of grafters also engaged the attention of the *Tribune* at this time. This was an intermittent warfare which lasted for years and resulted in many political changes and some penitentiary sentences.

In the national field the *Tribune* worked hard for the restoration of the silver dollar and thundered against Wall Street and the Eastern money lenders and bondholders, who were pictured as "Shylocks."

The religious world was shaken by the stand taken by the liberals, led by Henry Ward Beecher and supported in Chicago by Professor David Swing, against the teaching of an orthodox hell, a literal lake of fire. The *Tribune* sided with the liberals but at the same time warned science that it must not set up a new religion, only teach what it knew to be true. It could not, it was stated, at this stage of knowledge, prove that man had ascended the tree of life by the animal way alone. The heavenly spark must not be extinguished.

Thomas A. Edison's inventions were coming to world attention at this time, particularly the phonograph. Medill was a friend and admirer of the inventor and encouraged and aided him in many ways.

Contributors to the home department of the *Tribune* held a convention at Hershey Hall in the latter part of September. The ladies engaged briskly in politics and finally "Fern Leaf," one of the most popular contributors, was elected president.

The Fidelity Savings Bank crashed and the *Tribune* said that as confidence in savings banks was gone Congress should authorize national bonds in which the people could invest.

The sixth anniversary of the great fire found Chicago doubled in population and quadrupled in trade. Governor Cullom fired the West Park commissioners and the story was headed "A New Deal." Julia Ward Howe wrote regularly to the *Tribune* on "The Old World." The Chicago Historical Society moved into its new building at Dearborn and Ontario Streets.

Members of the "county ring" on trial for graft were found not guilty. "Such is their legal status," said the *Tribune*, "but the people don't believe it. The county ring acquittals tend to establish the fact that no man can be convicted in this county of any crime committed against the public. The law and the facts were impotent."

Republicans were urged to nominate good men for county offices. S. H. McCrea was named for county treasurer. The Communists were out with a workers' ticket that fall. The Republican party, the *Tribune* said, had responded fully to the demands of the property-owning and responsible classes.

Frances Willard, addressing a WCTU convention, said that during the year one out of every 14 inhabitants in Chicago had been arrested for drunkenness and one out of every 7½ was an applicant for charity.

Thomas Lynch was the Democratic nominee for county treasurer, around which office the political fight centered. During the campaign the Republicans were referred to in the *Tribune* as gentlemen and the Democrats as "bummers." Senator Morton's death was reported on November 1. The *Tribune* ranked him as among the great statesmen of the Republic.

Louisville and St. Louis dispatches told of crooked work among the baseball players, with evidence of the throwing of games. A special dispatch on the confessions of baseball crooks was printed on November 4, 1877.

Another "death blow" was dealt to the county ring in the November election reports. The entire Republican ticket was successful although the Communists were said to have been out in force. "The people cannot forever be hoodwinked and bamboozled."

A silver bill was before the House in Washington. The *Tribune* said that this bill with its free coinage of silver was the greatest and most promising hope of a restoration to a sound currency. It was opposed only by "Shylocks."

"Pop" Anson was Chicago's favorite ball player of the year, with a batting average of .325. The Field and Leiter retail store was destroyed by fire on November 15. Marshall Field watched the fire and then proceeded to lease the Exposition Building for a new store.

W. F. Coolbaugh, president of the Chicago Clearing House, committed suicide at the foot of the Douglas monument the same night. Quack doctors were exposed in an article of November 20, although the *Tribune* was still running many medical advertisments.

Jane Grey Swisshelm, *Tribune* special writer, in an article on co-education advised female students to leave off corsets, garters and high-heeled shoes. T. P. Keaton, another special writer, was in Japan.

The *Tribune* in December urged the restoration of the silver dollar as full legal tender, as the nationwide demand of the people. The President was expected to veto the bill. Mass meetings were called to influence the President and Congress.

The fall of Plevna, Turkish stronghold, was reported on December 11, leaving the road to Constantinople open to Russia.

A grand silver rally was held at the Tabernacle on December 13. William Bross was one of the speakers and the *Tribune* gave it a page under a heading "The Dollar of Our Daddies." "Gilded Shylocks" were denounced and a protest made against the intense selfishness of the bondholder and creditor class.

Mark Twain contributed two columns on Bermuda on

December 15. Henry Ward Beecher caused a sensation by coming out against the orthodox hell. He said he still believed in the Trinity but did not know anything about it. For the next few weeks there was a debate in the religion columns of the *Tribune* as to the reality of hell.

Congressman Carter H. Harrison returned home, remarking that it was his misfortune not to have a newspaper in Chicago which would give him support. The *Tribune*, he said, had called him a "demagogue and a Communist, which I am not." The *Tribune* said that an income tax measure which he had fathered justified the label.

The *Tribune's* annual business review of January 1, 1878, said that Chicago had had a moderately prosperous year amid widespread depression. The total trade was off 4 per cent. Trade in wheat, corn and canned beef had increased.

How to warm streetcars during the winter months was a problem discussed in the paper. It had never been tried. A national "blacklist" was reprinted from the *New York Sun*, listing thirty millions stolen in the United States during the last four years. This was a problem for the student of morals. The trouble in business, the *Tribune* said on January 5, 1878 was due to silver being taken away and the excessive value of gold. This was laid to "blood-sucking Eastern money lenders and bond holders."

Professor Swing rallied to the side of Dr. Beecher on the question — Is there a hell? Some of the preachers were still insistent on eternal punishment and a literal lake of fire. The views of sixteen clergymen on this issue were presented on January 15. The *Tribune* had its correspondents send in stories on the same subject and suggested as a theme for sermons the doctrine of the annihilation of the wicked, whether the survival of the fittest in nature applies to the destiny of man.

Local meetings were arranged and enthusiasm whipped up for "Our Dad's Dollar." Horace White, who was still in

Chicago, wrote a letter objecting to the remonetization of silver. The *Tribune* printed it and then took the other side of the argument. The remonetization of silver bill passed the House and Senate in February. The *Tribune* congratulated the country and those who had defied abuse and vilification to support the measure.

The peace dove appeared in Europe and a congress of the powers was in sight. Russian troops were near Constantinople and Gallipoli.

A column of railroad news became a regular feature of the *Tribune* and a market summary was put at the head of the editorial column daily. A national deficit of $4,969,219 was reported and the question was whether to increase taxation or reduce expenditures. The *Tribune* maintained that silver must be used as a compensation for the drain of gold.

"There is no virtue in economy of production," it was stated on February 15. "The world gains only by economy of consumption, and not even by this when it is carried too far. If the people consume less than is necessary to keep them well fed, well clothed and contented, their so-called economy is only wear and tear, since it eventually diminishes the power of production."

The city, too, was in financial difficulties. Sale of the lake-front park was proposed. In the criminal news column it was reported that "some unregenerate thief got away with a fine buffalo robe from Ald. Baumgarten's buggy."

The Senate took a final vote on the remonetization of the silver dollar as full legal tender, at 412½ grains. The vote was 48 to 21. The *Tribune* said on February 17: "THE CHICAGO TRIBUNE congratulates its readers that the protracted discussions of this subject have been brought to a successful issue, and, though there have been many hard and bitter things said, THE TRIBUNE, in view of the great popular victory, extends a hearty forgiveness even to the hardest hearted Shylocks, satisfied that in due time they will find it to the general benefit that silver has been restored to the money of the country." The House later passed this measure by a vote of 204 to 72.

The Philosophical Society in Chicago debated the acceptance of the doctrine of evolution. The *Tribune* gave this advice on what science must not teach:

"Science is becoming popular, almost fashionable. We are threatened with a religion of science. The mysteries of the origin of life, of the spanless abyss of the past, the viewless future, which religion, with its fables of Genesis and Gehenna, has failed to make clear, must yield to the universal solvent of science. There is complete absence of any connection between man and any other vertebrate animal, whether ape or ass. What shall science teach? Only actual knowledge. Today science must not teach doctrines of universal evolution, of the protoplast soul, of spontaneous generation, of mental physiology, of the animal origin of man. Some day it may find them true."

Blue ribbon pledges were becoming popular. Some included adultery and stock gambling, as well as liquor and tobacco.

The *Tribune* opposed the Wood tariff bill and stood for a tariff for revenue only. The National Greenback Workingman's party met at Toledo and called for a new income tax, unlimited issue of greenbacks and reduction of hours of labor. Carter Harrison's scheme to revive the income tax and reduce the tax on whisky was attacked in the *Tribune*.

The silver bill was passed again over the President's veto. "President Hayes discovers who the real sovereigns are," said the *Tribune*. "The victory is one of the people. It is a victory that was needed to remind the world that Wall Street no longer controls and dictates national legislation."

Russia and Turkey came to peace terms and a congress of powers was scheduled for Berlin. A five-column map of the new Turkish boundary lines was printed on March 5. The

Tribune was in controversy with the *Advance* and the *North-western Advocate,* religious weeklies, over proper kinds of advertising. A letter was printed from a subscriber who thanked the *Tribune* for taking the religious press to task.

"I am afar and live in Iroquois county, near Clifton. I believe in hell and hanging and THE CHICAGO TRIBUNE."

The *Tribune* wished the temperance reformers well, with exhortation and persuasion their weapons. "The moment government interferes with personal habits which are innocent in themselves and decent, it touches a private right which is more sacred than government itself. Persecution is never respectable."

The city won a victory in the effort to collect $507,703, the original deficiency of former city treasurer Gage, from the bondholders. Gage had loaned money to banks now closed and it was a question of how much could ever be collected.

The annual report of Coroner Emil Dietzch, a remarkable document, was given three columns in the *Tribune* of March 17. There had been 55 inquests during the year, with 28 murder and manslaughter cases. The coroner philosophized on love, suicide and education. The jails were filled with youthful criminals, he said, and compulsory education should be made the law of the land. He dilated on the leniency of juries and the hair-splitting sophistries of the law in murder cases.

Joseph G. Cannon, Illinois congressman, took a stand against government subsidies for the Pacific mail. The *Tribune* opposed legislation to give the mails a monopoly on newspaper distribution. It now used freight trains and other means, it was stated, to get to subscribers as soon as possible.

The daily weather report as observed by Manasse, optician at 88 Madison Street, was printed. A bill to put the government into life insurance business was called a Democratic absurdity.

Thomas A. Edison was interviewed in his laboratory at Menlo Park, New Jersey. He said he would have a phonograph working in a few days and also he was perfecting an aerophone, an instrument manipulated by steam and which pronounced words that could be heard ten miles.

Signal Office weather reports began to be printed late in March. Samuel J. Tilden was going to trial for failure to pay income tax. Thomas Carlyle's health was poor, it was reported, and he could work only two hours a day.

Edison's phonograph was on exhibition in Paris. When the machine presented its compliments to the Academy of Science there was a roar of laughter. The audience thought the sound proceeded from some concealed ventriloquist.

A new chapter in the history of John Brown was contributed by Horace White, who was still in Chicago. He sent the *Tribune* a letter from John Brown, Jr., authorizing him to publish testimony given by him (Brown) in the libel suit of Gerrit Smith against the *Tribune* in the summer of 1867. This showed that Smith was cognizant of every essential fact relating to the famous raid. This had nothing to do with the libel suit which had been settled out of court.

Too many "bummer aldermen" were elected in the April elections, the *Tribune* thought. There was apathy among the other voters, but the "bummers were astir."

An editorial on Mr. Edison's inventions was printed on April 3 as follows: "There can be no doubt that Mr. Edison, the inventor of the phonograph, is one of the most remarkable men of the present century. His improvements in telegraphic apparatus and in the working of the telephone seem almost to have exhausted the possibilities of electricity. In like manner, the discovery of the phonograph and the application of its principles in the aerophone, by which the volume of sound is so amplified and intensified as to be made audible at a distance of several miles, seems to have stretched the laws of sound to their utmost limit.

"At present the phonograph seems to be the most practical of all his discoveries, since it can easily be applied to common uses, and can be made so cheap and portable that every family can afford to have one. Mr. Edison is already at work to remedy the metallic tone which the disc gives off by the use of some sensitive material which will exactly reproduce the tone of voice talked into the instrument. One application of this quality will revolutionize the whole world of literature.

"Mr. Edison says that upon a disc of copper or tin foil, not over ten inches in diameter, the entire contents of an ordinary novel can be recorded, and that these plates can be sold cheaper than the books. Now, suppose that a publisher employs one of the most famous elocutionists of the age to talk one of Dickens' best novels upon a phonograph plate. By the stereotype process these plates are produced as fast as wanted, and much cheaper than books can be sold. The purchaser buys one of these plates for a mere song, takes it home of an evening, puts it in the machine, gets one of the children to turn the crank, and straightway Mr. Murdock, Mr. Vanderhoff, or Mrs. Dainty commences reading the novel to the delighted family. . . .

"Mr. Edison's aerophone is only a colossal telephone that conveys sounds for ten miles. The alarming capabilities of such an instrument when the reader contemplates an irate woman, whose husband is out later than he ought to be, in possession of a voice ten miles long and as big as a clap of thunder. . . . Such developments of domestic discipline are among the alarming possibilities of Mr. Edison's inventions. Nevertheless we are inclined to regard him as one of the wonders of the world.

"While Huxley, Tyndall, Spencer and other theorists talk and speculate, he quietly produces accomplished facts, and, with his marvelous inventions is pushing the whole world ahead in its march to the highest civilization, making life more enjoyable and proving the declaration of that old fogy, Solomon, that there is nothing new under the sun to be arrant nonsense."

A story of the life of Edison, written by George H. Bliss, was published on April 8, 1878.

An editorial on the D'Unger specific for alcoholism, much in controversy in medical circles, was printed on April 12, urging that this be given a fair trial. "The disease of intemperance, sweeping off thousands every year and leaving behind it social and moral ruin to thousands of others, breaking up homes, filling our prisons, and entailing untold pain and misery upon the innocent, is so terrible and devastating in its character that every suggestion for its cure ought to be welcomed and adopted, in the hope that it may prove the blessing for which the world has been praying so long."

The first full-page illustrated advertisment to be run in the *Tribune* was noted on April 12. It was that of Lawrence and Martin, importers of whiskies and cigars. The illustration was that of Chicago, represented as a Greek goddess, rising from a desolate scene of ashes, her eyes fixed upon a sunlit horizon of great temples. Four-year old Hermitage was listed at $2.50 a gallon. The next day, Sunday, Chapin and Gore had a first-page advertisment offering $3 a gallon for all four-year old Hermitage in first hand, free from chattel mortgage.

"Vesuvius Erupts Again" was a first-page headline of April 16, in which the Beecher scandal broke again. A letter was printed from Mrs. Theodore Tilton to her lawyer, Ira B. Wheeler, in which she asserted that the charge of adultery between her and Beecher was true, that she now desired to reaffirm this truth, leave it to God and return to her husband. Beecher in a special interview made a new and explicit denial. The reporter said he seemed to feel sorry for the woman, who was described as "a pretty little woman with rosy

The Chicago Daily Tribune.

VOLUME XXXII.   MAGNOLIA BALM.   CHICAGO, FRIDAY, JULY 27, 1877—TWELVE PAGES.   PRICE FIVE CENTS.

PITCHED BATTLES.

Steady War on the Southwest Side of the City.

Assault on the Burlington & Quincy Train—Turner-Hall Fight.

Battling for the Viaduct—A Series of Victories and Retreats.

Admirable Conduct of the Second—The Cavalry Charges.

Defeat of the Gang Advancing from the Stock-Yards.

Eight Persons Known to Have Been Killed during the Various Engagements.

Pretty General Peace in All Other Sections of the City.

Arrival of More Regulars—Organization of Ward Companies.

Scenes at the City-Hall, the Police Stations, and the Morgue.

The First Regiment Out for Service—The Company Talk Over the Situation.

THE BALL OPENS.

THE FIRST GUN.

AROUND THE VIADUCT.

UP AND DOWN.

A PORTRAIT-CLERK.

TURNER-HALL.

cheeks and bright eyes." "I declare her to be innocent of the great transgression," said Beecher.

The *Tribune* said next day that this would not change the situation, that those who believed in Beecher would not believe Mrs. Tilton and that the best thing for her to do was to keep quiet.

Dr. Galusha Anderson became the new president of the University of Chicago. The *Tribune* urged help toward the raising of an endowment fund and the financing of its debt of $174,000.

"Our Carter" came home for the congressional vacation. Asked if he were a candidate for re-election he said: "There is not fascination enough about Chicago newspaper abuse to make me anxious for the position. I am no politician."

"The Dangers of Communism" was a subject of editorial comment on April 24. "One of the most alarming dangers which threatens the future safety of this Republic is Communism. Its growth during the past 25 years has been so rapid that its disciples are found not only in the large cities, but in almost every town and village in the Union. The immunity which they have enjoyed at the hands of the authorities has emboldened them to give publicity to their pernicious sentiments, and to openly boast their hostility to society and their determination, when the opportunity comes, to assail and overthrow the rights of property."

The writer said that the plunder and misgovernment of cities formed one kind of Communism and spoke of William Tweed, who had just died in prison after having stolen six millions. "We are cursed with Communism in our county government. We have the same rings and corrupt system of jobberies, the same grabbing of offices at the hands of Communistic bummers. Its clutch upon the taxpayers can hardly be loosened except by a great popular revolution. It will be surprising if Communism is satisfied with public stealing. There are other elements of danger in it that only need

271

opportunity to come to the surface and manifest themselves in violence, sedition, incendiarism and mob rule. . . . The recent action of non-English Communists in this city arming themselves with guns in the hope of inducing discontented laboring men to join them in some sudden uprising, has the same object in view. Working men should remember that it was a similar rising against the government of France that led to the shooting of 20,000 Communists and the exile of a thousand more. If they shoot, they will be shot at. If they draw blood, their blood will be drawn. In the end the law will be vindicated and the government will prevail, though it cost the lives of the whole worthless herd."

The police worked up a Communist scare in Chicago at this time, talking about an uprising. They were not armed and Police Chief Hickey said every policeman should have a repeating rifle.

The Socialists, one of whose leaders was A. R. Parsons, and who had run under the Marxian slogan — "production belongs to the producer — tools to the toilers" — had polled about 8,000 votes in the last election. The *Tribune* bracketed them with the Communists. There were 52,000 other voters.

Frances E. Willard, sister of the late O. A. Willard, editor of the *Chicago Evening Post*, became editor-in-chief of that paper. She had been president of the Temperance Union and wore the white ribbon. She told a *Tribune* reporter of the moral tone she intended to put into the paper.

Police and firemen refused to accept city scrip for their January salaries. The issue of scrip had gone beyond the legal limit at the time and circulated at 8 per cent discount. The *Tribune* said the governor must protect property and the Illinois Supreme Court give relief.

An international exposition opened in Paris in May. It was covered in detail for the *Tribune* by Harry St. Michel.

So-called Communists made a disturbance at Belleville, Illinois, and the *Tribune* suggested that the army be increased to 50,000 and so distributed that any state governor would have 5,000 men on 24 hours' notice.

The National Greenback party met at Philadelphia. The *Tribune* called these, too, nothing but Communists. "The first and foremost aim of the Nationals is to use the government as an agent for the distribution of other people's money."

"New York is the natural home and birthplace of Communism in America," the *Tribune* said on May 11. "It lands there, like the cholera, when it comes from Europe. Whether in banquets, public meetings, mobs, politics, literature or demonstrations of any kind, New York has more genuine Communism than all the remainder of the country."

Longfellow's last volume of poems was reviewed and there was a whisky ring scandal in Cincinnati, "ex-porkopolis of the West." Theodore Thomas directed a music festival in Cincinnati, with a chorus of 700. The *Tribune* said that Chicago could only admire and congratulate Cincinnati on this festival and George P. Upton was sent to cover it.

General Grant, in an address in Paris reported June 1, estimated the Copperhead population during the war at 6,000,000, the total rebel force at 13 millions and the Union force at 14 millions. The Copperheads, he said, prolonged the war fully two years.

A new Congressional investigation, incited by Tilden Democrats, touching the Florida and Louisiana electoral votes, was regarded as a serious threat by the *Tribune* in June. When committee sessions began the *Tribune* said: "It is the fire-eaters reopening the Hayes case. Any effort to remove Hayes will be revolution and as such will be resisted as obstinately as if Grant were in the presidential chair."

A page was given to this investigation on June 2. Charles H. Dana, editor of the *New York Sun*, Tilden and Montgomery Blair, were called the chief conspirators against Hayes.

Henry Ward Beecher signed a contract for ten lectures at $1,000 each. Mrs. Tilton was reported to have told a friend that she felt much better after her latest confession and now "leaves it all to God."

Chicago was prepared to meet the Communists, the *Tribune* reported on June 2. The First and Second Regiments were in good shape and the police had been provided with 1,000 Springfield breech-loading rifles by the Citizens' Association.

The *Tribune* said on June 8 that its prophecy that the South would rush in to claim war indemnity and attempt to raid the Treasury had been fulfilled, and predicted that if the Democrats elected the next President and Congress that "Southern and Northern doughfaces will pay these claims and pension Confederate soldiers."

The *Tribune* argued frequently against the philosophy of Communism and said on June 10, 1878: "The time is coming when the force of events will compel all men to be for or against Communism."

Sitting Bull was claiming the Yellowstone and Big Horn country for his own and was roaming about threatening war.

The appropriation of government money for the purpose of giving men wages was opposed by the *Tribune*. It said on June 11: "That government is of necessity the most beneficially administered which interferes least with the business of the people, and which reduces the demands of popular substance to the minimum, which leaves each man the privilege of spending his own money in the most productive manner and which ignores to the greatest extent the wasteful policy of paternalism."

The plot against Hayes failed, it was reported on June 15. Congress had decided against the investigating committee and had passed a resolution that it had no power to revise the action of the last Congress or revise the electoral return.

A Communist parade and picnic at Ogden's Grove was

advertised on June 16. The *Tribune* advised all law-abiding citizens to stay at home. "Let the lunatics enjoy their lunacy exclusively." The picnic, however, was an orderly affair, with speeches by A. R. Parsons, Paul Grottkau and other Socialists. The attendance was about 3,000 and the *Tribune* reported it in three columns. At Market Square, on Randolph Street between Market and Desplaines Streets, the Lehr and Weber Verein turned out 136 men with muskets.

Illinois Republicans meeting at Springfield backed Grant for a third term. Two good terms deserve a third, was their slogan. Grant was in Europe.

There were 258,782 signers to the Illinois Blue Ribbon Temperance cause. A congress of powers at Berlin was partitioning Europe. The beer "schooner" was introduced in Cincinnati by a Chicago man. A trade union picnic at Ogden's Grove demanded shorter hours and more pay. "A rich man means much labor never paid," was one of their arguments.

The *Tribune* undertook to instruct these "misguided men" in the true value of labor. "They cannot demand $2 for instance, for something that no one will buy for more than $1.75. The only way out is to establish a legal price for what men shall pay for all they buy and consume."

A bit of Lincoln history in which the *Tribune* took part was contributed by John Lyle King, in a letter printed on July 9. In the latter part of 1859 he had organized a club in Chicago for Simon Cameron for President and Lincoln for Vice-President.

"Shortly after the organization of the Cameron and Lincoln club," he wrote, "in a conversation I had with Mr. Joseph Medill, editor of THE TRIBUNE, in my room, this gentleman with what seemed to me to be an impromptu suggestion of the moment, and as merely incidental, said in reference to the purpose of the club:

"'Why not reverse the order and have it Lincoln for

President and Cameron for Vice-President, and then it wouldn't be a kangaroo ticket?' Mr. Medill, as if kindling with his own suggestion, became quite animated with the thought. This was, so far as I know, the first suggestion of Mr. Lincoln's name in connection with the Presidency. A very few days after this I met Mr. Lincoln at the Tremont House, and said to him—'Mr. Lincoln, you have some friends in this city who are in favor of your nomination as President.'

"I have never forgotten the calm, thoughtful, earnest look of the man, as he seemed for a moment absorbed in silence, as though such a thought had never entered his mind. All at once he broke out into a hearty laugh and tapping me on the shoulder said: 'Keep it up, King, keep it up—that's a good joke.' It was not long after this that THE TRIBUNE proposed and afterward zealously championed Mr. Lincoln for Chief Magistrate."

Chapter Nineteen

"LET THERE BE MONEY"

THE PROLETARIAT was on its way during the latter part of 1878, making trouble all over the country and registering political progress in Chicago. Deep and troubled waters were ahead, possibly confusion and temporary anarchy, the *Tribune* editors felt, but they had a profound faith in the institutions of this country, in religion and education, and thought that the common sense of the majority would save the situation.

Investigations into the relations between capital and labor were carried on. The *Tribune* made little distinction between the demands of the Socialists and the easy money men, and the more revolutionary demands of the Communists. During this period it even called Ben Butler no better than a Communist, because he wanted to make money as God once made light. Butler was the same man it had once supported for Secretary of War in Lincoln's cabinet and whose contraband slave policy during the war received its highest approbation. But this old warhorse and Republican had now turned Democrat of the pinkest type. Dennis Kearney of San Francisco was another "Communist" to be fought with bitter words and ridicule. Demands for an eight-hour day, for the abolition of child labor and for compulsory education were considered impracticable at this time by the *Tribune*.

There was an outbreak of reminiscences on the part of those who had had a part in the nomination of Lincoln, and Medill took his pen in hand to give his view of the real cause of the nomination. He paid a high tribute to Dr. Charles H. Ray, *Tribune* chief editor in 1860.

James A. Garfield delivered an oration at Painesville, Ohio, which was published in the *Tribune* on July 10. It struck a responsive chord in Medill at least. Garfield spoke of the atheism of the times which, he said, was trying to expel God from government. "He will not be thus ignored," said Garfield.

As to the trouble between capital and labor, Garfield held that it stemmed from the Paris Commune and the International labor organization and all that was foreign to this country. Here, he said, every boy had an opportunity. His own life ("From Log Cabin to White House") was to be pictured later as a great example of this land of opportunity.

The Congress of Berlin was over and another seedbed prepared for war.

The *Tribune's* new folding and pasting machine was pictured and described on July 13. Until then papers had been folded by hand. "There are now three different types of folding and pasting machines," it was stated, "but only one had yet been granted a patent. This is the one invented by Mr. Conrad Kahler, superintendent of THE TRIBUNE press room, and its superiority to either of the others cannot be questioned."

The capacity of the machine was 12,000 to 15,000 papers an hour, folded and pasted. A second machine was being constructed and by August 1 all copies of the *Tribune* would be delivered folded and pasted. Kahler had been in charge of the press room for 23 years. When he went into the press room there was a single old-fashioned Hoe press capable of printing one side of 2,000 copies an hour. The *Tribune* at present, it was explained, required one Hoe and two Bullock presses, two engineers, four stereotypers, nine pressmen, a paper wetter, and eight mailers to dispose of the "immense edition" of the paper. It took six tons of white paper for the *Sunday Tribune* alone.

In a letter to the editor on July 14 Leonard Swett told the inside story of the nomination of Lincoln for President in 1860.

Lincoln's friends in Illinois had not expected success, he wrote. Judge David Davis of Bloomington asked Swett to go to work and said Lincoln could be nominated. The problem was to stop Seward on the early ballots and then get the Chase, Cameron and Bates forces to back Lincoln as a second choice. The best chance lay in Pennsylvania, with 48 votes. On Friday morning, in the Tremont House, the Cameron men agreed to come in on a second ballot, Swett said. They did so and this was the blow that disorganized the opposition. It was the good political work of the Bloomington friends of Lincoln that brought the nomination, according to Swett. There is no discounting the work of this group, but the *Tribune* took a slightly different view of the real force behind the nomination.

"Swett's narrative," said the *Tribune* on July 16, "begins with Monday and ends with the Friday of the nomination. On that Monday the great battle for Lincoln had been fought and won and when Swett and Davis entered the scene the most that remained to be done was ratification. No matter how the rule may be generally in conventions (politicians worship success) the nomination of Mr. Lincoln had been already decreed and demanded by the popular heart of the Republican party, although most of the politicians did not desire it and intended to defeat it. The nomination of Mr. Lincoln was the result of the education of popular sentiment in his behalf. It was not a sudden thought or act of bargain or inspiration on the part of the convention. Popular sentiment controlled the convention and overwhelmed the opposing candidate."

The *Tribune* continued with this account of Lincoln's rise to power, undoubtedly written by Medill:

"When Mr. Lincoln, who was the caucus nominee for United States Senator, was defeated by Judge Trumbull in 1854–55, the Republican party was not fully organized in this state. The campaign of 1856, which ended in giving the vote in Illinois to Buchanan, on account of Frémont's alleged radicalism, pointed out to the managing Republicans the necessity of a closer and better union of the old Whig element with the Republicans. The managers of THE CHICAGO TRIBUNE, who had witnessed the ability of Mr. Lincoln during the campaign of 1856, had reached the conclusion that that gentleman above all others was the best fitted to unite the Whigs to the Republicans and lead the party of Illinois to victory, and to remove all bad feeling among the old Whigs because of Mr. Lincoln's defeat for the Senate in 1854. In June, 1858, the memorable and historical canvass between Lincoln and Douglas opened, and was continued until election day in November following. During all that time THE CHICAGO TRIBUNE made extraordinary efforts in his behalf, not merely with reference to the then pending election, but to place the man prominently before the country as one fitted and worthy to be a great leader in the party, and to take the place of old statesmen who had yielded and were daily yielding more and more to the seduction of Slavery. Mr. Lincoln was not an extremist but he hated slavery, and, as he expressed it, desired to place it 'in the course of ultimate extinction.' He was a man of great natural ability, of tastes and habits commending him to the common people, while his personal character was beyond reproach or question.

"With the end of the senatorial canvass and the defeat of Lincoln, the managers of this paper did not lose confidence in him. The canvass with Douglas had been used by his friends to make him as conspicuous and familiar before the country as possible. The work of educating popular sentiment in his behalf for the Presidency thus begun by THE CHICAGO TRIBUNE never flagged; it was persistent, unremitting, and incessant. The story of Abraham Lincoln's life, his humble origin, his labors, his poverty, his grand courage in proposing to chain Slavery, his brilliant contest with the great Democratic leader, who was then expected to be the Democratic candidate in 1860, all this was kept constantly before the people. Lincoln, as the man certain beyond reason to defeat Douglas in Illinois and every Western state, was the constant burden of THE TRIBUNE song from the winter after the senatorial contest until the nomination in May, 1860. It insisted that he could carry Illinois, Indiana and Pennsylvania, which Frémont had lost, and that Seward could not carry any of them. It drummed this vitally important idea into the heads of multitudes of people and politicians.

"Dr. Charles H. Ray was then the directing head of THE

TRIBUNE; he was the personal and intimate friend of Lincoln, and was a great admirer of his integrity, moral courage and general character. He always spoke and wrote of him as 'Honest Old Abe.' Few writers of ability superior to that of Dr. Ray ever conducted a journal in this country, and he devoted his whole energy and time to the work of presenting Mr. Lincoln to the people of the country, and especially of Pennsylvania and the West, as the fitting man to be nominated by the Republicans as their candidate in 1860. The other editors of the paper heartily concurred in this course, and personally did all in their power to accomplish this end. The action of THE TRIBUNE received additional emphasis from the fact that the Chicago Democrat and the Chicago Journal, the other Republican papers of this city, both opposed Mr. Lincoln for the Presidency, and both energetically favored the nomination of Mr. Seward for the first place on the ticket.

"The Hon. N. B. Judd of this city, then state senator, was then a member of the Republican national committee, and an enthusiastic Lincoln man, and to his adroit and influential efforts was largely due the selection of Chicago as the place of holding the convention, giving Mr. Lincoln's friends in this state, Indiana and Iowa, and from all the Northwestern states, an opportunity to be present and swell the great popular demand for the nomination of Honest Old Abe. Mr. Judd captured the national committee by promising that the Republicans of Chicago would build a monster wigwam, capable of holding all the Republicans that might come. Holding the convention in Chicago was an important factor in promoting Mr. Lincoln's nomination. The storm in his behalf was irresistible. The popular sentiment all through the state was unmistakably for Lincoln.

"When the convention met, and when, as Mr. Swett described, he and Judge Davis appeared on the scene, the great battle for Lincoln had been fought and won among the people, and all that remained was to see that the convention was not misled or deceived by trickery or bargain into a betrayal of the popular choice. For that duty no persons were better fitted or more competent than Mr. Swett and Judge Davis, who undoubtedly did their duty ably and well. Yet we always understood that Jesse K. Dubois, O. M. Hatch, J. Y. Scammon, N. B. Judd, C. H. Ray and Ebenezer Peck put in considerable work where it would do the most good during the midnight conference of that interesting occasion.

"The convention consisted of 465 delegates, and the highest vote Mr. Seward received was 184, and that on the second ballot, and Lincoln had 181. Seward could go no higher and Lincoln was the second choice from the start of the Chase, Cameron, McLean and Bates delegates, who had among them 100 votes. The Pennsylvanians well knew their state could not be carried for Seward any more than it was carried for Frémont, and they came to Chicago with Honest Old Abe of the prairies in their minds as their second choice, for they knew he could sweep the Keystone state against any man the Democrats might put in the field.

"We have thought it proper, while so many eminent gentlemen are making history by stating the parts they took at the Chicago convention to nominate Mr. Lincoln, to call attention to the other fact, that the history of that nomination dates much earlier than they suppose; and that, without disparaging their services in the least, the work of preparation for the nomination covered several years, and, so far as the Republican party was concerned, the nomination was pretty much accomplished before the gentlemen put on their best clothes, and, in the full dress of lawyers, and judges and statesmen, met at the Wigwam to hurrah for Lincoln."

In this account Medill had overlooked, or perhaps forgotten, some of the more practical preliminaries of the Lincoln nomination, which are developed in the first volume of this history. It remains true, however, as shown by outside historical and political research, that the *Tribune*, through its news columns and editorials, and through the personal work of its editors, particularly Dr. Ray, was largely responsible for the nomination of Lincoln, and, in a lesser degree, for his election.

Thomas A. Edison came to Chicago in July, accompanying a party of scientists who were going to Wyoming to observe an eclipse. He was trying out a new precision device that he had invented.

"Mr. Edison is a young looking man," the *Tribune* reporter wrote, "with a smooth-shaven face which might be mistaken for that of a priest. He wore a straw hat and linen duster. Before talking he carefully lit a cigar and his painful efforts to keep it lighted during the conversation were the only drawbacks to an otherwise agreeable interview. He has a hesitating way of uttering his words, as if he were not quite sure that he is right, and is willing to be corrected if he makes any mistakes. He possesses the unusual quality of modesty — unusual to inventors — and like most people who are slightly deaf he speaks in a low tone."

Edison said he had 150 patents on inventions and that the phonograph was coming along finely, that it reproduced *The Last Rose of Summer* perfectly.

Chicago and St. Louis were rivals in heat wave casualties. Chicago's White Stockings were leading in the race for the baseball championship, with nine straight victories.

General Grant in Holland was asked if he was a candidate for a third term. He replied that if he thought that he would not go home at all. The *Tribune* said of him on July 23: "It is difficult to write of Grant and his deeds at the present time without being suspected of some secret alliance with a conspiracy to elect him for a third term and perhaps of deep design of paving the way for his repeating Caesar's folly. He has borne his honors with physical endurance, a moral patience and a simple republican demeanor that are characteristic of the man and creditable to the American people."

The *Tribune* accused the *Chicago Times* of stealing its story of July 23 on the eclipse to which it had given a page with maps. "Ye unwashed blackguards of the meretricious *Times* are at it again. Lying to them has become a second nature."

The English historian Macaulay had grave doubts about the permanency of the American democracy. He thought universal suffrage unwise and that it meant in time destruction of the government by the votes of the unwise. Commenting on this on July 25 the *Tribune* said: "We do not despair of the Republic. We still have faith that, with the blessings of education and religion, and with the untiring vigilance of the honest and intelligent members of society, the tide which now rushes so swiftly toward destruction will be stayed. It may require a desperate resistance, and the country may be precipitated into a confusion and disorder bordering on anarchy. The ignorant proletariat, led by these unscrupulous wretches, may commence its destructive work; the Government may find its very foundations trembling; but the misguided mob will meet its opponents arrayed against it as solidly as a wall of adamant. They will sooner or later discover that, in destroying currency, and contracts, and confidence, and establishing chaos, they have destroyed the demand for labor itself. Then they will turn and rend the demagogue leaders who have brought this distress upon them, and, returning to their senses, will help to reconstruct a fabric of capital and labor and bring about prosperity again. We may have to pass through very deep and troubled waters, but we shall arrive safely upon the other shore and stand upon firm land again."

Commenting on an alleged Grant interview concerning press criticism during the war, the *Tribune* said on July 29: "In a free country, the press will assert its right of comment and criticism in war as well as in peace; and, except in the case of disloyal newspapers seeking to embarrass the Government for disloyal purposes, we do not think the province of criticism was abused."

Professor Elias Colbert of the *Tribune* staff was in charge of a Chicago party of astronomers which took up a position in Denver during the eclipse of the 29th, and sent in a page story on it. Edison's heat-measuring instrument had failed.

In August the *Tribune* set to work to unhorse Dennis Kearney, the sand-lot orator of San Francisco, and "false apostle" of labor. He was in Chicago making speeches. The *Tribune* called him a nuisance and a public blatherskite. Ben Butler of Massachusetts, who was leading the easy money ranks, also came in for some severe words. "For personal meanness, selfishness, hoggishness and hypocrisy, Ben Butler may challenge comparison," said the *Tribune*.

An investigating committee in Washington delved into the depression and labor troubles. Horace White and Charles Francis Adams Jr. were among the witnesses called. White spoke against the protective tariff. The *Tribune* said the issue of the coming election was that of honest, sound currency, that the Democrats had been led astray.

Yellow fever spread its black wings over the South, with 2,000 prostrated in Memphis and 87 deaths in a day at New Orleans. Chicago raised a fever aid fund.

The fiat money fever extended to the Maine election and cut into Republican strength. "The new lunacy will have its little day and run its course like all other crazes," said the *Tribune* on September 10, 1878. Communism and Fiatism were twin sisters to the *Tribune*.

President Hayes visited Chicago. He was received by a committee of the Chicago Club and visited John V. Farwell and Henry Durand at Lake Forest, looking over their fine cows and grapes.

A machine to transmit power by wire was reported invented

by William Wallace of Ansonia, Connecticut. Edison, on a visit to the Sierra Nevada region, saw miners at work by hand drill and asked why the power of a nearby river could not be transmitted to these men. He talked of harnessing Niagara, and of making electricity a cheap substitute for illuminating gas.

The *Tribune* sent M. H. Tilden, a reporter who had been born in the South and who had passed through two yellow fever epidemics, into the stricken districts of Memphis. "He now takes his life in his hands for the sake of the news." There had been 2,250 deaths in Memphis, including 15 volunteer physicians. The people of Chattanooga had fled to Lookout Mountain.

The Republicans of Massachusetts were in a fight with "Communists and repudiationists, led by Ben Butler, candidate for governor." Butlerism, said the *Tribune*, would be the national issue in 1880. "It is a struggle in which revolution and anarchy are the aims of a large faction."

Butler said fiat money meant "let there be money, as when God said let there be light." The *Tribune* found in him an echo of Kearney's cry — "Corral the capitalists, and when you've got 'em corraled, grind 'em, God damn 'em."

"The end of Our Carter" was the subject of an editorial on September 27. "No more Congress for him. His career was brief, honest, funny, gentlemanly and speechy. We bid him hail and farewell."

The local Greenbackers met at North Side Turner Hall on October 3. The reporter at the meeting wrote: "I have seen many political gatherings but have never seen such a collection of howling, yelling, cursing, blatant, political browers as were assembled yesterday in the name of Greenbackism."

The death of Lewis E. Meacham, a member of the *Tribune* staff, was recorded and it was written of him: "In the course of a long connection with this paper he had won an enviable reputation as an authority in baseball matters and

The Chicago Daily Tribune.

VOLUME XXXIX.   CHICAGO, FRIDAY, MARCH 8, 1878.   PRICE FIVE CENTS.

THE NEW TURKISH BOUNDARY LINES.

A COMPREHENSIVE MAP SHOWING THE RESULT OF THE TREATY RECENTLY ENTERED INTO BETWEEN RUSSIA AND TURKEY.

Following its publication of its map showing the locale of the Russo-Turkish War, the Tribune kept readers informed by printing the map above illustrating the drastically altered borders of Turkey in Europe.

had come to be regarded in the West as a conservator of this branch of athletic sports in its best and purest estate."

A total of $92,000 had been raised in Chicago for the fever victims and the *Tribune* appealed to the people to help the South further; "not to stop in the work of well doing until the afflicted South is lifted to her feet and healed."

Despite the hard times the real estate editor reported that a frontage of five miles of houses and stores had been built in Chicago during the year. The Chicago Jockey and Trotting Club opened its fall meeting with $13,000 in purses, and a crowd of 35,000.

James G. Blaine began the fall campaign with an address on currency which the *Tribune* presented in full. The Congressional elections in Ohio, Indiana and Iowa were called a "fiat funeral," on first returns. "The corpse is as good as buried," said the *Tribune*. Indiana had to be consigned to "Democratic darkness," as the later returns came in. The elections on the whole meant a hopeless outlook for the Nationals, as the Greenbackers and allied factions were called, according to the *Tribune* view.

A survey by the *Tribune* showed that there was work in Chicago for all who were willing to work. Day labor was about one dollar a day.

It was reported that the revision of the Bible, which had been begun in 1870, was nearly half done and the New Testament would be published in 1880. The *Tribune* scolded the *Interior* for taking the attitude that the old wording, often in error, was sacred.

Cold weather came to the aid of the fever-stricken South. Samuel J. Tilden was in trouble over cipher messages relating to money offered or passed during the struggle for the electoral vote in the South and in Oregon. The *Tribune* took up the cudgels for "Honest John" Hoffman for sheriff against Charley Kern, the *Times* candidate.

Edison said that electric light was the light of the future

and gas stocks tumbled. General James A. Garfield, minority leader in the lower House, went on the stump for sound money. The *Tribune* supported him from the first. The Nationals, said the *Tribune*, were not only fiat men but Communists as well, for "they think working hours should be reduced by law and the government should employ all tramps."

The Republicans were confident as election day approached. "The bright dawn of victory is purpling the political east," said the *Tribune* on November 4. "Safe and Sound," was the report on November 6. "The popular heart is in the main true to Republicanism."

Cook County had again repudiated "bummerism" and ring rule. "Honest John" Hoffman and three Republican Congressmen were elected. Butler was beaten in Massachusetts. "It means," said the *Tribune*, "that the American people have taken a bold, definite and final protest against the heresy that government can create money by fiat."

A commissioner for the *Tribune* interviewed Sitting Bull in Montana territory, referring to him as "the old cuss." Another commissioner was on a tour of the Shenandoah Valley.

Later election returns did not present such a rosy Republican prospect. It was found that the "Solid South" had taken control of Congress. "This vassalage of the Northern to the Southern wing [of the Democratic party] is the bane of the politics of the country," said the *Tribune* on November 8. "Practically, the Republican party has been suppressed by force and intimidation in all the southern states. When the time comes for a presidential election for complete subjugation of all branches of government by the Solid South, there will be found, in all probability, a Solid North — firm, immovable, determined and aggressive."

It was found also that Chicago Communists (or Socialists) had elected four members of the legislature. Their vote was

288

about 6,500. "Some are for revolution and anarchy, as in Paris at the close of the Franco-Prussian war," said the *Tribune*, "but the majority have other views, or are moved by other motives, such as the eight-hour day, abolishment of convict labor, a law excluding children from every kind of employment, compulsory education."

There were hundreds of avocations to which children of 14 were adapted, the article continued. Compulsory education was generally favored by Republicans. The eight-hour law would ruin Illinois industry unless other states followed suit. The conclusion was that these demands were impracticable and there was no cause for apprehension.

Life insurance figures and tables were analyzed on November 11 to show policyholders what sums they had the right to demand on surrender of policies.

N. B. Judd, who had worked in close harmony with the editors of the *Tribune* for the nomination of Lincoln in 1860, was reported dead on November 12, 1878.

President Hayes was said to have revised his Southern policy, in view of election frauds and the murder of Negroes in the South. His new course would mean law enforcement instead of conciliation, it was stated. "Enforce the laws and quit temporizing with the South, no matter what the consequences may be," was the *Tribune's* advice to the President.

A company was formed in New York to introduce Edison's electric light when perfected, but there was considerable doubt expressed that he had solved the problem. Henry Ward Beecher was reported as saying there was no Adam or Eve, no Garden of Eden and no Flood — all were myths.

The *Tribune* which had opposed Tom Scott and his Texas Pacific railroad subsidy was accused of having taken $25,000 from C. P. Huntington, Southern Pacific president. The editor, in jocular mood, replied: "THE TRIBUNE always renders efficient service for any cause it espouses, whether it be fighting fiat folly, combatting subsidy grabbers or defending the money of the taxpayers from the beaks and talons of the lobby vultures and other unclean birds of prey. But we regret to say that he forgot to remit and we are still out the $25,000."

The *Tribune* thought a double standard in money was possible, with a ratio of 16 to 1. The progress of the Standard Oil Company toward a monopoly was described on November 26, 1878.

England was at war again and was fighting in Afghanistan. Gladstone said the war had been started without consulting Parliament. Mary McDonald, wife of the gambler and Democratic boss, Mike McDonald, was arrested for using a gun during a raid on their place at 176 Clark Street.

The first fat live stock show was held at the Exposition Building. Reorganization of the County Board was described under the heading "The New Deal." The Boston Oyster House offered clean, white table cloths instead of marble tops for diners.

James G. Blaine was regarded as a candidate for the nomination against the Grant forces. In a notable speech he attacked the election frauds in the South. "What are you going to do about it?" asked the Southern leaders. "National control of national elections," was the reply.

Chapter Twenty

"OUR CARTER" TRIMS THE TRIBUNE

Two political defeats and a war with the state legislature made the spring of 1879 a lively one in the *Tribune* office.

In Chicago, Carter H. Harrison came into power over the utmost opposition that the Tribune could muster. His election was tied in with national politics and the coming presidential struggle. The *Tribune* made the mistake, according to Harrison, of "waving the bloody shirt," while he, according to the *Tribune*, was wooing the saloon and gambler elements which put him in office.

In the state, the *Tribune* took an active part against the election of General John A. Logan as United States Senator. This old war horse, once the toast of the *Tribune* editorial writers, when he came up from Vicksburg to save the Republican war tickets and the Lincoln administration, now was pictured as a disgrace to the state. The Logan machine read the *Tribune* out of the Republican party and the legislature, after weeks of conferences in smoke-filled rooms at the Leland Hotel, elected Logan.

Possibly as an aftermath of this, the *Tribune* correspondent at Springfield, who had written of bribery in the legislature, was sent to jail for thirteen days for refusing to answer a question as to the source of his information. All the *Tribune* editorials, and legal aid, could not get him out of the Sangamon county jail, but his stories from there attracted wide attention, and the business of the *Tribune* continued to increase. Its politics did not seem to hurt the counting room.

The annual trade review of January 1, 1879, showed an increase in trade of 55 millions, touching every department. "The story of the growth of Chicago," said the *Tribune* in comment, "reads like a tale of the imagination. . . . An unbroken series of annual increases in all her business for 30 years is an evidence of her stability and offers reasonable grounds for the belief that the city is even now but in the infancy of the commercial greatness which is to be hers in the near future. . . . We might point to a somewhat corresponding advancement in her mental and moral status as a city, but that such notice would be foreign to the purpose of this review. . . . The year has closed with a victory of honest money — in remonetization of silver and to prevent repeal of the resumption act."

Neal Dow, founder of the political prohibition movement, criticized the attitude of the *Tribune* on this question.

"Can Neal Dow point to a single person who has been reformed by prohibition?" was the reply. "There is no difference of opinion between Neal Dow and THE CHICAGO TRIBUNE on the evils of intemperance. It recognizes them as fully and regrets them as keenly as he. We differ with him, however, as to the methods of arresting the evil. As between the two, THE TRIBUNE advocates moral 'suasion,' because it believes it to be the best, and it believes it to be the best because it sees definite results for good growing out of it, while not even on the showing of Neal Dow himself can it be seen that prohibition prohibits."

"Raconteur," writing from Washington, said the original female interviewer was Mistress Ann Royal, who resided on Capitol Hill for 30 years and who published a newspaper in 1823. Letters from "Gath," the old *Tribune* correspondent, were reprinted from the *Cincinnati Enquirer*, where he was now employed.

The *Tribune* on January 2 advocated the re-election of Senator Oglesby.

The so-called "literary bureau," or publicity agency for General John A. Logan excommunicated the *Tribune*, warning the Republicans of Illinois that the paper was false to Republicanism.

The Resumption Act went into effect the first of the year and the *Tribune* said that nobody was hurt by it. The public debt was $2,267,702,345. General Garfield said the resumption of specie payment ended a 17-year epoch of revulsion against the inflation and speculation that followed the war. The cycle had been inflation, delusive prosperity, then collapse and depression.

The *Tribune* on January 4 said the closing of the famous
Gold Room in New York was more properly the ending of
the war than was the event at Appomattox, for it signified
final recovery from the financial distress which the war had
brought upon the nation.

The *Tribune* was now printing 12 pages daily and 16 pages
on Sunday. Correspondent "H" in London sent a special
interview with Karl Marx, whom he called the "cornerstone of modern socialism." He described him as follows:
"He lives in a villa at Haverstock Hill. Your correspondent
has called upon him twice or thrice and each time the Doctor
was found in his library, with a book in one hand and a
cigarette in the other. He must be over 70. His physique
is well knit, massive and erect. He has the head of a man of
intellect, and the features of a cultivated Jew."

In this interview Marx explained the principles of Socialism
and defended the Commune. Religion would have to go and
blood must flow, he declared. If the system of capital and
labor did not go in this century it would in the next.

Interest centered in the senatorial contest at Springfield.
Two weeks of what the Springfield correspondent called
"indefatigable chinning" at the Leland and other hotels followed. The *Tribune* attacked Logan's candidacy nearly every
day and went into his record in 1859 to show he was the
author of the Illinois Black Act, which made it a crime to
feed, clothe or shelter a Negro.

Logan was finally nominated in the Republican caucus on
January 18 and the *Tribune* said: "This was brought about
by disreputable and degrading means. We protest, in behalf
of intelligence, principle and public interest, against this outrage upon the people of Illinois and the Republican party of
the state and country."

The Logan supporters at Springfield called a meeting and
read the *Tribune* out of the party again. Long Jones, pension
commissioner, who led the Logan machine, came in for

Tribune attention. "He is out to make it party heresy to patronize this journal. THE TRIBUNE says it can't be read out because it doesn't belong to Long Jones' machine, and can't be influenced morally, nor be bulldozed politically, nor be affected financially, by anything which can be done or left undone by the machine itself and much less by a common and hired stoker like Long Jones.

"Long Jones is a member of a gang that is fond of cherishing the delusion that THE TRIBUNE and independent Republican journals generally, have no influence. They ignore the important part played by these journals in rescuing the Republican party from the Credit Mobilier, and the salary grab, and Whiskey Ring scandals, by helping to expose and denounce them. They have not the sense to understand that there would have been no Republican party today if these same journals and other purifying influences had not forced the Whiskey Ring and the runners of the machine to the rear in the last presidential election. The Springfield Ring, of which Long Jones has constituted himself the spokesman, may prevail for the time being or it may not; but its temporary success will only the more surely impress upon the majority of the Republican party the necessity of unloading it."

The Teller Committee in Washington was taking testimony on Southern elections and the Tribune asked Henry Watterson what he thought about it. His reply was described as nothing but a "sportive blue grass pastoral."

A music hall was projected at State and Randolph Streets, with a $10,000 organ and an auditorium for the Sunday use of Professor Swing.

General John C. Black was nominated by the Democrats for the Senate, and Logan's election was reported on January 22. The *Tribune* said that the discussion was now ended and suggested that he pay back the salary grab of $5,000 which he took in 1873.

The Democrats were saying that Grant for a third term would be the end of our form of government. The *Tribune* said this was an unreasoning and croaking opposition. "Grant's election, if nominated, seems sure enough. Some Republicans fear he would call a set of rapacious rascals about him, as before, but it seems he would be better able to protect himself. If the Confederates continue to disfranchise and persecute the blacks there may be a demand for a third term for Grant."

A. M. Wright was slated on February 16 to succeed Monroe Heath as Republican mayor. Carter Harrison was said to be considering running. The *Tribune* political writer said "the great unwashed [Democrats] haven't a ghost of a chance." Wright snuggled up to the German vote and the *Tribune* said the Republicans would not take a chance again of going with the professional prohibitionists on Sunday closing and "turn the city over to the bummers again." Medill had had a lesson in this that he never forgot.

The committee on Southern elections reported on February 28 that Negro Republicans had no rights in Louisiana and South Carolina, that there was no such thing as free speech, that all ideas not approved by the Democracy were classed as incendiary. It was recommended that Congress provide free and fair elections for its members and not rely on state governments which did not prosecute violators.

On the question of Grant and a third term the *Tribune* said: "The Grant talk comes largely from ex-office holders under him. It is an open question for the convention. Grant must be taken, as any other man must be chosen, for what he is able to accomplish for the country in the future, and not because of his great military service in the past. The Republican party cannot live upon its old war record any more than the Israelites could live upon old manna, though it was supposed to have descended from Heaven."

Exclusion of the Chinese became a political issue that spring.

The Pacific coast was aroused by Hayes' veto of an exclusion act.

Professor Swing talked of the things God has concealed from men and suggested that in one hundred years, if alive, he might see men making rapid progress in the air from continent to continent, or whether "night should not be made as light as day by electric lamps, hanging like dewdrops upon each tree, along even the country roads, lights fed from the subtle fluid that pervades all space."

The editors of the *Tribune* found a gloomy look ahead in the "vicious control of Congress by the Democratic party, ex-Confederates and Copperheads uniting, and an unpopular President makes it worse."

The debate in Congress to pension Jefferson Davis was almost too much for the editor. He issued a fresh warning to "vipers and Copperheads." He had hardly expected to live to see such a day. Zach Chandler's speech in the Senate on this subject was heartily applauded by the *Tribune*. The Michigan Senator spoke of the effort of "the bullying, roaring rebels" around him to make a saint of Davis, "a living Rebel, whom every man, woman and child in the North believes to be a double-dyed traitor."

The *Tribune* said the ex-Confederates were trying to cripple the army. "The South is treading upon dangerous ground. It mistakes the temper of our people. It may raise a storm if it crowds too closely."

Carter Harrison was given a rousing welcome on his return from Washington, chronicled March 7. A crowd of a thousand gathered in front of his residence, lighted tar barrels, had music and made speeches. They were mostly Democrats, the reporter wrote, but "not a few Republicans who admire him as a man."

Harrison said he was a plain citizen again. He had labored in Congress for seven years. The Democratic party, he said, was the party of the people. The tendency in the Republican party was to centralize all power in the seat of government at Washington. In the Democratic party power was held to be lodged with the people in the states, where the Constitution placed it. "If we allow the Republican party to continue its centralization," he said, "we will have a nation, it is true, but a nation whose master will sit in Washington."

Harrison assured his friends that he had come back home and never would hold office again by his own will. He predicted a Democratic President, House and Senate in 1880. Then he added: "Come in and have something, boys." Most of them did, it was reported, as there were plenty of bottles and cigars about.

The Democrats were hard up for a candidate for mayor and the next day the *Tribune* political reporter said that the Harrison surprise party was no surprise. "It was a put up job, arranged in advance, and his talk of never again running for office meant nothing."

Samuel J. Tilden's "bar'l" was said to be behind Harrison for mayor, and a Tilden paper, the *Morning Herald*, was to be established at 2 cents.

"The Democrats seek to repeal the national election law," said the *Tribune*, "and they are reviving the old state sovereignty issue. This is shown in Harrison's talk. State sovereignty and the freedom to stuff ballot boxes. It is the same thing, the aim of the party. The Democrats threaten to stop the wheels of government. This is the old issue, the right of secession, the right to stuff ballot boxes, and it is to be the governing political issue in 1880. Harrison has started the ball in Chicago."

The next day the city Greenback party, led by M. M. ("Brick") Pomeroy nominated Harrison for mayor. The Republicans nominated A. M. Wright on March 12.

Harrison was nominated by the Democrats on March 15. Circulation of the *Tribune's* Sunday edition of the 16th was 54,400.

Harrison accepted both nominations and the campaign was on. An extra session began in Washington with the South in the saddle. The Chicago campaign hinged on what candidate Wright described as "the revolution of the southern brigadiers." The *Tribune* called the Democratic party the party of revolution and robbery but "strong, persistent and dangerous." It appealed to Chicago to remember the good administration of Heath and the Republicans. Daily the editorial page thundered at Carter. General Garfield's speech raking the Southerners for attempting to starve out the government unless they got the legislation they wanted, was in demand as a campaign document. "A vote for Carter Harrison," said the Tribune on March 31, "is an endorsement of the sentiment that the character of Jeff Davis is as pure and grand as that of John Hampden and George Washington."

Such a vote also, the *Tribune* argued, meant a return to the conditions that prevailed under Colvin, "dishonesty, profligacy and bummerism."

On election eve the *Tribune* again emphasized the national significance of this vote. "A vote for Harrison is a vote in favor of the party that having failed in 1861–65 to shoot the Union to death now proposes to starve it to death." (The Southerners were holding up appropriations in Congress.)

On April 2 the *Tribune* mournfully reported that Harrison and his ticket had been elected by majorities of about 5,000 and only the South Town district of the city was left as a small reminder of Republican hopes. Editorially the opinion was given that local issues won for Harrison, with the aid of wealthy German brewers, and that Chicago was still Republican on the great issues that divided the parties. The Democrats, it was stated, were shaping things toward the nomination of Tilden and the Harrison election would be used as part of this machine.

Mayor-elect Harrison said that he would divorce the police

and fire departments from politics and give a good business administration. The opposition papers, he said, made a mistake in "hollering about the bloody shirt." He said he would favor Democrats, if that could be called a machine. The vote was Harrison 25,604; Wright, 20,440. Socialists elected four aldermen.

Helena Modjeska (Countess Bozenta) was at Hooley's theatre in *East Lynn*, a great triumph.

The *Tribune's* spotlight swung to Springfield, for on April 5 its correspondent there, Frank E. Nevins, was arraigned before the House for refusing to answer a question before a bribery investigation committee. "A plucky journalist, who prefers a dungeon to dishonor," said the *Tribune* headlines. "Stick it out, Frank. THE TRIBUNE will never go back on you."

A member of the legislature had told Nevins he knew that a certain other member had received $1,500 for desisting from pushing a certain measure. He refused to tell the name of his informant. A resolution to put him in the Sangamon County jail unless he answered the question passed the House. The story which caused the trouble had been printed on March 21, 1879. Called before the bar of the House Nevins again refused to answer. "I have no reason to change my mind or my answer," he said. "The answer is no."

The story of March 21 said in part: "A large number of strangers are in the city today hanging around the legislative lobbies. These men are interested in various measures pending in the general assembly, those relating to insurance, ticket scalping, militia and liquor license laws being the immediate objects of attention. The lobby is neither small nor inactive and it may be said that it is effective, from the fact apparently well understood in a certain circle, that a rather prominent member of the House, whose name is known, pocketed $1,500 last week as an inducement to him to let up on a certain measure he is pressing.

"It is creditable to the assembly, however, that the ring of thieves is confined to about five senators and no more than two or three representatives. The balance of the body is measurably honest."

The *Tribune* reprinted the Nevins story editorially and denounced the action of the House as outrageous and cowardly.

"It was only in the firm conviction that he would not betray the name that the action was taken. The remedy is in the libel laws. It is time the laws and practice of the courts should fully recognize the principle of the inviolability of professional secrecy in the case of journalists as well as physicians and lawyers; but, until they do so the newspaper men themselves will protect the principle, and the people will sustain them in its assertion. As a matter of course Mr. Nevins will have the support of THE TRIBUNE which employs him, and the assistance of the best available legal talent, in resisting this petty exhibition of malice."

Editorials, however, did not keep Nevins from jail and he was put in a cell with some St. Louis tramps where, he reported, his journalistic labors proceeded somewhat unevenly. The *Tribune* printed a first-page story of his life in jail, and the affair produced a sensation. Nevins wrote a "card" to the legislature in which he said that he had not by any means told all the truth about the members, but perhaps enough had been said for the present, adding:

"It is a well known fact that the dens of vice with which this city is crowded are nightly filled with members of your body. It has been said by a member of the House that THE TRIBUNE has always been engaged in stirring up investigations, that Mr. Medill, its chief editor, would never forgive this legislature for electing John A. Logan to the United States Senate. It seems strange that the honor of this House should be so suddenly wounded when it is notorious on the streets of Springfield that acts a hundred fold more disreputable than anything that has yet been published are occurring, and when the current opinion escapes criticism that the Speaker of the House bartered his vote for Senator for the seat he now holds."

Former Governor John M. Palmer was engaged as special counsel for Nevins and a writ of *habeas corpus* was applied for. The House appointed managers to resist and the commitment was held valid. So Nevins stayed in jail, writing stories daily. He wrote about the "lichen-covered, vermin-haunted, disease-breeding, vapory old structure where he was confined." He told of breathing an air of bean soup and consorting with thieves and rats. He kept a dairy and received visitors and attracted more attention than any other news interest of the day.

The *Tribune* said on April 8 that "if Nevin, who is only an employe of THE TRIBUNE, feels a contempt for the legislature, how much greater contempt must THE CHICAGO TRIBUNE itself feel for them. It should have directed its vengeance at THE TRIBUNE."

F. K. Granger of McHenry came forward with the statement that he was the man referred to in the Nevins story and the bill in question was a gas bill, No. 327. A committee, reported that the accounts of bribery and corruption Nevins remained in jail. On his thirteenth day there, P. T. Barry of Cook County, chairman of the investigating committee, reported that the accounts of bribery and corruption started by the *Tribune* were without foundation. A resolution was offered that Nevins had been sufficiently punished and he was discharged by a vote of 103 to 12.

"May it be long," Nevins wrote on April 17, "before I am called upon to endure such a penance again. The town appears quite excited and rejoiced over my release, the opinion being strongly grounded that it was an original outrage, with supplemental vindictiveness. A warm bath, a change of undergarments throughout, a 'freshener' at the Leland House water tank, and Richard is himself again. Anyone who thinks it is a pleasant experience to entertain a contempt for a legislature and get imprisoned thirteen days in the Sangamon county jail, with all the appurtenances thereto belonging, hasn't judgment enough to run a garbage wagon."

The *Tribune* said the Nevins case would become of great historical importance, as it involved personal rights and the powers of a legislature, and promised to take the case to the Supreme Court.

Another investigation at Springfield was of special interest to the *Tribune* this springtime. This concerned an alleged attempt at blackmail by Sam H. McCrea, Cook County treasurer, who had been named a West Park Commissioner and whose confirmation was held up in the Senate. The question of blackmail was in connection with publication of the delinquent tax list, over which McCrea had control, in Chicago newspapers. There had been two grand jury investigations, with no results. A Senate committee took up the charges. Samuel J. Medill, managing editor of the *Tribune*, was one of the first witnesses called. He told of the political support the paper had given McCrea as a Republican. McCrea made no promises about the publication of the tax list, said other papers were hounding him but he expected the *Tribune* to get the work. Medill did not know much about the matter but Alfred Cowles, business manager of the *Tribune* and one of the stockholders, had more information.

Cowles testified, according to the *Tribune* of April 11, that he had known McCrea a year and in February a year ago had called on him regarding the publication of the list. In March following, he said, M. A. Hapgood, a bondsman of McCrea, called on him (Cowles). Hapgood said that McCrea's expenses in the election were $7,000 and as his salary was only $5,000 he would have to have a share of the profits. One paper, he said, had offered $15,000. Cowles told Hapgood, he testified, that if the *Tribune* got the job it would pay 25

THE TRIBUNE'S NEW LIGHTNING FOLDING AND PASTING MACHINE.

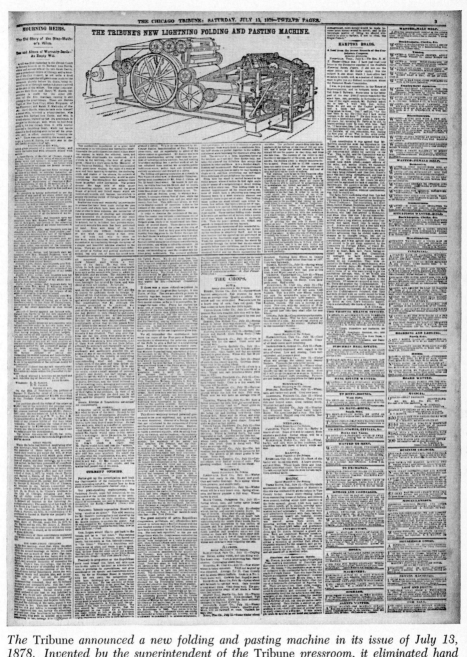

The Tribune announced a new folding and pasting machine in its issue of July 13, 1878. Invented by the superintendent of the Tribune pressroom, it eliminated hand folding copies of the newspaper.

per cent of the profit, which would be about $7,000. On April 3 following Hapgood said it was not enough, that it should be $12,000. A man named Robinson informed Cowles later that it would take $14,000 to get the job. Cowles said he assented to the proposition and made an appointment for the next day. He was to pay the $14,000 and get McCrea's order for the work. He wrote an order for McCrea to sign. In the meantime he got the sentiment of the members of the *Tribune* Company and found that the other stockholders would have nothing to do with the transaction. Without waiting for Robinson to present the order he told him that he would have nothing to do with it. He telegraphed to Joseph Medill, who replied that he would not allow the office to be blackmailed one cent. The witness said he saw McCrea afterward and he insisted that he knew nothing about the matter. Joseph Medill returned and sent a note to McCrea and the application for the printing was withdrawn.

It developed later that the *Chicago Journal* had printed the list and was paid $44,000. The *Journal* witnesses denied having paid McCrea any money. The *Tribune* offer, made to intermediaries and then withdrawn, was the nearest the committee could come to showing blackmail and McCrea was confirmed on April 24 by a vote of 40 to 4.

The *Tribune* continued to poke fun at "Our Carter," particularly on account of the stuffed eagle he took around with him on campaigns, but said this of the new mayor on April 13: "Leaving out his views on politics, which are somewhat erratic, he is a man of pure personal character, justifying the belief that he will not only be honest himself in office but will require others in offices under his control to be equally honest."

The police administration had something to account for, according to a news story in the *Tribune* of April 20, 1879.

"Bold faced vice has never been so rampant in Chicago since the palmy days of the Colvin administration. From Jackson to 12th street the west side of State street is lined with Italian restaurants, saloons where the women of the town and boys of 16 are the chief customers, dives of every variety and houses of ill fame. Even in the afternoon no man can walk along Clark street south of Harrison without being compelled to hear the solicitations of the vile women who inhabit the unsavory thoroughfare, and in windows where they sit in more or less undraped loveliness, tout for custom, irrespective of decency and careless of consequences."

It was on this note that Harrison was inaugurated mayor for his first term. In his inaugural address he said:

"Some persons fear an organized resistance to authority in Chicago. I do not. I do not believe that there is in our midst any considerable body of men mad enough to attempt such folly, for they must know that they would be but chaff compared to the solid masses who love our institutions and are determined that law and order shall reign. If, however, there are any so ignorant as to think differently or so rash as to attempt violence, they will quickly find that they have made a fatal blunder. Our honest citizens and brave police can and will protect the city."

Chapter Twenty-One

GRANT COMES HOME — THIRD TERM DEBATE

GENERAL GRANT's return from his world tour and the boom for his nomination for a third term, were the chief political developments of the latter part of 1879. The knotty problem of Southern elections, in which the Republicans were being driven from the field, was tied in with the question of the Grant nomination, in the opinion of the *Tribune*. The third term and disfranchisement of Negroes in the South were about equally distasteful to the *Tribune* editors, and it was thought that things might come to a pass where Grant's iron hand would be needed again. The great threat was the ascendancy of the ex-Confederates in Congress, and the possibility of a Democratic President. All local politics in Chicago was pointed toward the presidential race of 1880, and November found the *Tribune* in the seat of triumph for the moment.

The country was emerging from hard times and the only cloud on a clear prospect for business was the influence of what the *Tribune* designated as demagogues and "Communist quacks." The depression had bred Communist leaders in the ranks of labor and the unions were gaining new strength. Employers sought to uphold their right to hire and fire without regard to union membership. The first eight-hour day law was passed in Chicago, applying to employes of the department of public works. This was attributed to Communist influence by the *Tribune*.

In view of the presidential election of 1880, Southern elections kept Congress in heated debate, and caused much editorial comment in the *Tribune* through the spring and summer of 1879. The army was kept out of the polls in a bill which was finally passed. The President vetoed the bill. Another similar measure was passed and this also was vetoed. Thus Hayes made his record. It was one of which the *Tribune* approved.

Senator David Davis won the enmity of the *Tribune* for his speech on the army bill, in which he supported the Democratic viewpoint. "Senator Davis is an imposter and a fraud," said the *Tribune* on April 26. "He has been nothing but a Democrat of the meanest type ever since he entered the Senate." His actions, the editorial continued, "were shameful and dishonoring to the memory of Lincoln," who had appointed him to the Supreme Court. "He was never a lawyer, just a jolly old bar-room story teller."

Mayor Harrison began his "New Deal" in the City Hall by appointing standing committees without consulting the council. Alderman Ed Cullerton was among those who took exception to this innovation. *Tribune* reporters informed the new police administration where gambling was in progress.

Russia was under martial law that spring, in a gigantic effort to suppress Nihilism.

Joseph Medill was in California, writing of the new state constitution there. He said it would not hurt the people much but might hinder mining stock gambling, one of the curses of the state. If Communistic features, such as discrimination against capital, had been omitted, he said, it would have passed by 100,000 instead of 10,000.

The Chicago and Alton railroad was formally opened for traffic, with an unbroken line to Kansas City. The *Tribune* on May 10 printed a large map of the system. A *Tribune* "commissioner" who signed his article "R.W.P." toured the South on the causes of the Negro exodus.

Henry Ward Beecher in a lecture described the newspaper as the record "where man is shown in all his nakedness, a panoramic view in each issue of all the greatest, best and meanest in the rapidly forming record of the deeds of mankind."

Editor Storey of the *Chicago Times*, it was reported, intended to retire, and had built himself a "hennery" of ornamental marble. The *Tribune* in May began to print a 12-page daily. The constant building, activity in real estate, new business and increased sales, led to the confident prediction that Chicago was destined to be the great city of the continent, possibly by 1925.

In a final exchange of compliments with the legislature the *Tribune* said on May 27: "One of the last acts of

the lower house – very much the lower – of the Illinois legislature, whose session may now be considered at an end, was
to denounce THE CHICAGO TRIBUNE for the vigorous
manner in which it has expressed the sentiments of the people
of Illinois regarding the delectable gathering of blackmailers,
corruptionists and incapables. For every howl of malignant
spite uttered yesterday concerning it THE TRIBUNE has
reason to rejoice, because the hatred of these whipped curs is
the highest compliment they can possibly pay."

The Democrats won the June judicial elections in Chicago.
Mayor Harrison at a council celebration congratulated the
party and said the election meant that the Socialists had
come into the Democratic party. Within the Democratic
party, he added, the Socialists could win "not only a mere
principle but practical results as well, for the Democratic
party will take care of the poor man."

A two-page digest of all the acts passed by the legislature
was printed on June 7. Two messengers of the Illinois Central railroad were robbed of $10,000 at Wabash Avenue and
Washington Street by a bandit who threw red pepper into
their eyes and escaped in a buggy.

The *Tribune* wanted to know what was the matter with
Harrison's police force. Reporters toured State and Clark
Streets at night to get information for the Mayor and the
police. Prostitutes were found in full possession of State
Street, which was lined with 43 dens of vice between Monroe
and 12th Streets. In each place, it was reported, there were
half a dozen lewd women. Vile liquor was being consumed
and assignations made, and "the general work of the Devil
progressing finely." Special attention was called to the Eagle
saloon on State Street just south of Harrison Street, to Jerry
Monroe's dive at State and Polk Streets and Jim Fitzsimmons'
place on Clark Street near Van Buren. A carnival of gambling
was reported and the mayor was asked what he was going
to do about it all.

Gilbert and Sullivan's *H.M.S. Pinafore* was performed by combined church choirs at Haverly's theatre on June 15, stirring much clerical criticism. The Rev. Robert Collyer accepted a call to the Church of the Messiah in New York. Billy Emerson's minstrels were at Hooley's theatre.

In comment on a proposed general strike for the eight-hour day, the *Tribune* said this meant a 25 per cent increase in costs just at the time the country was recovering from depression. "It is an idea of fools that will end in failure."

An eight-column interview with Sitting Bull, dated in his camp via Fort Buford, was printed on July 5. The old chief would never consent to go on a reservation and become a farmer, it was reported. There was a vivid description of life among the Indians. Sitting Bull was described as having a remarkable face, broad and fleshy but with determined lines about the mouth, and eyes wide and black and piercing.

Wells Street property owners objected to a proposed elevated railroad to Evanston. The West Side Elevated Railroad Company had just been incorporated.

Mayor Harrison had become a spoilsman, the *Tribune* said on July 21. "Mr. Harrison has run his brief course as the patriotic citizen-mayor of Chicago. He now enters upon the second act of his drama, a puppet in the hands of an unscrupulous gang of desperate politicians bent upon the restoration of the Democratic party to power in the whole country through the aid of spoils, backed by the well-known Democratic practice of shoulder hitting and ballot box stuffing."

Alderman Meier, a "Communist," according to the *Tribune*, introduced a resolution making eight hours a legal day's work for employes of the Public Works Department. It was passed by a vote of 17 to 16, the first breach in the wall of opposition to this new order of labor.

James A. Garfield, speaking at a Republican party anniversary at Madison, Wisconsin, said: "If one truth blazes out of the fire of our war more clearly than another, it is this,

— that this is a powerful and mighty Nation. And yet a rebel Senator tells us it is not a nation but a confederacy of states."

A Congressional committee on labor and industry came to Chicago late in July. Strikers in furniture factories were trying to build a co-operative.

The *Tribune* said that genuine co-operation was not desired by the Communists. "They advocate the most sweeping revolution of government and society. They would have the manufactures, the labor, the transportation, even the land, controlled by a sort of universal parental authority, and all men treated alike, without consideration for individual worth, energy, application, frugality, skill, ambition or the other qualities which enter into individual success. It is a scheme of universal pauperism.

"We are now coming out of the depression caused by war and the future looks to a solid, substantial and enduring prosperity if the agitators and quacks can only be repressed," the *Tribune* said on August 2, 1879.

This theme was continued on August 4. "This is an age of iron and the revival of the iron industries throughout the country means that the hard times period has passed. . . . The country is on the high road to prosperity and before the presidential convention of 1880 shall have been held the present strong indications of a general revival of business will have crystallized into an active commercial and industrial campaign. The Socialists and Communists — the rank and file — will have found constant employment and they will have no time to listen to the wild and foolish harangues of their demogogical leaders. Make way for the iron horse."

General Grant was in Tokio where his reception was unprecedented in Japanese history. Tokio spent $50,000 in entertaining him. He talked with the Emperor several times and advised him to have a firm, independent spirit and resist the aggressive policy of the British.

Tribune advertisments began to have woodcut illustrations more frequently; a can of baking powder, for instance; a stove, a bookcase.

A *Tribune* correspondent took a walk in the woods with James Whitcomb Riley and sent in a delightful two-column story about his poetry and comment thereon.

Professor F. A. March addressed the Philological Society on the necessity for reformed spelling, a reform in which the *Tribune* had taken leadership. "Silent leters which are uterly useles are dropt in speling this adres to save space and sho what a great degre of simplification mite be adopted at any time."

A sensational news story came from San Francisco on August 24, when Charles De Young, one of the owners of the *Chronicle*, shot the Rev. I. S. Kalloch, workingmen's candidate for mayor, in the breast and thigh in front of the Metropolitan Temple. It was stated as the cause that Kalloch had called Charles De Young and his brother, Mike, "two bastard sons of a prostitute." Mike went to jail with Charles for protection and the *Chronicle* office was defended. The *Tribune* said the universal verdict would be that it served Kalloch right.

The *Okolona* (Mississippi) *Southern States*, a newspaper in the Yazoo country, took the attention of the *Tribune*. One Henry Dixon had desired to be sheriff of the district but when he tried to run as an independent he was forced to withdraw. He had the unanimous backing of the Negroes. Criticized for this by Northern papers, the *Southern States* replied: "Mississippi is a Nation and no foreign state shall lay a finger on her royal robes without suffering the consequences. The plan is to give the Negro no vote. Tell him to stand back, his usefulness is in the cotton patch. Our people possess the old Cavalier pride of blood and race and will revolt with hot, grand hauteur against subjection of virtue and intelligence to ignorance and vice. This is settled."

The old battle would have to be fought all over again. "If

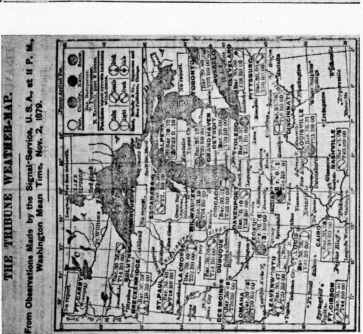

As a service to its readers, urban and rural, the Tribune made many efforts to print reliable daily weather forecasts. The first map to be printed pictured above, appeared in the Tribune of November 3, 1879.

This cartoon, one of the first in the Tribune, appeared November 5, 1879. The picture of the American eagle shaking a plucked rooster was inspired by a Republican victory in Cook County.

the existing mob rule in the South continues much longer it must be put down by the government of the United States or it will eventuate in civil war," the *Tribune* said.

Grant was on his way home across the Pacific and great plans were being made for his reception in San Francisco during September. The third term controversy continued, despite Grant's alleged disclaimers of any such ambition. It was much like the discussion caused by Coolidge's "I do not choose to run" statement in 1927. On August 30 it was said that Grant might take the presidency of the American-Nicaraguan Inter-Ocean Canal Company. The *Tribune* preferred to take Grant at his word and said:

"There is reason both to commend and congratulate General Grant on the stand he has taken. His fame is as radiant now as it ever can be unless some new danger shall threaten the Republic during his life, and in that case the American people will turn to him with such unanimity and confidence that he will be in no doubt as to his duty. He will leave the Republican party free to unite on the most promising candidate and make a vigorous fight on the living issues of the time, without defending any of the mistakes of the past."

A two-column first-page advertisment, the largest of this kind to appear in the *Tribune*, was taken by The Fair department store on August 31.

Thomas A. Edison told a science association at Saratoga, New York, that before long a person making a speech in New York could be heard through the electro-chemical telephone by a hall full of people in Saratoga. Dr. Kalloch recovered and was elected mayor of San Francisco. The *Tribune* started a campaign against milkmen who watered their milk.

General Butler, again a candidate for Governor of Massachusetts, was visited at the Palmer House by a *Tribune* reporter. His opinion of the *Tribune*, it was reported, "was

expressed with a big big D and other words of evil sense."
"General Butler," the *Tribune* said, "is the most pestiferous
demagogue who has ever appeared in American politics. He
is a social bully and a political blackguard, whose election as
governor of Massachusetts would be as great a calamity to
that state as that of Blackburn has been in Kentucky."

Governor Luke P. Blackburn of Kentucky had come in
for much criticism in the *Tribune*. Henry Watterson had
supported him, which was enough to put the *Tribune* against
him. It was charged and later admitted by the *Louisville
Courier-Journal*, that this was the same Dr. Blackburn who
had sought to spread yellow fever through the North during
the war by means of infected clothing from Bermuda. "It is
no joke," said the *Tribune*. "Kentucky wears the brand of
shame."

"Home Again" was the big news of September 21. The
bay and hills of San Francisco were alive with welcoming
throngs as Grant came home from his tour of the world. The
big boom was on. He was to come east through Omaha and
Galena. The *Tribune* announced that its telegraphic correspondent in San Francisco was authorized to state that
Grant was not a candidate for the nomination for President
in 1880.

However, John Russell Young, newspaper correspondent
who had accompanied Grant on his tour and who had the
best inside information, said that Grant did not know what
he would do, that he would not decide until the nomination
was made. "He acts only when the moment for action
comes," said Young, "and never blows a fog horn." Young
had talked with him almost every day for three years.

President Hayes came to Chicago and a *Tribune* "ambas-
sador" met him at Grand Crossing station, nine miles south
of downtown Chicago. The President's reception in Chicago
was cordial. The *Tribune*, in commenting on this, September
24, said: "The President's vetoes against the Southern efforts

to reinstate the states rights doctrine [the army bill] have done this. Radicals and conservatives alike are grateful to him."

On the Grant reception the *Tribune* said: "In the presence of this grand demonstration, this spontaneous outpouring of patriotism and affection, partisanship is hushed and the American people, as a unit, receive back to their bosom and confidence the beloved General who beat back the waves of rebellion and saved the Nation."

A special First ward election late in September aroused the *Tribune*. Arthur Dixon had long been the Republican leader there but his candidate in this election was defeated by the Democratic "bummers," despite the efforts of the *Tribune* to get the voters to the polls. Apathy was at first supposed to be the cause of the "regrettable" result, but later fraud reared its head. The *Tribune* which had been so scornful of "shotgun elections" in the South, said on September 26: "The First ward election held scenes that would cause the waters of the bayous of Mississippi and Louisiana to blush with shame." A list of "suspect" voters was printed. The Republicans appointed an investigating committee. Mike McDonald and the Mike Evans gang were blamed for the frauds.

Grant's slow progress homeward was page one news daily. The *Tribune* interviewed 50 political leaders on the Grant boom and reported on October 2 that they agreed on the strong probability of Grant's nomination, and were unanimous in his support if nominated. There had been a change of sentiment about the third term because of the intervening four years.

"The boom is booming," said the Tribune. "It depends on the Democrats. If fraud, intimidation, violence, murder continue in the South, if the Nation's right to supervise national elections is to be repealed, if this Solid South hatred and intolerance continues, and the state sovereignty issue is up again, with threats of seizing the Congress and the Presidency, then Grant will be nominated and elected — then the country will turn to Grant with one accord, and he will be elected with the aid of thousands of Democratic votes in every Northern state."

Grant had just used a telephone for the first time in his life.

On *October* 8 the *Tribune* published a full-page map of Colorado. It was taken from an original published by Rand, McNally & Company, and was said to be the most elaborate map that had ever appeared in any newspaper. Chicago capitalists had invested millions in Colorado gold mines and there was much local interest in the area. The map gave many details of the mining regions and the scene of the Ute War. Mount Bross, named after William Bross, who had done a lot of geological exploring in that section, was shown near Hot Sulphur Springs.

On October 10, the *Tribune* published a small political almanac, possibly the forerunner of the modern newspaper yearbooks. It gave results on all elections, dates of conventions, tickets and platforms, for all the states during 1879. The Republicans won the fall elections in Ohio. The *Tribune* thought this of national significance and that it would infuse new life into the Republicans of the South.

A Tobey Furniture Company advertisment had a picture of a lady in a hoop skirt letting down a folding bed. Willoughby, Hill and Company, clothiers, pictured a Board of Trade man, with whiskers and cane, going after his winter overcoat.

Preparations were made to entertain Grant in Chicago in November. The Army of Tennessee was to hold a reunion. The *Tribune* called on Republicans to get busy in Chicago on the elections for treasurer, judges, etc. Mayor Harrison, they said, was working to strengthen his party for 1880. "How do Republicans like the idea of contributing toward the prospects of Confederate presidential success in 1880?"

"Fern Leaf," the prize contributor of the *Tribune's* Home Department columns, came to the defense of high school girls who were being abused for banging their hair and pasting it down, flirting and other sins.

Senator Zach Chandler of Michigan, who had made a "rip-roaring," Republican speech in Chicago on the previous Friday, was found dead in the Grand Pacific Hotel on November 1. Senator Chandler said in his last speech at McCormick Hall: "You are going to hold an election next Tuesday that is of importance far beyond the borders of Chicago. By your verdict you are to send forth a greeting to the people of the United States, saying either that you are in favor of honest men, honest money, patriotism and a National government, or that you are in favor of soft money, repudiation and Rebel rule."

The *Tribune* began printing its first weather maps on November 3. They were two-column maps, four inches deep, containing reports of weather from the United States Signal Service for a district extending from Cleveland to Des Moines and from Nashville to the Canadian border.

The election results, reported November 5, were headed: "A Solid North. This is a Nation and don't You Forget It." "Chicago and Cook County redeemed from the bane of Democracy."

The story was illustrated by one of the first cartoons to appear in the paper. It depicted the American eagle standing on a flag-draped crag and giving the Democratic rooster, a plucked bird, a thorough shaking. The *Tribune* said of the result: "It was the most complete sitting down on the played-out dogma of states rights that has been seen in the city since war times. It means simply this: we met the enemy and they are ours, from Rebel Brigadier to camp followers. We got 'em and we propose to keep 'em where the hair is short."

The entire Republican ticket was elected with majorities of 5,200. Grant's arrival home at Galena, escorted by 10,000, was given a big play on November 6. Henry Watterson in the *Louisville Courier-Journal* said that Kentucky never would swallow such large doses of reform and civilization as the editor of the *Tribune* suggested. He quoted the *Tribune* as follows: "They must quit the use of whiskey as a staple drink. They must renounce the odious dogma of state sovereignty. They must abolish caste. They must treat the Negro as a man and brother. They must quit shooting and carving each other for fancied offenses. They must go to church and be good Christians."

The *Courier-Journal* continued: "Brother Medill would refuse us the luxury of nigger killing; when he knows that a plump, colored baby, roasted brown, is the most valued delicacy upon the true Kentuckian's dinner table. He would refrain us from what he calls 'illicit distilling'; when he knows that whiskey to be good, must be hid in the bushes and pay no taxes. He would even have us go to church. O Lord, O Lord! Then, such is the rigor of his disciplinary injunction he wants us to learn to read, in order, we suppose, that we may subscribe for The Chicago Tribune and become such Christians as that pious saint, Roscoe Conkling."

The Southern editor continued in this vein, wondering why lightning did not strike the *Tribune* building and melt the type therein and "strike the editor dead at the feet of the Goddess of Liberty." "But stay," he concluded, "we grow excited. We would not harm our brother . . . we leave him to his conscience."

The *Tribune* suggested a political invasion of the South in the coming campaign, a Republican crusade. "Insist on the right to preach Republican doctrines everywhere, just as the editor of the *Okolona Southern States* [Col. A. Harper] spoke his mind in McCormick Hall. If freedom of speech is not possible in the South the sooner we find it out the better."

There was trouble at the stockyards early in November. The men wanted a raise. The packers met and agreed to act in harmony with each other in employment of labor and especially in the right to hire or discharge any man as they saw fit regardless of any union or association of labor. Twenty packers signed this agreement. The Butchers' Union withdrew its demands for the time.

The November 12 edition was nearly all a Grant welcome. A two-column illustration of the returning hero was printed on page one, with a map of the globe showing his trip and a map of the city showing where the grand procession would march. There were poems on Grant, sketches of his career, stories of his life and trip and no other news, and no advertisments, until page six. It was a remarkable issue and the *Tribune* promoted it as a souvenir, with an unlimited printing.

On November 13 there were six pages on the Grant reception in Chicago. Every window of the *Tribune* building for five stories was draped with red, white and blue and festooned with evergreens. A large evergreen shield reached from the roof to form an arch in front of the building, surmounted by gilt eagles standing on a globe holding streamers of color. There were three other arches in front of the building, with figures of Washington and Lincoln. The display won the admiration of the crowd and the various units saluted as they passed in procession. Grant also saluted from his carriage. There was a reception at the Palmer House, with the Army of Tennessee in charge and E. B. Washburne the speaker. The next day there was a grand banquet, with Sherman and Logan present. Mark Twain was also there, and made an address on "Babies" which held the crowded tables in uproar. It is said this speech is not included among Twain's regular publications, but it is in the November 14, 1879, issue of the *Tribune* in full. There was a reception that night at the home of Colonel and Mrs. Fred Grant, 781 Michigan Avenue. The society reporter noted that Mrs. Potter Palmer was attired in an elegant costume composed of garnet velvet over white brocaded silk, court train ornaments and diamonds.

Mrs. Alfred Cowles wore an elaborate toilette of Nile green silk, embroidered in colors and caught up with a bouquet of pansies.

All this did not tend to clear the question of Grant's nomination. All factions were awaiting some authentic indication, the *Tribune* said on November 19, of the wishes and intentions of Grant with regard to his candidacy. General Benjamin Harrison said Grant was too much of a patriot to accept a third term. The *Tribune* blew hot and cold on the question and said on November 22 that there was no impropriety in his becoming a "candidate de novo, after a period of retirement and instruction," such as the last four years had afforded.

There was a meeting of those interested in forming a Union League Club on November 21. It was to be constituted of "those who believe in the unity of the states and the supremacy of the United States government, and who pledge themselves to aid in sustaining its authority against all its enemies, both at home and abroad."

A rise in freight rates led the *Tribune* to criticize the railroad combination of Vanderbilt and Gould and to say that the interest of the producers demanded a maximum rate and prohibition against rebates. This was the beginning of the agitation that led to the Interstate Commerce Bill.

A "gastronomical" column was begun by the *Tribune* on November 29, with suggestions for menus and how to prepare food.

The 46th Congress opened on December 1. President Hayes congratulated the country on the success of resumption and recommended the suspension of silver dollar coinage.

A mass meeting was held in Chicago in sympathy with the people of Ireland, who were staging a tenants' war. Joseph Medill, who was in New York, sent a letter of sympathy, hoping that Ireland would be rid of the "juggernaut of landlordism." The Chicago City Railway men formed a union.

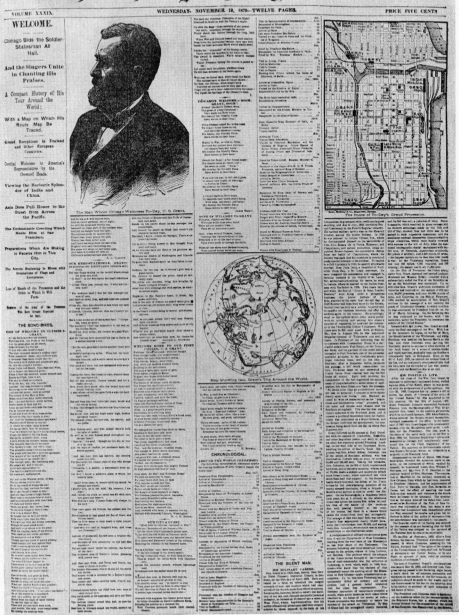

In honor of Grant's visit to Chicago, the Tribune gave over the front page of its issue of November 12, 1879, to poems of welcome, a portrait and maps. Inner pages contained the complete story of Grant's life and travels.

The company objected and called on the men to take an oath they would not become members.

How the President's message was printed in advance of presentation to Congress was the subject of an article in the *Pottsville Miners' Journal* on December 7. It had been sold to the *Cincinnati Enquirer* in the first place, then resold to the *New York Times* and the *Chicago Times*. The *Tribune* got an early copy of the *New York Times* and had the message telegraphed on fourteen wires and set up 20,000 words in less than four hours, thus checkmating the *Chicago Times*.

E. M. Haines contributed an article on December 7 on the origin of baseball. The *Tribune* of December 7 consisted of 20 pages totaling 140 columns, 46 of which were advertisements. The circulation was 46,440 copies.

It was reported on December 8 that there were three thousand licensed saloons in Chicago and a thousand more where liquor was sold without license. The *Tribune* printed a feature on the feet of the prominent men of Chicago, with outline drawings and measurements. They started with "Long John" Wentworth's feet.

The Republican National Committee on December 18, 1880, selected Chicago for the next convention. Senator J. Donald Cameron was named chairman. A mining stock exchange was established in Chicago with Jesse Spalding as president.

A Tribune representative visited Horatio Seymour at his home at Utica and interviewed him on his possible nomination by the Democrats. A strike began in the stockyards over the employment of non-union men.

As the year closed it was reported that Edison had at last solved the problem of electric light. Dispatches from Menlo Park told of a little lamp about the size of an orange, and a strip of paper the shape of a horseshoe. This lamp, the *Tribune* said, might be almost as magical as that of Aladdin. " The flash of the Edison paper horseshoe marked a moment of time from which epochs in science will date."

Chapter Twenty=Two

WHY DANA FAILED IN CHICAGO

THE presidential campaign of 1880 came close to the *Tribune* office in the spring, when, after attacks on the candidacy of Secretary of the Treasury John Sherman, the charge was made that Medill had sought to have Sherman nullify the Resumption Act of 1879. Editorials and Medill's personal files were gone into to disprove this, and the *Tribune* gave the history of its position on currency questions.

While friendly to General Grant, as always, the *Tribune* doubted the wisdom or the necessity of his nomination for a third term, and took much criticism from other Republican newspapers.

The electric light was on the way and the *Tribune* aided and encouraged Thomas A. Edison, in this experimental period, in every way. Medill and Edison were personal friends.

The *Tribune* appeared in a new typographical garb on January 1, 1880. The new dress was said to be the "plainest, prettiest and clearest ever worn by a Chicago newspaper." The new type, made by Barnhardt and Spindler of Chicago, was larger and therefore carried fewer words to the column. The *Tribune* reporters had to begin to write down their stories.

The January 1 edition carried an eight-page trade review, showing that Chicago had taken the lead in grain shipments. The total increase in trade over that of the preceding year was 17½ per cent, a substantial progress. The demand for the review was great and an extra edition was printed.

The *Tribune* prospectus for 1880, printed January 4, stated:

"THE TRIBUNE is the chief business medium and commercial exponent of this city and is undeniably the strongest and most influential Republican newspaper in the West. A President is to be elected this year and on the result of this issue will turn the peace, harmony and well being of the country. If the Republicans win, the great truth that this is a Nation, and not a Confederacy, will be forever established, and the pestilent heresy of 'state sovereignty' will be entombed in its grave, to rot and be forgotten.

"Politically THE TRIBUNE is a stalwart Republican newspaper; and will remain so until every man in the South, irrespective of race, color or politics, shall enjoy the right to vote and be voted for, and have his ballot honestly counted, without bulldozing or cheating, and until civil liberty and political liberty for black Republicans as well as white Democrats, is as firmly established in the South as in the North.

"The redemption of legal tender greenbacks in coin, and the remonetization of silver have contributed immensely to the restoration of national confidence, industrial revival and good times experienced during the past year; therefore the present sound and satisfactory money system should be let alone.

"THE TRIBUNE will strenuously oppose any Wall Street and Shylock schemes to demonetize greenbacks and silver, and produce contraction, for the benefit of money lenders, to the ruin of the industrial masses."

Special features advertised were: *Farm and Garden* by "Rural Jr.," *Horticulture* by "O. L. B.," and *Field and Stables* by "Veterinarian." The *Tribune* during this period frequently carried one-word headlines.

The stockyards strike ended in the middle of the month; the labor supply was too great. The *Tribune* commented on the foolishness of the strike and its Communistic background.

"The yards strike," it was stated on January 18, "furnishes additional instance of the abuse of the trade unions. Strikes which aim at something beyond the laws of supply and demand for labor, such as the demand for the surrender by an employer of the control of his own business, must of necessity fail."

General Grant was on his way to Mexico City, where he was to be a guest at Chapultepec Castle, in the storming of which 33 years before he had won his first distinction as a soldier.

President Hayes' feeble efforts to abolish polygamy were criticized by the *Tribune* on January 22. "It is worse than useless to dillydally or temporize any longer with this crying sin against Christian Civilization and this bold defiance of law."

A new debate over money started in Congress. The *Tribune* argued against "the enormity of the scheme to demonetize greenbacks and reduce the legal tender money of the United States to such a limited quantity of gold as may happen from time to time to be in the country."

Henry George's *Progress and Poverty* was reviewed in the *Tribune*, which predicted it would "stir up a hornet's nest." "E. B. W." wrote from Washington about a proposed Interstate Commerce bill to prevent railroad extortions. "R. W. P." wrote from Washington on the presidential situation and the candidacies of Blaine, Sherman and Washburne.

The business revival had not helped the newspaper publishers, the *Tribune* said on February 2. Advances in wages and prices had made hard times for them. White paper was up 33 to 50 per cent. Some Chicago papers had dropped in size, others had raised prices. The *Chicago Times* had gone up to 6 cents. The *Tribune* said it had omitted part of its supplements but would retain its old price. The daily edition was still 12 pages.

On the question of what Edison had accomplished, the *Tribune* said on February 3:

"The mistake that is made by an impatient public is in demanding too much of Mr. Edison in too short a time. It was scores of years after Watt discovered the motive power of steam that it was brought into anything like its present practical uses. Electricity is even a more subtle agent than steam and yet it is expected that Mr. Edison will introduce his lamps at once into general use. He has solved the great problem of making them burn continuously and now time should be given him to perfect details of his machinery so as to make them as practical and economical as possible. That he will accomplish this no one who knows his indomitable perseverance, courage and industry will even doubt."

Senator Cameron was pushing the Grant candidacy in Pennsylvania, but the *Tribune's* Washington correspondent said the Grant wave was losing strength.

The *Tribune* declared that the navy was obsolete and utterly inefficient and that a number of ironclads, torpedo boats and other fast vessels should be built.

A new weather map appeared in the February 5 edition, said to be superior to any weather chart published in any American newspaper. It covered the area from Winnipeg to Mobile and from the Atlantic to the Rockies.

Grant won the endorsement of the Pennsylvania Republican convention, but his majority was small and the *Tribune* said that he was unlikely to become a candidate of a faction. Blaine's strength was growing. A "Letters and Science" page was introduced in the Saturday *Tribune*. The Eastern press, said the *Tribune*, was impotent in connection with the scheme to demonetize the country's legal tender. "They represent the brokers of Wall Street. The Western papers represent intelligent communities. That is the difference. THE CHICAGO TRIBUNE and papers generally of the West represent productive capital, the energy and labor of the country."

323

At the President's reception in the White House, Mrs. Astor wore $800,000 worth of diamonds and was attended by detectives. The correspondents said they did not have to enter by the back stairs any more but ranked with captains and lieutenant commanders.

The *Tribune* reverted to an earlier size by becoming an eight-page daily on February 12. A Chicago company was incorporated to use the Edison light patent whenever it was in working condition. General Booth and his Salvation Army were the sensation of London.

Thomas Carlyle said that England was retrograding rapidly and predicted that America would be the future great power if she kept herself free from entangling alliances and "from the humbuggery of agitating foreign mountebanks." This was good advice, but hardly needed, the *Tribune* said, as this was America's firmly implanted policy.

Among the improvements of the future predicted in the *Tribune* was that of introducing steam into business houses and private residences through pipes laid under streets and alleys from a common producing center.

The *Tribune* was friendly to Blaine's candidacy and opposed that of Secretary Sherman. Replying to criticism on its opposition to a Grant nomination the *Tribune* said on February 25: "THE TRIBUNE did not boom for a third term in 1876 and because it is not booming much for a third term in 1880 it is charged with inconsistency by the Conkling, Cameron, and Logan conduits. It will have to stagger along as well as possible under their obliquity, and struggle for life even in their cold shade."

The troubles of the Irish were being agitated in this country by Charles Stewart Parnell. Concerning a Parnell meeting the *Tribune* said:

"THE CHICAGO TRIBUNE, in broad contrast to the press of New York, was the first among American daily newspapers to expose to the people of the West and of the country, the real cause of Irish starvation, poverty, misery, rags, wretchedness, expatriation, discontent, insurrections, rebellions and the illiteracy with which the Irish people are reproached. This was the horrid system of feudal land robbery."

On the demand of the Grant supporters for "a strong man" for President, the *Tribune* said on February 28: "The strong man cry too often implies belief in a weak people. It will be a sad day for Republican America if she is ever compelled to confess that one man alone is strong for her, and that without him the perpetuity of her free institutions would be imperilled."

A page was printed on the life of Elihu B. Washburne on March 6, indicating that the *Tribune* looked with favor upon his candidacy.

Grant was still in Mexico and the *Tribune* said on March 7: "When General Grant returns from Mexico and becomes acquainted with the deep and widespread hostility to a presidential third term, and the means by which whole delegations have been coerced to vote for him, it is more than probable that he will decline a candidacy which lacks that popular support which alone could induce him to be a candidate for a third term."

The London correspondent sent in a story about the *London Times* as "a college of invention and discovery in the newspaper world." This characterization might be applied to the *Tribune* also.

A newspaper gallery was established in Washington by the committee on rules. Ex-members as lobbyists were given free range of the House.

An improvement in the *Tribune* was noted at this time. It had always been slack in giving initials or first names of persons in the news. The writer assumed that the reader knew these. A new order appears to have gone out calling for something more in line with modern news practice.

Pictures and elaborate descriptions of the "Four Great Stalwarts," Grant, Blaine, Washburne and Senator George F. Edmunds of Vermont, were printed on March 27. An Illinois canvass showed Blaine first and Grant second.

A sketch of St. Thomas Aquinas, his life and teachings, was printed on March 28, as Pope Leo XIII had issued an encyclical requiring Roman Catholic bishops and professors to teach the principles of scholastic philosophy.

Secretary of the Treasury John Sherman, whose presidential aspirations had been strongly opposed by the *Tribune*, entered into a controversy with Joseph Medill on March 29. He made the statement that in the winter of 1877–78 Medill had called on him in the Treasury Department and in a violent manner had demanded a pledge that the Secretary would nullify the Resumption Act (redemption of greenbacks in coin) pleading that it would break banks and ruin the country and especially the editor of the *Tribune* who was grievously burdened with debt.

Medill answered this by saying that he was in Washington that winter and had called on the Secretary but nothing was said about resumption. Medill said that it had never entered his head that the Secretary had such power, and that he must have imagined a conversation with some other person.

This attack, it developed, had been fostered by W. M. Bateman, chairman of Sherman's "literary bureau." The *Tribune* continued its attacks on Sherman, showing how he was using Federal employes in political work for himself. His nomination, the *Tribune* said, would mean the defeat of the Republican party, but they saw little danger of the nomination.

"Sherman Story Exploded," the *Tribune* said on April 1. A letter was printed which Medill had sent to James W. Sheahan, *Tribune* chief editorial writer, on March 9, 1878, from Arlington House, Washington, in which Medill gave orders which show the exact opposite of the stand which

Sherman said he had taken. Instead of wanting repeal of the Resumption Act, Medill said in the letter: "THE TRIBUNE must put a little stiffening into the Senate, or it may give way and pass the House repeal bill [of the Resumption Act] and the President is reported to be so demoralized over the result of his silver veto that it is not certain he will stop its passage. And this, said the *Tribune*, "at the very time Sherman declares Medill was demanding of him a promise to nullify the law. Was ever a grosser falsehood attempted to be fastened on any man?"

The *Galesburg* (Ill.) *Register* came to the defense of Medill in a story headed "The Befouling Fiends Are After Mr. Medill of The Chicago Tribune."

"The History of a Machine Organ" was the subject of an editorial on April 2. The occasion was the end of a suit which Charles A. Dana had entered against the stockholders of the old *Chicago Republican* and which was now decided in his favor for $10,388. The *Tribune* said:

"In 1864 and '65 THE CHICAGO TRIBUNE refused, as it had always done previously and has done ever since, to be a personal or 'machine' organ. It refused to acknowledge allegiance to any person, or clique, or faction; it refused to be the mere mouthpiece through which any man could trumpet his own praise; it refused to be the instrument on which any man, or ring, or confederacy, or gang of jobbers could play or perform any tune which commended itself to their profit and the public's loss. It refused to be the conduit or escape pipe through which any corrupt or scheming gangs could vent their destructive poisons and dishonest appeals. Hence in the winter of '64–65 there was a gathering of the corruptionists of Illinois at Springfield, and it was then and there decided to establish an 'organ' and destroy THE TRIBUNE. The handsome sum of $500,000 was subscribed and 20 per cent cash was paid down and in April, 1865, the paper was called into existence."

Theodore Tilton was first sought as an editor, it was stated, and then Charles A. Dana was induced to take the position. The article continued:

"It is unnecessary to relate the subsequent proceedings in detail. Somehow or other THE TRIBUNE didn't fail in the least; it was not broken down; the rings and the cliques at the state capital waited anxiously and hopefully to be informed that THE TRIBUNE had suspended issue, but the news hung fire somewhere on the road. The paper continued to be published and the people bought and read it, and its earnings seemed to be undiminished, notwithstanding the new 'organ' was printed in Chicago. The organ itself did not progress, though it had a legion of godfathers, including all the men who ever had or whoever expected to fatten on the spoils at Springfield. All the men who had tasted public plunder during the war in the shape of army contracts, cotton smuggling and other spoils, and whose gains incited in them hopes of future distinction, — all worked for the new paper which was to command the Northwest and dictate its patronage. The spring and summer and part of the winter passed away, and the $100,000 cash was nearly exhausted. Mr. Dana was hampered by the multitudinous character of the spoils ring of proprietors, and he was helpless; the machine men who were disappointed because THE TRIBUNE had not been crushed out of existence laid the blame on Dana. They called him a failure. Orders were issued for the collection of another assessment on the machine stockholders. Dana took that occasion to resign and escape. He sold his stock, — subject to the lien, pocketed the cash, shook the dust of Chicago from his boots and dissolved his partnership with the Illinois ring and robber combinations. The 'organ' was out of tune. Other stockholders soon followed his example. Eventually the control of the stock fell into the hands of a wealthy banker at Springfield who had made his fortune out of the war. Then a number of young men who had been employed on THE

TRIBUNE were seduced into putting their cash capital into the ring's organ. It became a high protection and subsidy advocate. The manufacturers of the Eastern states were appealed to and were bled freely and mercilessly, and many thousands of dollars were thus obtained and sunk. In the meantime the central capitalist at Springfield was subjected to regular demands for more money, and he had embarked so much that he could not afford to let the thing go down, though THE TRIBUNE was still living and flourishing, which made the machine fellows green with envy and red with choler; but THE TRIBUNE still lived and actually declared and divided cash dividends from its earnings, while the 'organ' made its owners bleed at every pore to keep the breath of life in its emaciated frame. Thus some years more were consumed, the 'organ' repeatedly changing hands and forever sinking money. One of these rotation editors is now running the St. Louis Third Term Boomer. We can't remember all the others. Several of them are still out of jail and a number have gone where the woodbine twineth.

"At last the fire of '71 consumed the material part of the establishment, and some time later the entire property, charter, franchise, etc., were sold for $10,000, with which the three managers went off and bought a paper in one of the rural towns. Up to the time of the fire it may safely be assumed that $500,000 of good money taken from the stockholders and blackmailed from manufacturers and from cheap but aspiring politicians, were irretrievably sunk; sunk, — forever and hopelessly lost. On the ruins of the 'organ' of 1865 was erected another 'organ' whose life has been shockingly checkered, whose management has been varied with each change of the moon, and which now enjoys the proud journalistic eminence of being an advocate of all subsidy schemes, swindling rings, and everything that has 'money in it'; and that politically it is the personal organ of a Senator, bearing the same relation to the official that the tail of a dog does to the canine that wags it.

"During the fifteen years of diversified labor and expenditure to establish and maintain a personal ring and machine organ in Chicago, and to destroy, break down and annihilate THE CHICAGO TRIBUNE, nearly $1,000,000 of money has been sunk and lost to stockholders, patrons and creditors, and the 'organ' still languishes, while THE TRIBUNE still lives and it has flourished so bravely that, while the $1,000,000 has been lost to the corruptionists and monopolists, THE TRIBUNE has added to its property and made some dividends to its proprietors.

"The days of mere 'organs' have passed, never to return. The world has moved away from that kind of narrow and disreputable journalism. An 'organ' is of itself positive evidence of weakness and corruption on the part of its master, and its degradation is fatal to the concern itself. An organ with one tune is necessarily monotonous and wearisome. The people want something better, — something in keeping with the progress of the age, something free and independent, which can call its soul its own. The world to them contains more than one man, and has higher aims than the personal aggrandisement of one and generally an indifferent person. It wants a journal reflecting the great interests of mankind, and not the personal schemes of a single officeholder or a professional office-broker."

The anti-third-term movement was spreading, it was reported in the *Tribune* on April 4, 1880. An article on the furniture trade in Chicago said it centered around John M. Smyth, who had inaugurated the time payment system. There was a division of sentiment among the Yale faculty as to the teaching of Herbert Spencer's *Study of Sociology* by Professor Wilbur G. Sumner, because of the manner in which the issue between science and religion was treated.

Republicans elected 10 members to the new city council,

In 1880, when the fastest city transportation was provided by horse-drawn cabs and streetcars, State Street, Chicago's main shopping thoroughfare, appeared like this looking north from Madison Street.

the Democrats 5 and the Communists 2. Swayne Wickersham, a Democrat, was elected in the First ward.

Horace White, president of the Independent Republican Club, spoke in New York on the third term. The *Tribune* gave six columns to this. In the course of his argument Mr. White said: "It would perhaps be said that the candidate for the third term does not want a fourth and would refuse to run again. That would not make the case any better. Let the barrier of the forefathers be broken down — let the precedent cease to exist — then any ambitious future President is privileged to be a candidate as many times as he chooses. The Republic is switched off on a new track. Nobody knows whither it leads."

Medill in Texas gave an interview to the *Galveston News* on his war with Secretary Sherman. "Mr. Sherman has announced himself as a candidate for the Presidency," he said, "and organized his Literary Bureau and set it to work in his behalf. The business of such an institution is to tab rival candidates by starting injurious rumors about them and falsehoods about editors who do not boom for the owner of the bureau. I have exasperated Mr. Sherman undoubtedly by saying that a man holding and advancing his anti-silver and greenback and sweeping contractionary principles would be an unsafe and unavailable candidate for the Chicago convention to nominate. This has aroused his ire and instead of retracting his obnoxious and destructive views he pours out his little bottle of wrath upon my head. He concocts the anti-resumption bulldozing interview with me. No cock and bull story of that sort will serve his purpose. The issues he must meet are those of his own making, — destruction of the greenbacks as debt paying money, and the abolition of silver tender coin, and therewith I leave him and his little boom to be dealt with by the people."

The *Tribune* said on April 13 that it had no personal objection to the nomination of Grant, but doubted that he was the most available man. It pointed out that it had opposed Blaine in 1876 because it did not think he could be elected and added:

"THE TRIBUNE has as high an appreciation of his [Grant's] great ability and of his personal rectitude, and also of his great services to the nation, as is entertained by any of the blatant shriekers who denounce all persons who question the expediency of his nomination. It cannot be ignored that the sentiment of the Republican party so unanimously expressed in 1875-76 against the election of any person to the Presidency for the third time has found a deep lodgement in the popular heart. The objection to a third term among Republicans is so strong that there are thousands in every state who will prefer the defeat of the candidate rather than submit to the establishment of any such precedent. For this reason, we urgently appeal to the Republicans of the Northwest, and especially of Illinois, whether it is advisable to court defeat, and to invite a wholesale defection from the party, by a blind determination to establish a third term precedent."

Workingwomen's Union No. 12 said that sewing women in Chicago were no better than slaves, getting from $2 to $3 a week.

Grant was on a Southern tour, which was said to have for its object the securing of convention delegates. A mass meeting for Grant was held in Central Music Hall on April 16, with Senator John A. Logan the chief speaker. "Senator Logan saws the air and outrages the English language," was the *Tribune* headline on this report, which, however, gave the speeches in full.

In England the Liberals under Gladstone had come into power. In Germany Bismarck was increasing the power of the state. The *London Times* objected to exclusive United States control of the proposed interoceanic canal.

Professor Elias Colbert, commercial editor of the *Tribune*, began the publication of astronomical tables daily showing the rising and setting of the moon and the official time for lighting the first street lamp in each circuit of the city during the week. It was said later that this saved the city from $30,000 to $40,000 a year in the expense of lighting.

The Boston *Advertiser* said that the *Tribune's* policies on financial matters were a "baneful influence." The *Tribune* in answer to this said on April 20, 1880:

"The great crime and offense THE TRIBUNE has committed was the successful support of the remonetization of silver. The successful legislation of silver coinage defeated one of the most deep-laid and infamous conspiracies against popular rights and against the industries of the country that was ever attempted. [Silver was demonetized in 1873.]

"After the inauguration of Hayes in March, 1877, THE TRIBUNE began the discussion of the silver subject and from that time until a year later when Congress passed the bill remonetizing silver over the executive veto, this paper never omitted any proper occasion or proper argument to urge and advocate the remonetization of silver. All other questions were subordinated to that. We carried on the discussion editorially and with the aid of communications from many of the ablest writers of the country. We treated the subject as one of National policy, not as a Republican, but as an American policy in the success of which the whole country was deeply interested.

"The Resumption Act provided for the redemption of the legal tender greenbacks in coin. Under the law as it then stood the only coin possible to be used in redeeming the greenbacks was gold. The amount of gold in the whole country did not exceed 100 millions. The construction placed upon the Resumption Act by all the eastern Republicans and Democrats was, that upon redemption the greenbacks were to be withdrawn. The Secretary of the Treasury, though often appealed to, refused to negative this construction. The greenbacks being withdrawn and the silver being demonetized, there would after January, 1879, be no legal tender money in the country save gold, in which dear and scarce metal all debts, public and private, including banknotes, would have to be paid.

"Under these circumstances THE CHICAGO TRIBUNE advocated not only the remonetization of the silver dollar, but also its free coinage, as something essential to the resumption of specie payment in January, 1879. We urged the impossibility of resumption in gold alone. We denounced the contraction of the currency by the redemption and the withdrawal of greenbacks, and of the necessity of the bank currency, and of the general wreck of business and property by the attempt to make gold the exclusive legal tender and debt paying money of the country. We urged the impossibility of resumption in 'gold alone.'

"These views were presented in this paper day after day, the one leading idea being that the remonetization of silver was an absolute necessity for the resumption of specie payments, and that without silver it would be impossible to resume specie payment at the time named in the law. We were conscious of the powerful influence exercised by the money lenders and the money shavers, and urged that, when Congress met, if it was found impossible to remonetize silver and provide for the largest possible coinage of silver dollars, then the date fixed for resumption should be postponed, because it would be impossible to resume specie payments in gold alone. . . . Congress followed THE TRIBUNE's argument that to attempt to resume in gold alone would be a disastrous failure. It vetoed the scheme to redeem and retire the greenbacks, and, to make specie payments practicable and easy, it remonetized the silver dollar and provided for its immediate and continuous coinage.

"Congress in all this adopted almost to the letter, and despite the wild and frantic protests of the Secretary of the Treasury, and the veto of the Executive, and even the cultured solicitations of The Advertiser, the policy so long and persistently advocated by THE CHICAGO TRIBUNE.

"So far as this paper aided in bringing about the result, THE TRIBUNE claims to have labored for the best interests of the country, although it regrets that The Advertiser considers it as having exercised 'the most baneful influence on financial questions of any paper published in this country.'"

Chapter Twenty=Three

"THE THIRD TERM THING IS BEATEN"

THE BATTLE against the third-term precedent, involved in the nomination of General Grant, was the chief political event of the latter part of 1880. The *Tribune* had no candidate in this presidential struggle, but fought hard against the third term. With the nomination and election of General James A. Garfield it was considered in the *Tribune* office that the third term idea had been killed forever, and also that the principle of nationality had been established beyond dispute. The South, in other words, was beaten again and this time for good. The Democratic party was defunct and a long period of prosperity under Republican rule was in sight. It still could not see, however, how Republican votes were going to be counted in the South, which presented a stone wall against Negro political equality, despite constitutional law.

The *Tribune* was accused during this campaign of seeking to injure General Grant personally, but it said that General Grant's friends would acquit it of that untrue charge. They regarded his fame as immortal and looked upon those who sought to nominate him for the third term as false friends, selfish men who had disgraced his administration once and would do it again.

The theological world was in ferment over the question of salvation by faith or by works, and a new heresy trial was about to begin over the question of eternal punishment. Edison brought household electric light nearer and the *Tribune* thought that science was bringing new light into religion. Isolationism became a subject of debate between the *Tribune* and the London *Spectator*.

As the spring advanced the presidential situation became more intense, with the Grant boomers active and insistent. The *Tribune* saw no chance of getting any Southern electoral votes and said Grant was being boomed by the "Senatorial spoils syndicate." Grant had not yet indicated whether he desired the nomination. He was waiting until it was necessary to act. The *Chicago Journal* said that the *Tribune* would not "get the smell of an office" under a third term regime and the *Tribune* replied that it was not on the scent of any office.

A national school fund, to be raised largely from a liquor tax, was suggested by the *Tribune* on April 24. There was particular need for this in the South, it was stated.

San Francisco contributed another news sensation on April 24, when Charles De Young, one of the owners of the *Chronicle*, was shot and killed in his office by I. M. Kalloch, son of the mayor of San Francisco. This had grown out of a campaign and a shooting previously recorded.

Susan B. Anthony called a convention of suffrage workers for June 2 in Chicago. The site of the new Pullman car works was fixed at Kensington. The Chicago Spelling Reform Association met at the Sherman House. The secretary read letters from educators approving the efforts of the *Chicago Tribune* in spelling reform.

The Cook County convention of May 9 gave a victory to the anti-third term Republicans, but the Grant faction bolted the convention, which listened, according to the *Tribune*, "to long and windy speeches from hired third term lawyers." Illinois became a battleground for the third termers, with Long Jones and Senator Logan managing the Grant forces.

Tennyson's *De Profundis* was published in May. Sir Edwin Arnold's *Light of Asia* was given much notice and Ernest Renan's lectures were printed. The *Tribune* world was not all politics.

"There is just one safe and honorable escape for General Grant from the scramble for a presidential nomination in which selfish and insincere friends have placed his name," said the *Tribune* on May 7. "This is a personal withdrawal from a contest to which he has never yet given a public assent."

The *Tribune* reported that its circulation had increased steadily since January. The Sunday circulation was just under 50,000. "We accept this as a token of improving activity in all departments of trade and proof of the continued growth and prosperity of Chicago. No first class journal west of New York equals THE TRIBUNE in circulation, and it is doubtful if any two together have as large an advertising patronage." The paper had ten branch offices in the city.

Lincoln Park, which had been improved, was patronized by a Sunday crowd of 40,000 visitors. Chicago was in the lead for the baseball championship. An abatement of the smoke nuisance was called for by the *Tribune* on May 18. The *Tribune's* own plant had an Orvis smoke consumer which had reduced smoke to a minimum.

Potter Palmer sued the *Tribune* for $25,000 on May 18 because of alleged libel in a story of his activities in voting colored men from his hotel in the First ward. The Palmer House was described as the "headquarters for the third-term bolters."

337

The Grant third-term bolters were seated at the Springfield Republican convention and the *Tribune* said that the Republican congressional districts were as thoroughly disfranchised as the Negroes in Mississippi. "For the first time in the history of Illinois this state has a boss — Boss Logan."

Of the 42 votes of Illinois in the national convention, Grant had 22. The *Tribune* said this result would be appealed to the convention and prophesied that there would be 457 anti-Grant votes in the convention. "The Third Term thing is beaten," it was declared on May 23.

The *Galena Gazette* said that Grant would not withdraw and would accept if nominated.

The *Tribune* announced a set of spelling reform rules to go into effect in its office, a part of the American Philological (Filological) Association rules, listing such words as "infinit" and "favorit."

On May 25 there was a description of a musical soirée at the home of Cyrus H. McCormick, who had built a palatial residence at Rush and Huron Streets. The house was of three stories, built of Lake Superior sandstone and decorated by Marcotte of New York. The occasion of the housewarming was the 21st birthday of Cyrus, Jr.

Anti-third-termers met at Central Music Hall and overflowed into Farwell Hall. The *Tribune* said this was an evidence of the people's voice raised in anger, and that the Springfield style of politics was not fashionable — "and don't you forget it, John Logan, Long Jones, Emory Storrs, etc."

"Gath" was back in the *Tribune*, writing a lead for the convention news. Ten Illinois districts were in contest as the convention time neared, and news was carried of a country wide protest against the third term. There were pages of politics but one could still read Swinburne's new poems, or about women, or solve a puzzle in the puzzle corner of the *Tribune*, or read of a trip through the Gunnison country on snowshoes.

The Grant boom was weakening, but it was still formidable, "Gath" reported on May 30. "The Republican convention," said the *Tribune*, "will assume a terrible responsibility by inviting and provoking and defying a deep rooted and widespread hostility to the election of any third term candidate." The *Times* said the *Tribune* opposition to Logan was personal. The *Tribune* denied this, and said it was fighting "his Southern Democratic practice of bolting, fraud and bulldozing in order to impose his preference on an unwilling majority. The third termers are whipped," was the theme of *Tribune* editorials on the eve of the convention.

There was much excitement in town that first week in June. Barnum's circus was there, as were the comic opera *H.M.S. Pinafore*, and Susan Anthony's suffragists. The Grant men took an advertisment in the *Tribune* and printed the names of 500 vice-presidents of a Grant mass meeting. Roscoe Conkling, Matt H. Carpenter and Senator Logan were the chief speakers. Colonel Bob Ingersoll and other notables were in town. There were ten Illinois delegate districts in contest and the credentials committee made big news. All the contestants were finally admitted except one district, and the Grant campaign news was printed under a heading "The Lost Cause." On the question of the currency platform, the *Tribune* said that Wall Street wanted to go to gold but advised the convention to "let the best currency the world has ever seen alone."

General Garfield, who had been favorably regarded by President Hayes as an available candidate, began to look like "a very great favorit" (Tribune spelling), according to the June 5 leading article.

The balloting began and it was seen that neither Blaine, Grant nor Sherman could win. They would not go to each other and so they went to Garfield. On June 9 the Republican rooster was crowing again over the *Tribune* political news. "The Battle Won—The Tribune Eats Spring Chicken

—The Long Agony Over and The Republican Party Saved From Destruction," were the convention headlines. General Garfield and Chester A. Arthur had been nominated. Press comments were carried from all over the country and the *Tribune* said: "Never was a nomination made that has been received by friend and foe with such evidences of hearty respect, admiration and confidence. That he will be elected we have no question."

To General Grant's friends, the *Tribune* had this to say:

"In the rejection of General Grant as a candidate, a great, and we now believe a lasting, principle of American institutions has been vindicated. There has been no fight against General Grant personally in all this bitter strife. Many persons interested in his candidacy have sought to spread the impression that THE TRIBUNE and other Republican journals opposed to a violation of the unwritten constitution of the Nation, have abused General Grant pending the contest. So far as THE TRIBUNE is concerned, there is not even the semblance of truth in this charge, and we believe that the honest friends of General Grant will acquit it of the unfounded imputation now that the long agony is over. . . . THE TRIBUNE has deprecated the return of certain selfish and scheming men to power, which would have been implied by General Grant's election to a third term after having secured the nomination by the aid of some of the very men who disgraced his second administration. But THE TRIBUNE has never sought to snatch a single jewel from the crown of fame which General Grant so justly wears as the conqueror of the Rebellion and the first citizen of the American Republic."

There was an outburst of campaign songs as Garfield started home. A typical anthem began:

Run up the banner, boys, for Liberty and Law!
For Garfield and for Arthur, boys,
Hurrah, hurrah, hurrah!

The Greenbackers next took the stage, with Dennis Kearney, the sandlot orator, as leader of one wing. The Democrats nominated Lyman Trumbull for governor. The *Tribune* suggested that General Grant be sent to the United States Senate. Carter Harrison, home from a visit with Horatio Seymour in New York, was said to be a candidate for Vice-President. His lightning rod, said the *Tribune*, was three stories high. Tilden withdrew from the Democratic race and General Winfield Scott Hancock of Pennsylvania was nominated, with William English of Indiana as his running mate. Southern Democrats had dictated the nomination, according to the *Tribune*.

As a military commander in Louisiana and Texas under President Johnson, Hancock had carried out the Johnson policies. He deferred to the ex-rebels, the *Tribune* stated, and failed to protect the Negroes. This was his reward. English was pictured as a penurious man, a hard landlord and a note shaver.

Garfield, on the other hand, was given high moral qualities and great patriotism. His letter of acceptance was " a statesman-like document," while that of Hancock was said to have been written by somebody else, " as he is not capable of it." Such was the character of the campaign that took shape in July.

Chicago population was 503,000, according to the new census. St. Louis was sore and the real estate men were happy. Chicago had counted ghosts and convention visitors, according to the St. Louis wail.

The *Tribune* stated its political views and campaign plans in a " Card to Working Republicans" on July 17 as follows:

" The presidential campaign has now fairly opened. The Republicans have a magnificent standard bearer, at once a statesman, scholar and soldier, who is worthy of the cordial support of every Republican in this broad land. Every man who is proud of the patriotic record of the Republican party,

341

and devoted to the honor and welfare of his country, cannot hesitate to support General James A. Garfield and the whole Republican ticket.

"The Demo-Confederate candidate is wholly ignorant of political and civil affairs, as his whole life has been spent in military routine; he is utterly unfit to discharge the delicate and difficult duties of the Presidency, and if elected will be nothing more than a nose of wax in the hands of the crafty, unreconstructed, State-supremacy Brigadiers of the South. It is not safe to elect such a man Chief Magistrate of this great Republic.

"The Republicans must confront the Solid South by a Solid North. Congress must be recovered from the hands of the Confederates and their dough-face allies; and the government must be kept in control of the party that saved the Union and made a free country; that preserved the fiercely assailed National credit, restored the currency to par, filled the channels of trade with gold and silver, reduced the public debt and the rate of interest, and established general prosperity. The business interests of the country cannot afford to be tampered with or experimented upon by currency quacks or reckless demagogs. General Garfield will give the public a pure, able, economical, and efficient and patriotic administration. In electing him there are no risks to be taken, as his wisdom, experience and record are known to all men.

"In support of the Republican party, its candidates and principles, THE CHICAGO TRIBUNE will make a lively campaign. No agency will contribute more to the success of the Republican cause than a wide dissemination among the people of this journal."

Mayor Harrison took a walk along State Street and was surprised. In a letter to Police Captain Fred Ebersold he said:

"State street from Van Buren to Jerry Monroe's place is a disgrace to the city. It seems to have been given over by landlords to prostitutes. These women live upstairs and at

June 9, 1880, was a happy day for the Tribune, not only because the Republicans had nominated James A Garfield but because by so doing they had put the party on record against "third-termism."

night make unseemly calls from the windows. They run down to the streets and turn the sidewalks into open bagnios. They go into the saloons, drink with the men and even fight. I have been loathe to believe all I have heard on the subject [much of it from The *Tribune*] but last night I made a personal observation and found that the picture had not been overdrawn. In a city like Chicago we cannot prevent prostitution, but we can and must, prevent its being made an open calling."

A series of scholarly and finely written articles on the life of Ernest Renan began in the *Tribune* of July 17. They were written by Henry D. Lloyd, who had been on the *Tribune* staff since 1872 as literary editor, financial editor and editorial writer. William Bross wrote on science news for the Saturday supplement.

Ratification meetings were held by both parties. The Republican meeting, the *Tribune* said, was like a brilliant electric light to the farthing candle of the Democratic meeting.

Horace White, interviewed on the merits of the candidates, said that Garfield was the better man but that General Hancock was a brilliant soldier, a true patriot and a polished gentleman. There was no humbug about him. He was not a statesman and never said he was.

The murder farm of Kate and John Bender in Kansas provided a sensation in August. Many travelers had been killed there and dropped through a trap door. Another sensation was Dr. Mary Walker, woman's rights leader, who insisted on wearing trousers. The *Tribune* suggested that a suitable music hall be erected so that Theodore Thomas might be induced to leave Cincinnati for Chicago.

Thomas Hughes, English writer and reformer, led a group of young Englishmen to establish Rugby Colony on the Cumberland plateau of Tennessee. They entered upon this Utopia with high hopes, practicing a sort of Communism. Manicuring was introduced into Chicago by a pupil of Mad-

343

ame Thalie of Paris. This young woman proposed to visit the better homes to practice her art.

Robert G. Ingersoll caused a new controversy in theological circles with his lecture on salvation. A perfect practice of charity was all that was necessary, he argued. The *Tribune* urged the clergymen to reply to this, whether salvation could come by works and deeds rather than by faith. Ingersoll said that Matthew had never mentioned salvation by faith. Nearly three pages were given to the preachers on this subject on September 27, 1880.

"If the Democratic party is successful in November it will be the South that is successful," said the *Tribune* on October 1. "If the Democratic party rules this country it will be the South that rules it. Are the people of the North ready for that rule?" Accounts were given of the disfranchisement of voters by state laws in the South.

The Republican rooster flapped his wings at the top of the political column on October 13, for Indiana and Ohio had gone Republican in state elections. "No such gratifying news has been spread before the American people since the wires announced the fall of Richmond and the capture and surrender of Lee's army," said the *Tribune*. "This is a Nation and Don't You Forget It," was the political heading. The Stars and Stripes was shown triumphant and the state sovereignty flag a rag in the dust.

"It is now an ascertained fact," said the *Tribune* next day, "that General Hancock can in no event be elected President. The weight of the Solid South, because it is the Solid South, will bear him to the earth in every Northern state. A Republican Congress is almost assured. . . . THE CHICAGO TRIBUNE extends its kindest condolence to the Democracy, especially of this city and county. It has many friends among the respectable members of that party, and to them it extends its heartiest sympathy in this time of bereavement. It invites them into the Republican ark for the November flood."

344

The Rev. Hiram W. Thomas, a liberal Methodist clergyman, announced in the course of a sermon that he did not believe in eternal punishment. The *Tribune* commended him, saying that he voiced what many believed, that this was the age of progress in the religious world, an age of sifting and analysis in the light of science. A resolution was offered at the Rock River conference that Dr. Thomas should withdraw from the church, as his doctrine was at variance with the historic theology of the church. The resolution was adopted by a vote of 107 to 47. Dr. Thomas, however, refused to be kicked out and a heresy trial was in prospect, like the Swing case. The Rev. R. M. Hatfield was chosen to prosecute the case, and formal charges were to be drawn. Dr. Thomas began to preach at Central Music Hall. The *Tribune* said this would be good for young people, as there was little hope of progress among their elders.

The *Tribune* began a "Lost Cause" column late in October. The Louisville *Courier-Journal* was quoted: "Satan and the Republican party have triumphed. The bloody shirt and money and imported fraudulent votes did win. We have lost nearly everything save honor."

"A Dying Snake—the Copperhead Writhing in Its Last Hideous Agonies," was the heading over the political story of November 1. Illinois, it was said, was aroused beyond precedent. Mayor Harrison was warned to give the people a fair election. Four hundred special policemen had been appointed. The *Tribune* called them "roughs" and said: "Mayor Harrison threatens to bring lasting disgrace upon the fair name of Chicago tomorrow. It will be the duty of all law and order loving citizens to take care that the purpose of this bold bad man is frustrated."

It was reported on November 2 that Mayor Harrison had begun a $50,000 libel suit against the *Tribune* for printing his speech at Hershey Hall in which he was said to have advised the Democrats to take over the polls and defy United

States supervisors. The *Tribune* said no libel suit had been started, but if it was it should be against the *Times*, which had printed the speech and from which the *Tribune* had taken its account. "If his purpose is to bluff or intimidate THE TRIBUNE he will fail miserably."

Lists of names to be challenged at the polls were printed in the *Tribune*.

November 3 — "Victory. The Great Battle Decisively Won. Glory Hallelujah! The Solid South was battered and scattered and shattered by the Solid North. The second rebellion against freedom and nationality put down by five million Union ballots fired yesterday. Twenty more years of Republican rule assured."

These were the triumphant headings beside the crowing rooster. The Republican majority in Illinois was 50,000. In the city and county the Republican majority was 10,000. There had been no disturbance at the polls.

"The election," said the *Tribune*, "will convey a lesson to the Democrats of the North and of the South which they can study with profit. It has made Nationality a fundamental principle of American government, and a principle no longer to be questioned or disputed."

A vast crowd gathered in front of the *Tribune* bulletin boards. "At 10:30," it was reported, "upon receipt of the first news from New York, THE TRIBUNE building suddenly blazed into pyrotechnic glory. Rocket after rocket rushed riotously zenith-ward like winged serpents, grew less and less in the airy deep, hovered a moment — dazzling Bengal lights through the entire line of the building made night like day with vari-colored splendor, while through the black above darted volleys of swift stars from Roman candles in ceaseless fusillade, issuing from a cascade of ruby sparks that fell thick as votes for Garfield, hot as Democratic rage, and perished as fast as the hopes of the rebel Brigadiers." A rather neat bit of political pyrotechnics.

Victory poems and editorials appeared for a few days and then the news world settled back into the normal. The *Tribune* thought that the great problem for the Garfield administration was to see how Republican votes could be counted in the South. The mayor appealed to the public in a "card" which the *Tribune* published. He said that the speech which the *Times* and the *Tribune* had published as his was not his, that no reporter was present and that someone had told it to a reporter as a joke. He had not started a libel suit.

At the annual meeting of the Western Associated Press in Detroit, November 23, Joseph Medill declined re-election to the board of directors, on which he had served for fifteen years. This resolution was adopted: "That the thanks of this association are hereby tendered to the Hon. Joseph Medill for the unselfish zeal he has shown, for the interest he has manifested in the association, an association of which he was one of the founders, and for the ability he has displayed in the affairs intrusted to his charge."

Three years later, however, Medill was elected president of the association, at the nineteenth annual meeting in New York, and was re-elected in 1884 and 1885. He was active even while out of office and in 1879 took action to improve the press telegraph service to the West. In 1882, on motion of Melville E. Stone, the board of directors was instructed to call him to their assistance.

Edison was reported to be making great progress with electric light lamps. The *Tribune* said this was being watched with great interest all over the country as his success would tend to lessen the price of gas and break a great monopoly. "Meanwhile it is impossible not to admire the patient, courageous and hopeful manner in which Mr. Edison keeps to his task in the face of numerous obstacles."

Congress was called in special session in December and new debates began on money. The Rev. Robert Collyer, speaking in New York on the modern newspaper, said that a great and good newspaper was as sacred in its own way as the Bible.

The *London Times* issued a fanciful "1980 Edition," giving news of the House of Peeresses, flights to other planets in balloons, etc. "They may not be so far out of the way when 1980 comes," the *Tribune* commented, "at which time it is to be presumed the editors of THE CHICAGO TRIBUNE will look with pride at their ancestor of 1880 and will contemplate with satisfaction that the paper has not retrograded, since in 1980 as in 1880 they will see it still distances its contemporaries."

In a final message to Congress, President Hayes said that polygamy as practiced by the Mormons was the great disgrace of the United States. The Baltimore and Ohio railroad advertised palace sleeping cars to Washington: "Leave Chicago 4:55 p.m. Arrive Washington 9 p.m. next day."

Henry Watterson said the Republican party was very bad, but also smart and strong, "and all the keen rascals in the country have contrived to get in it." He was looking for a "principle" on which to beat them.

Endymion by Lord Beaconsfield (Benjamin Disraeli) was the most successful novel of the year.

The incoming administration would devote itself to internal improvements and development, the Washington correspondent of the *Tribune* said, describing the time as "an era of universal good feeling," with the Solid South and the Democratic party "defunct."

Sarah Bernhardt was in New York and William Winter was criticized for getting "too ecstatic." On December 21 the *Tribune* announced it would print a list of the ladies who would "receive" on New Year's Day. This was the form: Michigan Avenue — No. 1112 — Mrs. Smith and the Misses Smith.

Police telephones had been in use three months and had proved satisfactory.

The *London Spectator* commented on American prosperity. It said that America was doing nothing for the world involving self sacrifice, but was "practicing selfishness and isolation." So this was the beginning of the isolationist debate.

The *Tribune* said of this article on December 28, 1880: "In other words because the United States is rich and powerful the Spectator would have it pause in its great work of feeding, sheltering and educating the refugee oppressed of all nations, and start out, like another Don Quixote, upon a crusade for the settlement of political questions at issue between nations, to pull down this people and build up that, to get into all sorts of entangling alliances, and to reform everything that needs it. . . . How would the Spectator like it if we undertook to reform Great Britain first in her persecution of weaker peoples?"

INDEX